IMAGES
of America

Historic Cemeteries of Long Beach

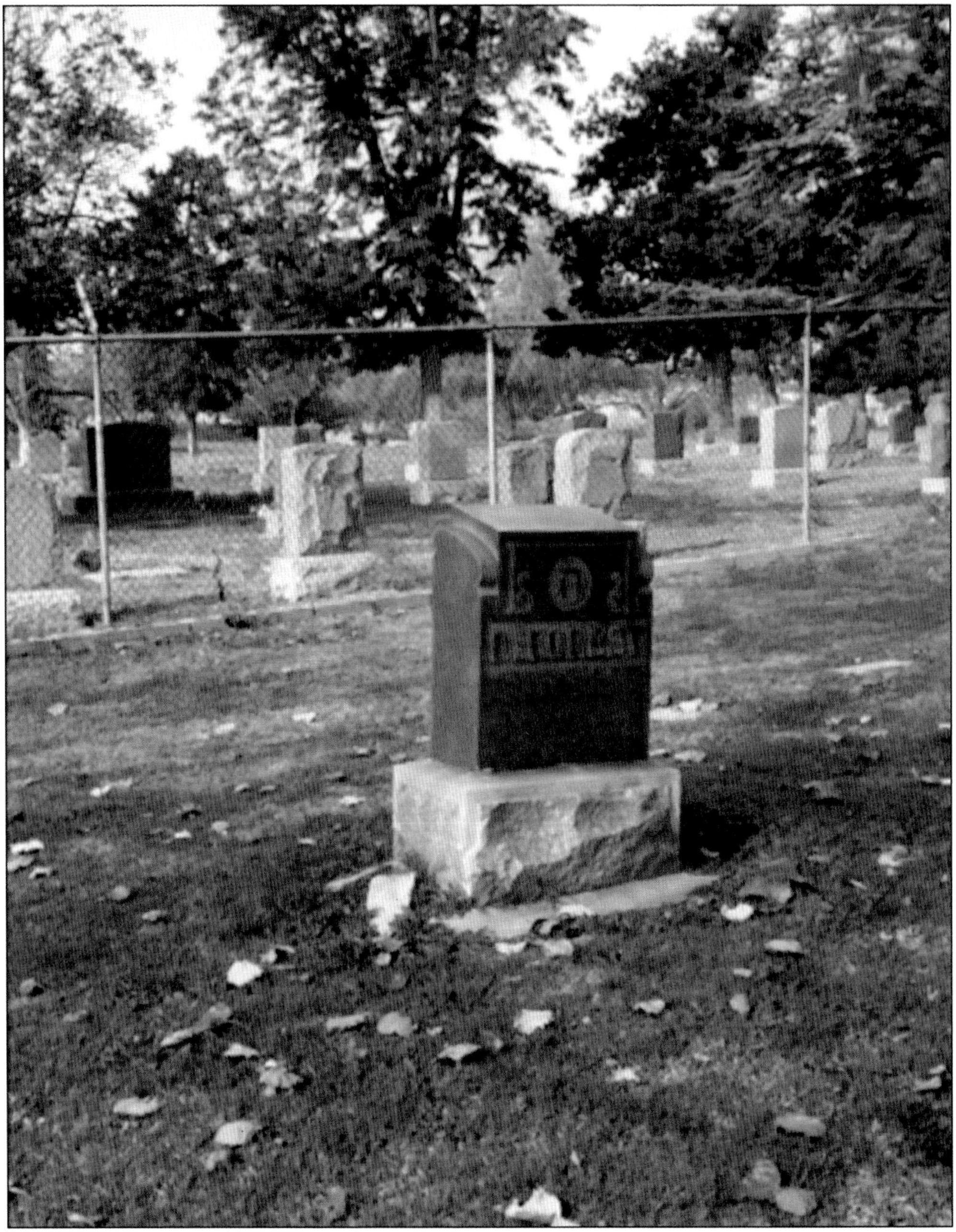

A chain-link fence separates the Municipal and Sunnyside Cemeteries—the two oldest non-native burial grounds in Long Beach, California. Both are located on Willow Street on the sloping land of oil-rich Signal Hill. The "Second Sunnyside Cemetery" is several miles to the north and today is known as Forest Lawn Long Beach.

On the Cover: Ansel Adams made the "Angel of Sorrows" famous in 1939 when he took pictures of the statue against a background of hundreds of oil derricks. The author's photograph shows that most of the oil derricks are gone, but the statue remains atop the 1907 grave of Dr. Albert Rhea in Sunnyside Cemetery.

IMAGES
of America

HISTORIC CEMETERIES OF LONG BEACH

Gerrie Schipske

ARCADIA
PUBLISHING

ISBN 978-1-4671-1713-5

Published by Arcadia Publishing
Charleston, South Carolina

Printed in the United States of America

Library of Congress Control Number: 2016941976

For all general information, please contact Arcadia Publishing:
Telephone 843-853-2070
Fax 843-853-0044
E-mail sales@arcadiapublishing.com
For customer service and orders:
Toll-Free 1-888-313-2665

Visit us on the Internet at www.arcadiapublishing.com

To Flo Pickett, my partner in life, who listened so patiently as I told these cemetery stories over and over again. Thank you.

Contents

Acknowledgments 6

Introduction 7

1. The Earliest Burial Grounds in Long Beach 9
2. Coffins, Caskets, and Burial Rituals 19
3. The Long Beach Signal Hill Cemetery 33
4. The Most Valuable Cemetery in the United States 53
5. The Other Sunnyside Cemetery 73
6. Tragic Burials in Long Beach 93
7. The Blue and Gray Club 109

Additional Information Sources 127

Acknowledgments

A sincere thank-you to Michael Miner, a board member of Friends of Sunnyside Cemetery, who made records and access so readily available. The preservation of Sunnyside Cemetery is a labor of love for him, not only because he has family buried there, but because he understands that it is one of the remaining sites that provides a glimpse of early Long Beach history. Thank you also to Long Beach city manager Patrick West and Dustin Borrelli of the Public Works Department for providing access to city records. Unless otherwise noted, all images are from the author's collection. The following sources were also used: LOC (Library of Congress), LBPL (Long Beach Public Library), LAPL (Los Angeles Public Library), and the University of Southern California Digital Collections.

INTRODUCTION

Long Beach may contain some of the earliest burial grounds in California. Home of the Tongva natives, the eastern portion of Long Beach contains a dozen or more archeological sites that are believed to be ceremonial and burial sites.

The non-native cemeteries of Long Beach came in the late 1870s and early 1900s and are the final resting places of those born here and the many more who came in search of a better, healthier, and calmer life. They were doctors, bankers, real estate developers, teachers, politicians, lawyers, farmers, writers, evangelists, activists, entertainers, and veterans. They were their spouses, siblings, and children.

Some died within their first few minutes or years of life. Some were taken by disease, murder, accident, or suicide. Some have no marker to provide clues to their name and history. Most lived the long lives they hoped they would after leaving other states and coming to Long Beach.

One chronicler of cemeteries remarked in a 1921 edition of *Park and Cemetery* that Long Beach was a "two grave town" due to more than one half of the population being elderly retired couples who moved to Long Beach to live the remainder of their lives. With children living elsewhere, they only needed a two-grave lot.

Many early residents, some of whose names are immortalized as streets, parks, schools, and historic areas of the city, lie in one of the four cemeteries: William E. Willmore, whose American Colony eventually became the city of Long Beach; Col. Charles Heartwell, one of the first city water commissioners whose vision for use of water property led to the development of one of Long Beach's largest parks; F.W. Stearns, a prominent real estate developer whose father, T.P., served in the Civil War; and Dr. William Lawrence Woodruff, who promoted good health through his Woodruff Sanitarium. There are also a number of other prominent families, including those of Buffum, Bixby, Walker, Bush, Teel, and Shaw.

The history of these cemeteries parallels the changes in public attitude toward death and burial. Early cemeteries were removed from churchyards and placed in rural areas and made park-like. Funerals were no longer conducted in family parlors, but by those who would "undertake" the tasks in their own funeral parlors. Coffins became caskets to emphasize that the dead were "only sleeping." Headstones, once stark and small, became ornate and large to indicate wealth.

There were no crematoriums or community mausoleums in Long Beach until 1922, when the second Sunnyside was opened. Before then, families wishing cremation or entombment went to other cemeteries.

Two of the Long Beach cemeteries are located on Signal Hill. These were originally farm lots in the American Colony and were thought to be largely unusable land because of the slope. In its earliest days, the Municipal Cemetery was known as Signal Hill Cemetery. It is not known for certain who is buried in the Municipal Cemetery because burial records were not required to be kept before 1905, and a fire destroyed much of the records in 1936. A headstone marking the 1878 death of 17-year-old Milton Neece appears to be the oldest in the cemetery.

The records for Sunnyside Cemetery are much more complete. The first plot purchased in 1907 was for Dr. A. Rhea, a retired Civil War physician who was deaf and was hit by a trolley while bicycling.

Both Sunnyside and the Municipal Cemeteries contain hundreds of Union and Confederate veterans of the Civil War, including Abraham Cleag, a former slave who served as a private in Company A of the 1st Colored Heavy Artillery Regiment in Knoxville and later as a janitor in Long Beach City Hall. Nelson Ward, a Union Medal of Honor recipient, is buried in Sunnyside Cemetery, as is Confederate Alexander Lawson, who served as the city's third prosecutor. Long Beach Post 181 of the Great Army of the Republic, an organization of Union Civil War veterans, was one of the largest. Only Sunnyside has a dedicated Civil War section on its Westside.

The 1921 discovery in Signal Hill of one of the largest oil fields in the world sparked an intense and long battle for oil drilling rights in and adjacent to the two cemeteries as thousands of oil derricks surrounded them. A second Sunnyside Cemetery was opened in 1922 several miles to the north with advertisements offering to remove and rebury those in the older Sunnyside Cemetery.

Famed photographer Ansel Adams was so intrigued by the surrealism of a cemetery surrounded by oil derricks that, in 1939, he photographed the white marble "Angel of Sorrows" that sits atop the grave of Dr. A. Rhea in Sunnyside Cemetery with the derricks in the background. The photograph appeared in *Life* magazine.

The new, ornate Sunnyside Mausoleum and Memorial Park attracted many families who liked the idea of an elegant funeral that cost little more than burial in the deteriorating Municipal Cemetery and older Sunnyside cemeteries.

In 1960, Forest Lawn purchased Sunnyside Mausoleum and Memorial Park and made extensive restorations and improvements. In 1974, an area was designated Rose of Sharon Memorial Gardens for the burial of those of the Jewish faith. Today, Sunnyside Mausoleum and Memorial Park are known as Forest Lawn Long Beach.

A Catholic cemetery was established on the acreage across from Forest Lawn in 1950. The church lifted its ban on cremation in 1963. All Souls Cemetery includes a crematorium, columbarium, crypts, and ground burials. Former city attorney Gerald Desmond is buried there. A major bridge linking Long Beach and San Pedro is named in his honor.

In 2000, the city council designated Sunnyside Cemetery as a historic site. The older Municipal Cemetery remains undesignated.

This book is by no means exhaustive. It is meant to give the reader a glimpse into the cemeteries that hold those who made and lived in early Long Beach. Hopefully, it will serve as a catalyst for people to appreciate the history contained in these cemeteries and become involved in their preservation.

One

The Earliest Burial Grounds in Long Beach

The Tongva natives inhabited the area now known as Long Beach many years before 1542, when the European Juan Rodriguez Cabrillo "discovered" this special land on the West Coast. The Europeans left the Tongva alone for more than 200 years after Cabrillo's excursion. When the Spanish returned, the Tongva were pressed into slavery by the Catholic missionaries. Eventually, the Tongva (which translates as "people of the earth") were renamed San Gabriel Mission Indians or Gabrielinos after the Mission San Gabriel Arcangel, where they were forced to work the land and tend cattle and sheep.

The priests who founded the 21 missions in California copied the European tradition of including cemeteries on church grounds. According to archeologists, the earliest Tongva utilized funeral pyres (*ahtochgnah*) to cremate their dead. The bones and ashes, called *kooseerok*, were then scattered to the east. Burial sites were called *koonasga*. A deeply spiritual people, the Tongva participated in a Tongva mortuary ceremony. Every one to four years, the tribe would hold a "cry" ceremony lasting for 16 days for the people who died since the last ceremony. They would dig a hole and place a fire at the bottom. Bones of the dead would be placed in the fire hole and then covered. Cremation and Tongva mortuary rites were considered pagan by the Catholic missionaries and were forbidden.

The eastern portion of Long Beach contains a dozen or more archeological sites, including what is believed to be an ancient sacred Tongva village known as Puvunga (also called Pubuna). It is debated whether or not Puvunga is a burial ground, even though human remains and artifacts suggesting burial have been found there. It is clear that the land is considered to be sacred and the birth place of the Tongva lawgiver and god Chungichnish. Puvunga is on the land of California State University Long Beach and the Rancho Los Alamitos historical site, which are adjacent to the now covered Bouton Creek, a tributary of the San Gabriel River that flowed into Alamitos Bay.

In 1542, Cabrillo and his men sailed into what is now San Pedro Bay and reported seeing a "bay of smokes and fires" (Bahia de los Fumos y Fuegos) caused by the tall grass fires set by the Tongva to drive out small game for hunting. The Cabrillo landing monument is located at the tip of Point Loma in San Diego.

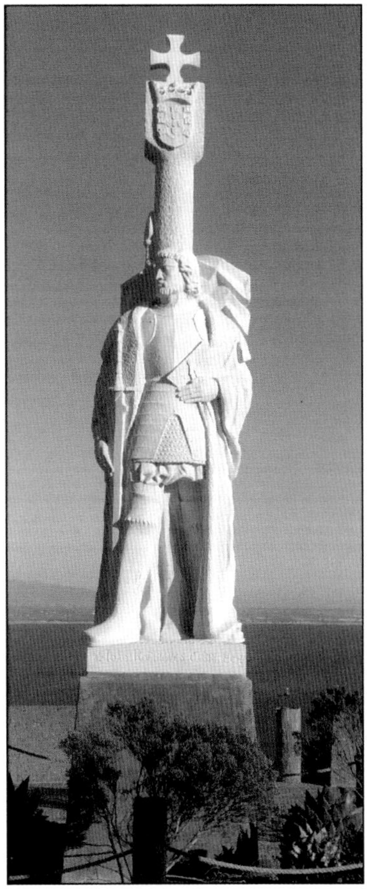

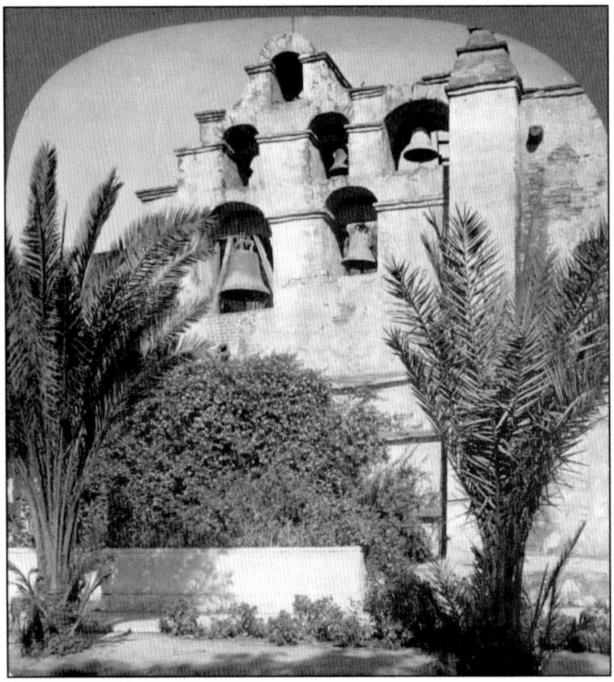

The Tongva were left alone for more than 200 years before the Spanish returned and pressed them into slavery at the local Catholic missions. The Tongva were renamed San Gabriel Mission Indians or Gabrielinos after the Mission San Gabriel Arcangel (shown in this 1909 photograph), where they worked the land. (LOC.)

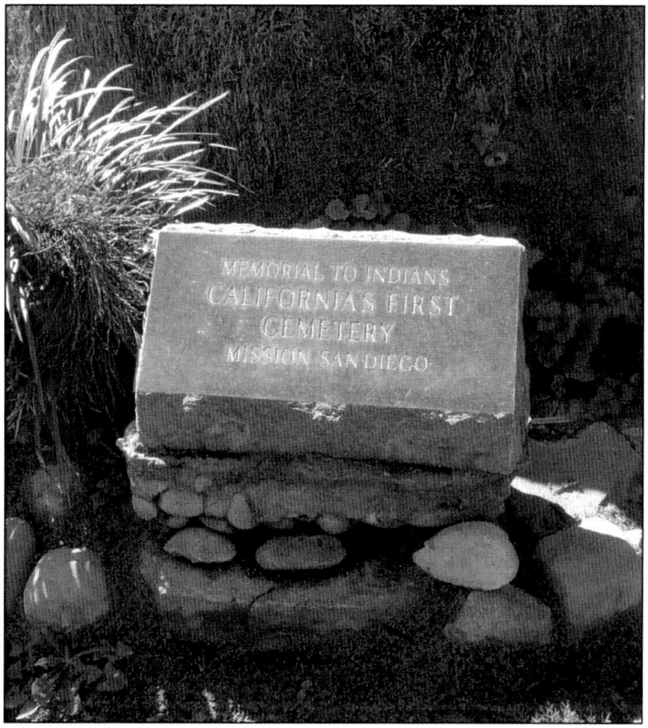

Mission San Gabriel Arcangel is one of 21 founded by Spanish Franciscan priests. Mission San Diego de Alcalá, established by Fr. Junipero Serra on July 16, 1769, contains California's first and oldest Catholic cemetery. These cemeteries contain the remains of hundreds of native Americans who were baptized into Catholicism but buried in unmarked graves.

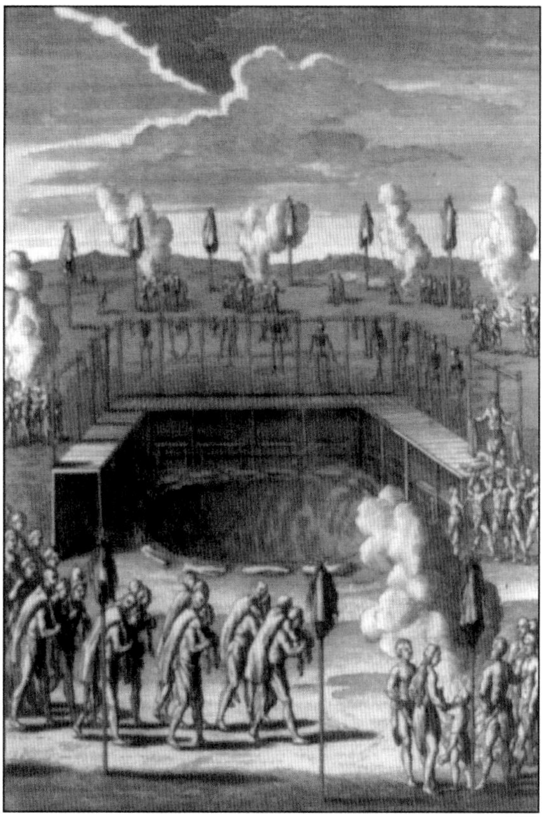

The cry (or mourning) ceremony was used by Southern California Indians at the death of a person and often on the anniversary of their death. This 1724 engraving shows a mortuary ceremony of Native Americans, who are carrying bodies over their shoulders to fires. (LOC)

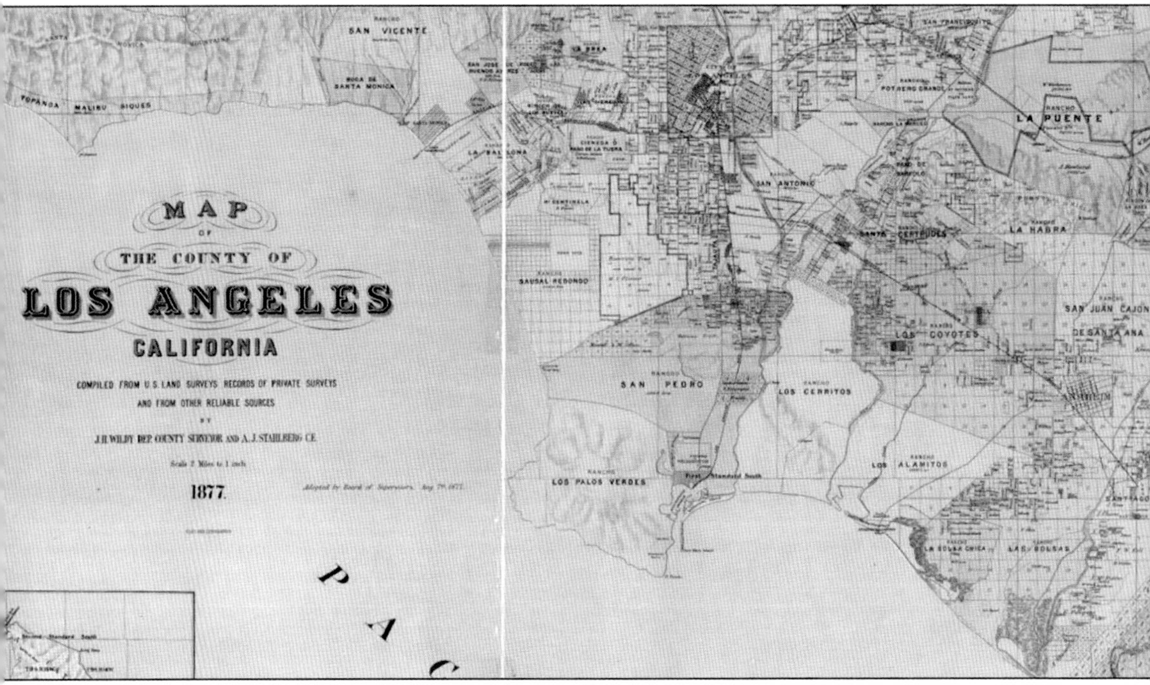

This 1887 map details the land once occupied by the Tongva on and near what is today Long Beach, which was taken by the Spanish and distributed as land grants to friends of the king of Spain. Subsequently, these land grants were divided into five ranchos: Los Coyotes, Los Cerritos, Santa Gertrudes, Las Bolsas, and Los Alamitos. Rancho Los Cerritos ("little hills") and Rancho Los Alamitos ("cottonwoods") eventually became Long Beach. Jotham Bixby purchased Rancho Los Cerritos. He sold cattle and wool to Union troops. Starting in 1879, he sold off areas of the rancho for settlement to Civil War veterans and others who were in search of land on which to grow citrus fruit and nuts. The discovery of artesian wells helped market the land for farming. Much later, a rich oil deposit was found on Bixby's land. (LOC.)

Jotham Bixby was a member of the railroad-backed California Immigrant Union, which advertised for white Europeans and East Coast residents who could bring at least $1,000 to settle. William E. Willmore, an Englishman and teacher, arrived around 1870, and in 1881 contracted with Bixby for land to start the American Colony, which was renamed Willmore City at the suggestion of a reporter from the *Los Angeles Daily Star*.

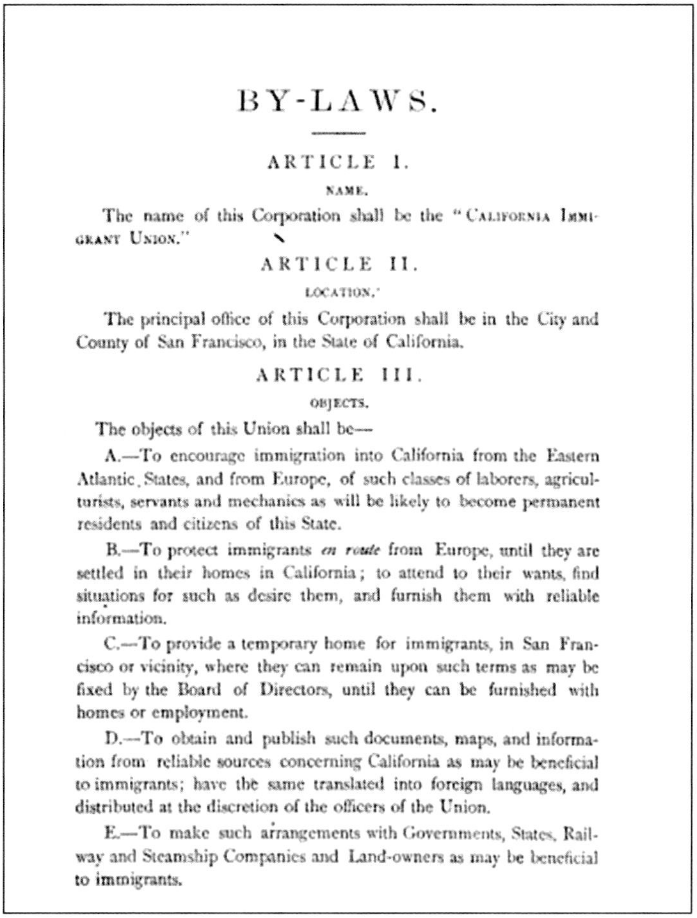

BY-LAWS.

ARTICLE I.

NAME.

The name of this Corporation shall be the "California Immigrant Union."

ARTICLE II.

LOCATION.

The principal office of this Corporation shall be in the City and County of San Francisco, in the State of California.

ARTICLE III.

OBJECTS.

The objects of this Union shall be—

A.—To encourage immigration into California from the Eastern Atlantic States, and from Europe, of such classes of laborers, agriculturists, servants and mechanics as will be likely to become permanent residents and citizens of this State.

B.—To protect immigrants *en route* from Europe, until they are settled in their homes in California; to attend to their wants, find situations for such as desire them, and furnish them with reliable information.

C.—To provide a temporary home for immigrants, in San Francisco or vicinity, where they can remain upon such terms as may be fixed by the Board of Directors, until they can be furnished with homes or employment.

D.—To obtain and publish such documents, maps, and information from reliable sources concerning California as may be beneficial to immigrants; have the same translated into foreign languages, and distributed at the discretion of the officers of the Union.

E.—To make such arrangements with Governments, States, Railway and Steamship Companies and Land-owners as may be beneficial to immigrants.

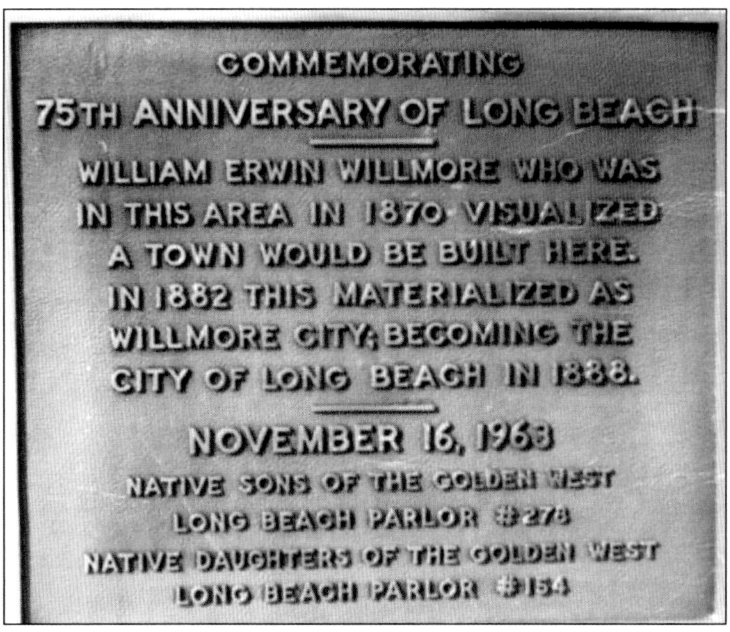

Capt. Charles Terraine Healey plotted out the American Colony. In 1884, Willmore relinquished his rights and left for an investment scheme in Texas. He returned in 1901, penniless and dying, to a city that had been renamed Long Beach at the suggestion of Belle Lowe. The city incorporated in 1896 and unincorporated over the issue of legalizing alcohol, then reincorporated in 1897.

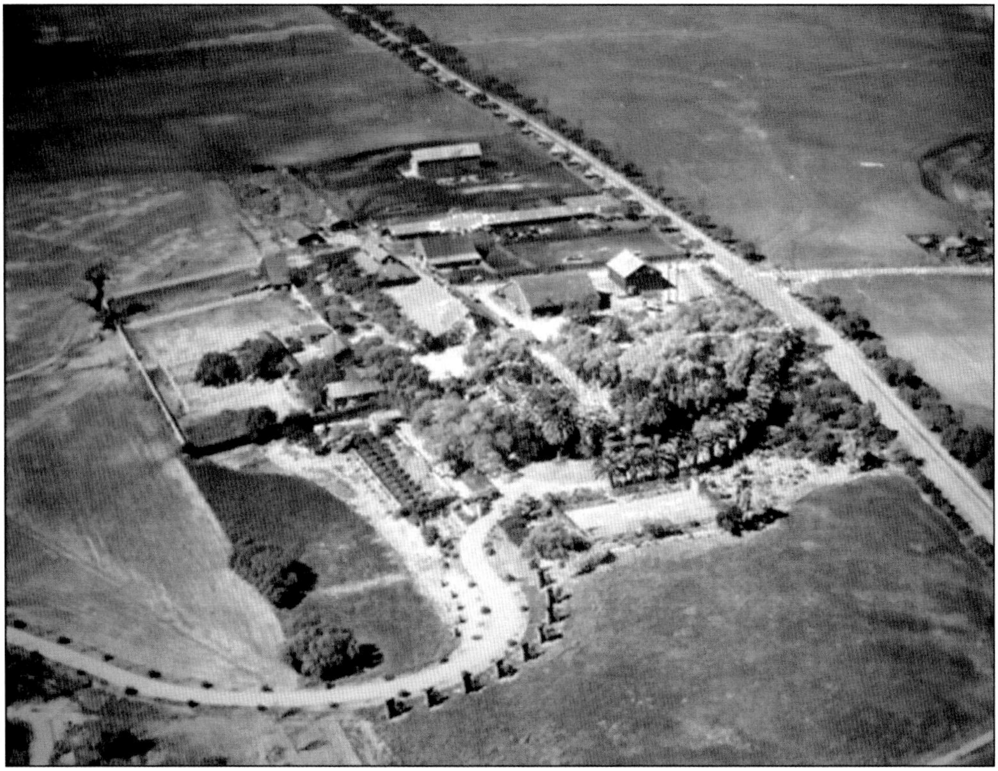

Rancho Los Alamitos (pictured in 1936), located in eastern Long Beach, is designated as a National Historic Landmark. Originally owned by Don Abel Stearns, the rancho was a farm and cattle ranch until a severe drought killed the crops and the cattle. John Bixby purchased the rancho in 1878. He plotted out Alamitos Beach and chose the Spanish names of the streets still in use. (Rancho Los Alamitos Foundation)

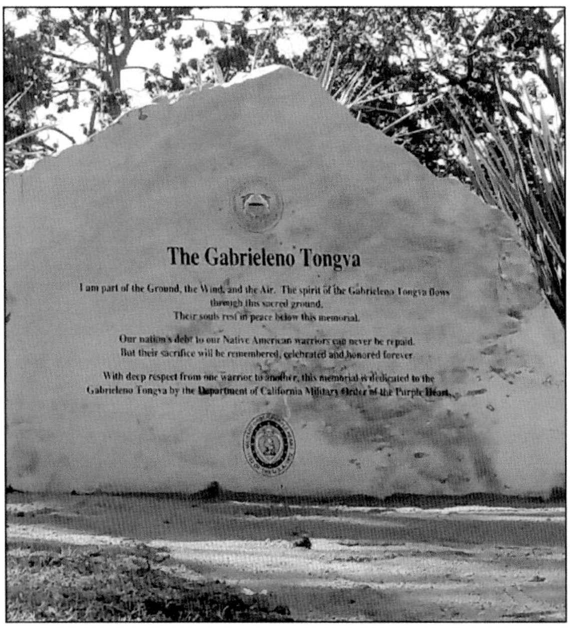

Rancho Los Alamitos is currently the site of California State University Long Beach (CSULB), the Veterans Administration Medical Center, and a large residential area. It is also the site of the ancient Tongva sacred village known as Puvunga, which was listed in the National Register of Historic Places in 1974. A tribal memorial was placed in Purple Heart Park on the grounds of the VA medical center.

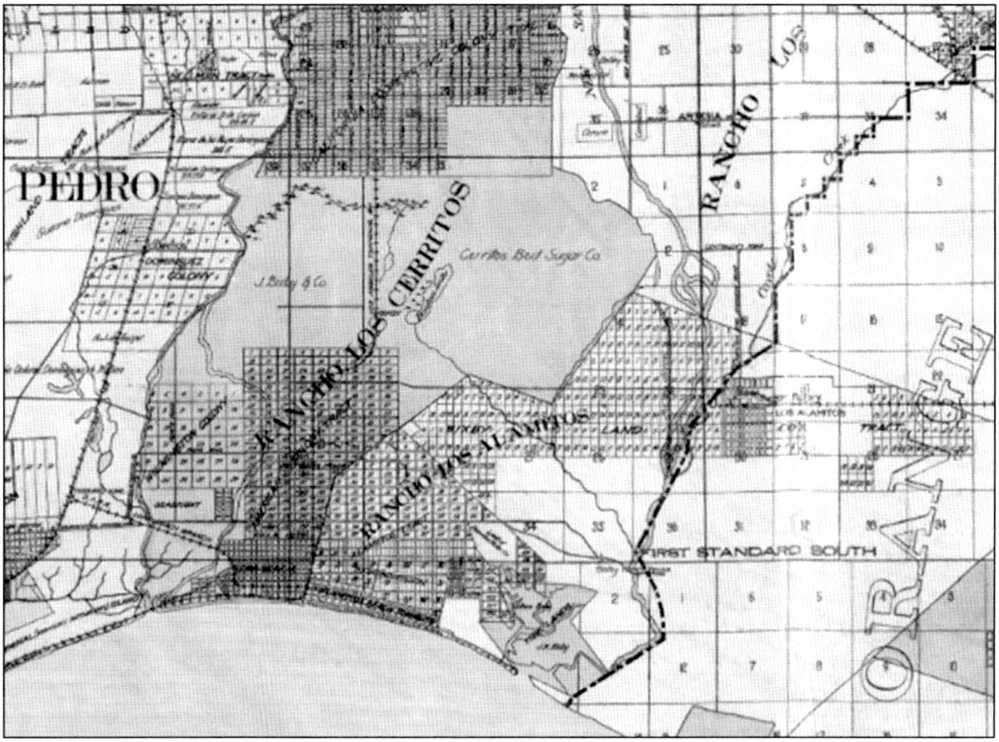

Tongva settled along areas adjacent to water. This 1898 map shows the location of the two ranchos and the creeks that flowed and connected with the San Gabriel River, including Bouton Creek, which was a tributary of the San Gabriel River. The creek ran directly through the Bixby Ranch and the site of Puvunga. (LOC.)

In 1953, CSULB archaeologist Ethel Ewing removed human remains found underneath the Los Altos shopping center. Bones of 21 individuals and evidence of cremation were stored in the Liberal Arts 5 building for many years. During a renovation of Los Altos shopping center in 1996, public art was installed, including the pictured representation of the artifacts found in the soil at Puvunga.

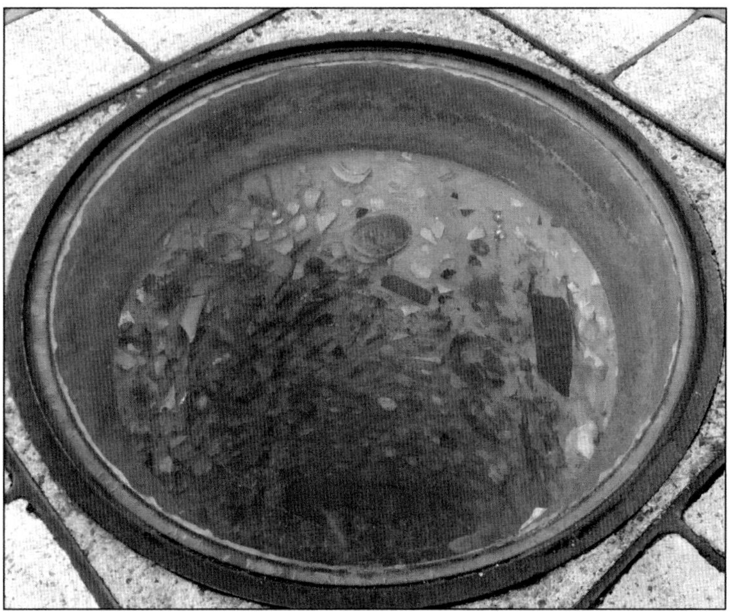

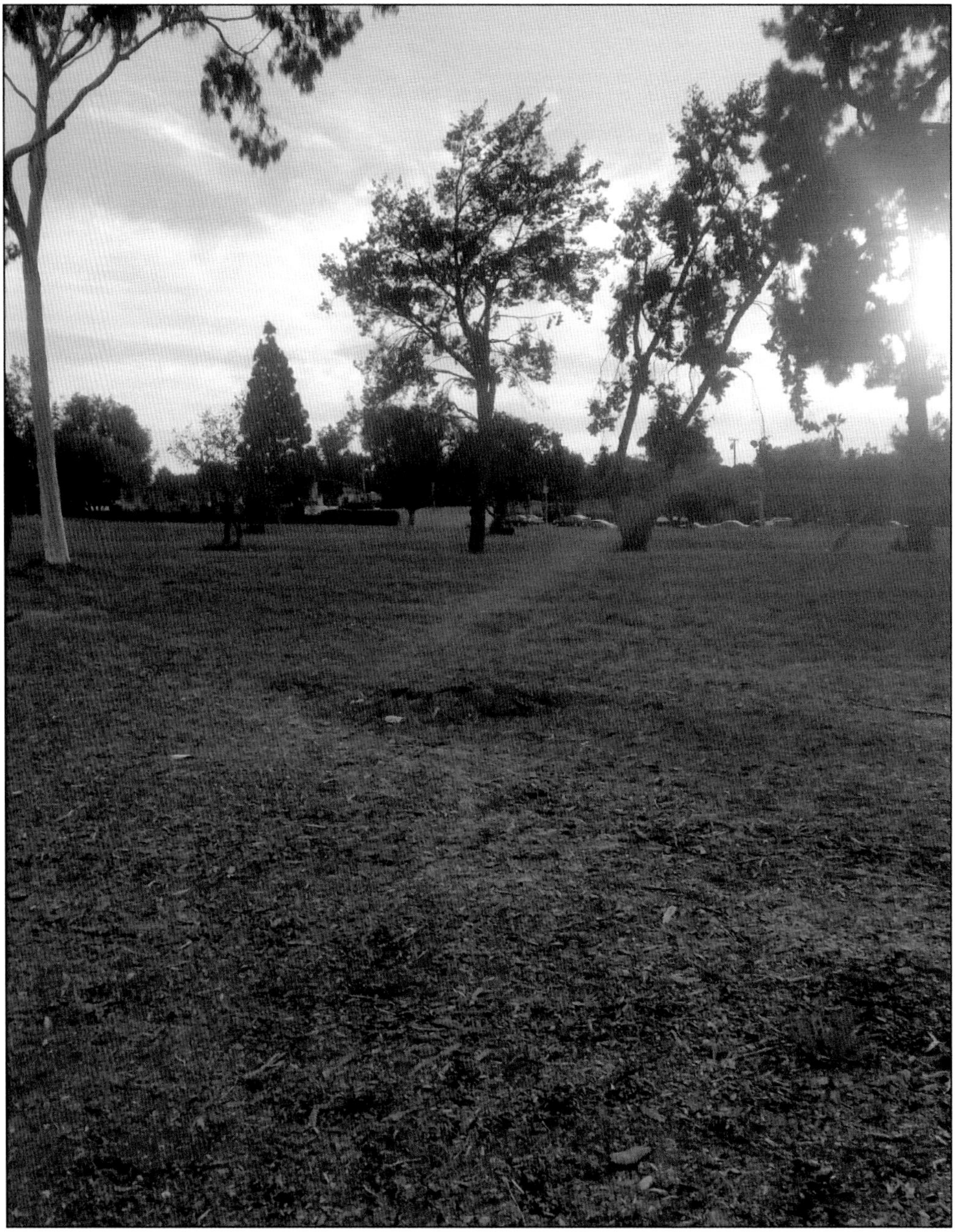

In the 1990s, CSULB officials planned to develop an open field on campus into a mini mall. The plan was stopped when tribal members and others sued to protect the site. Flyers declaring "Save It, Don't Pave It," and "Go Dig Up Your Own Grandmother!" were used to rally opposition to the development. Several college students claimed that this field where remains were found is haunted. The area, located near the Japanese gardens on campus, is often covered with a fog layer in colder weather. While excavating ground to build a new parking structure at CSULB in 1994, more than 1.25 metric tons of shells, bone fragments, bone tools, and pottery shards were unearthed, resulting in what archeologists consider to be the best dated find of prehistoric pottery in all of California.

DIED.

FUNERAL NOTICES ONE DOLLAR.

BIXBY—At Los Alamitos Rancho, May 6th, after a short illness, John W. Bixby, aged 39 years.

Funeral services at the house of Jotham Bixby, Long Beach, to-day, Sunday, at 12 o'clock. Interment at Evergreen Cemetery, after the arrival of Long Beach train at Commercial street station (4:20 P. M.) Friends are invited to attend without further notice.

Many of the early settlers of Long Beach were buried in cemeteries nearby. As shown in this 1887 funeral notice in the *Los Angeles Daily Herald*, the Bixby family chose Evergreen Cemetery in the Boyle Heights area of Los Angeles. Evergreen was a considerable distance away from the Bixby ranchos. In 1877, the Los Angeles Cemetery Association established Evergreen Cemetery. Evergreen provided 70 acres. With the advent of the electric trolley in the early 1900s, Evergreen Cemetery became even more accessible to the public, as pictured below. (Below, Security Pacific Collection, LAPL.)

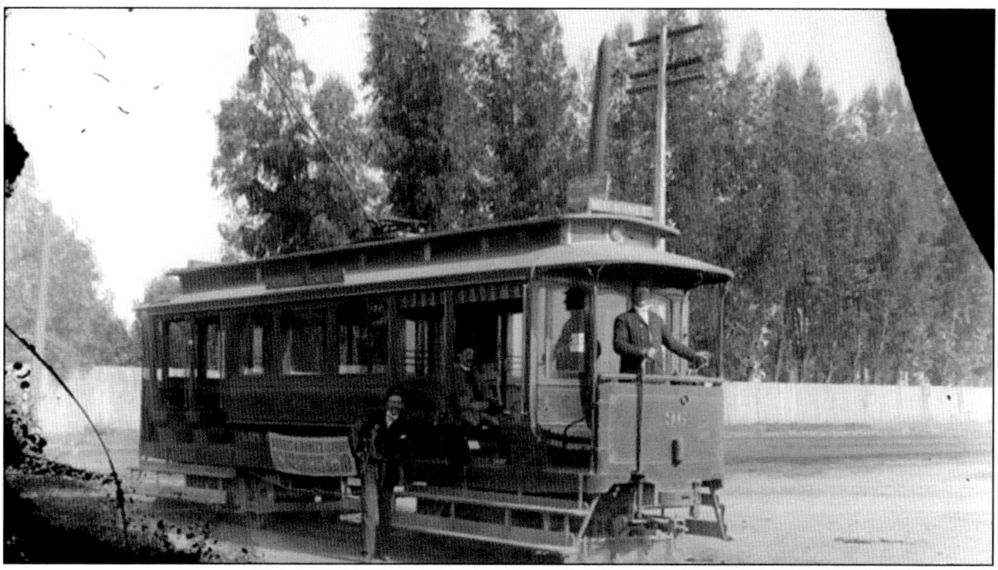

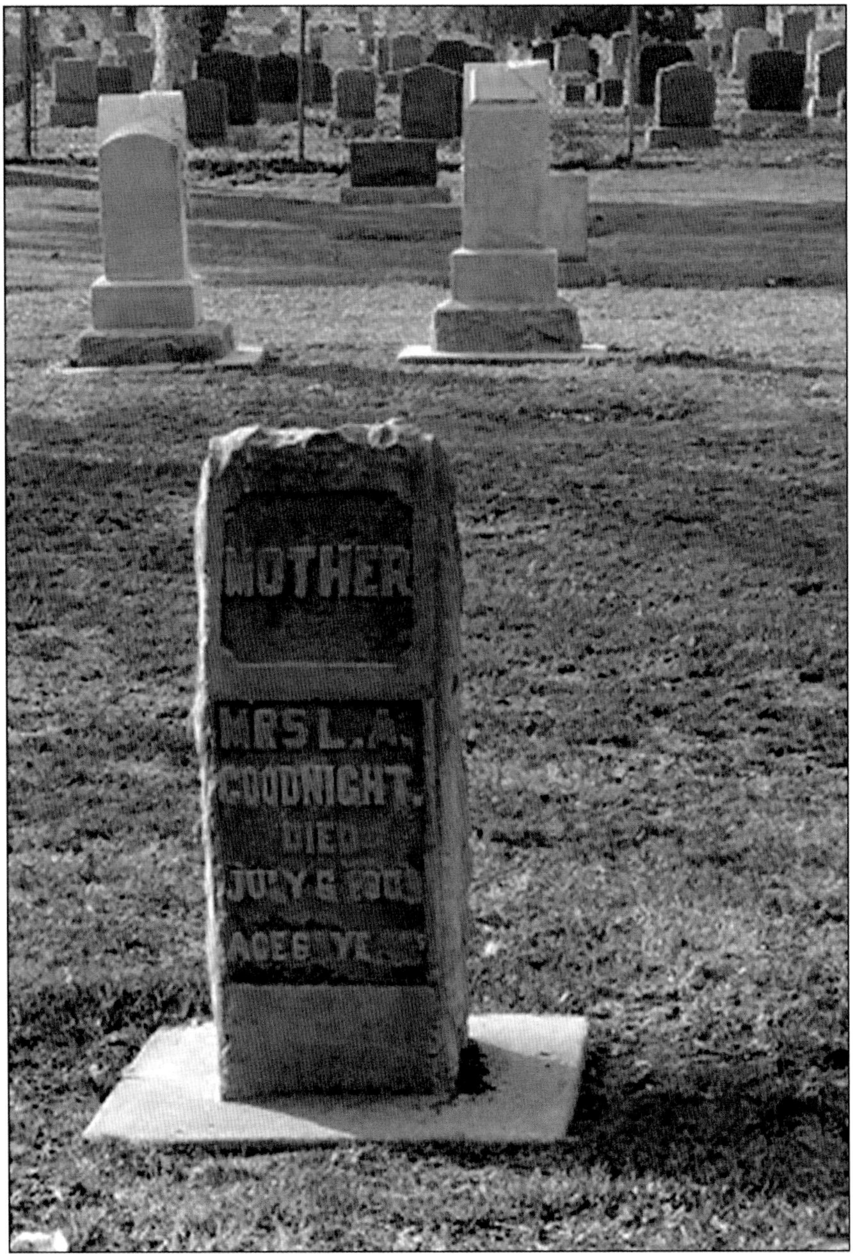

Researching the location of those buried can be somewhat difficult as burial records were not well maintained before 1905. Newspaper archives contain many obituaries about Long Beach residents. Unfortunately, cemetery records often do not exist for these burials. Additionally, information and spellings on headstones sometimes do not match the burial record or newspaper account. Tracing the full names and backgrounds of women who died in early Long Beach is also problematic. Newspaper articles refer to the married women under their husbands' names, as in "Mrs. L.A. Goodnight." Headstones are etched with "mother" or "wife." Women's maiden names can be found in early census records that can be checked first under the husband's name or through marriage records. Historical records can also be found on www.familysearch.org, which is maintained by the Church of Jesus Christ of Latter-day Saints.

Two

Coffins, Caskets, and Burial Rituals

As Long Beach was beginning to grow as a city in the late 1890s, the ways in which people dealt with death changed dramatically. Up until then, most families washed, groomed, dressed, and displayed their dead in their own front parlor and held a wake, or a "watch," to ensure that the departed were really dead and that no harm came to the body before burial.

The body was placed in a six-sided wooden box, a coffin, which comes from the Latin word *cophinus*, for "basket." Coffins were made by family members or local carpenters. A coffin carried on the shoulders to the church graveyard was referred to as a pall, and those who carried it as pallbearers. The term *casket* originated in the 1860s for a coffin with four square sides made to look more like a bed inside, giving the appearance that the dead are sleeping. Graveyards and burial grounds were no longer viewed as stark depositories of remains, but instead as cemeteries, or "sleeping places," where the departed waited for the afterlife.

The Civil War and the death of Pres. Abraham Lincoln changed public opinion about embalming. In the 1850s, Dr. Thomas Holmes was dubbed "the Father of Embalming" for his techniques. Civil War surgeons embalmed the bodies of thousands of fallen soldiers so they could be transported home from the battlefields. Families paid for embalming and shipment of the bodies by train. The professions of embalmer and undertaker (persons willing to "undertake" the tasks of retrieving bodies from trains) flourished as the United States buried tens of thousands of fallen soldiers. Cities like Long Beach soon found these professionals listed in local business directories. Cemeteries, which had few staff, worked closely with these new professionals.

Embalmers came to the homes of the deceased until the early 1900s and then established funeral parlors in their own residences. The directing of funeral preparations became complex and expensive. Embalmers passed along the costs of new paraphernalia to the families of the deceased. The funeral business remained largely a male profession, but employed female attendants to help alleviate concerns.

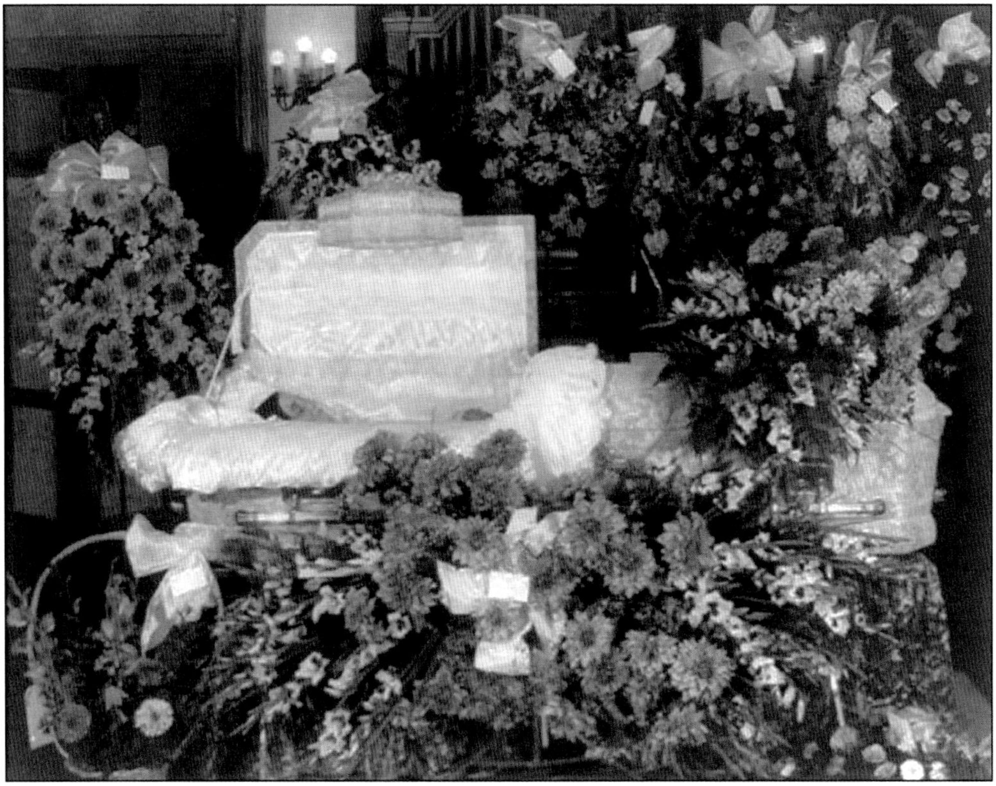

Until the early 1900s, families took care of funeral preparations in their own homes. They would wash, groom, dress, and display their deceased in the front parlor. Coffins were surrounded by flowers to mask the odor of the decomposing body. The 1914 song "I Go to the Garden Alone" popularized the concept that burials should take place in garden-like settings. (LOC.)

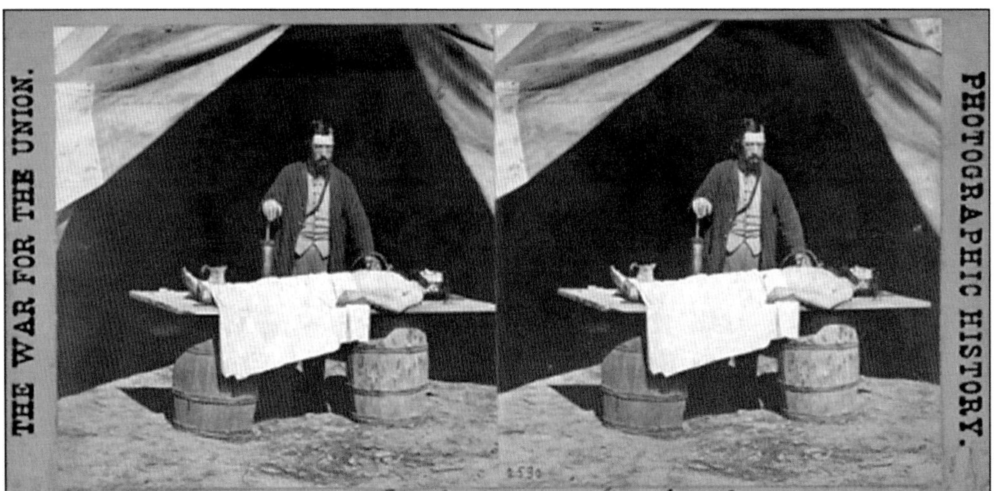

For most burials, there was no need to preserve a body for the short time it would be displayed in a front parlor of a home and no need to embalm. During embalming, bodily fluids are removed and replaced with chemicals such as arsenic, mercury, and formaldehyde. This stereograph depicts Civil War surgeon Dr. Richard Burr preparing a body for shipment home on the trains. (LOC.)

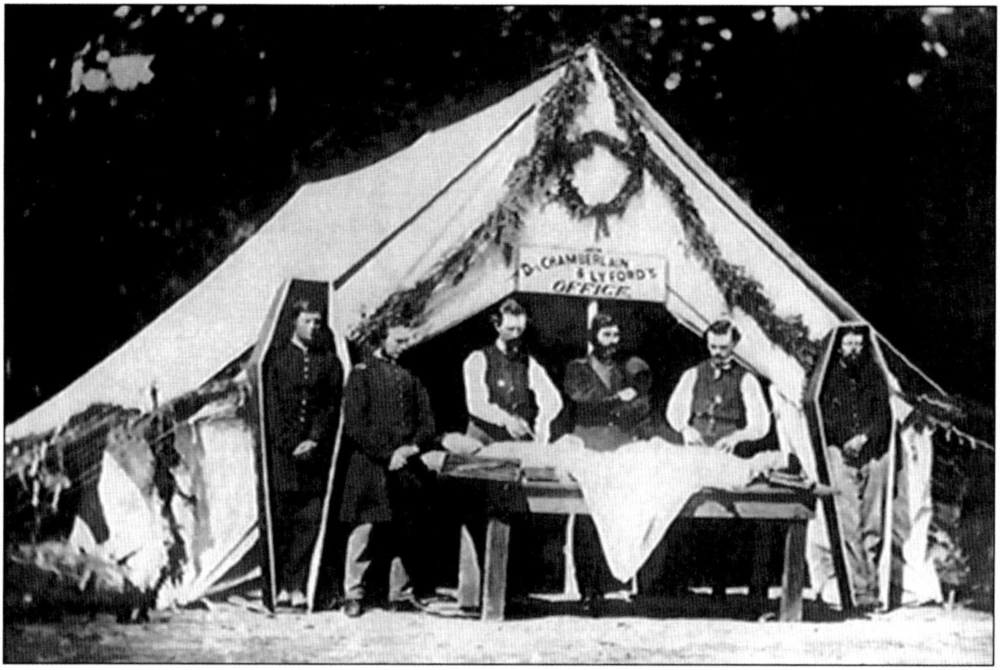

Civil War surgeons Chamberlain and Lyford demonstrate techniques in front of an embalming tent. Families paid for embalming and shipping in wooden coffins. Two embalmed Union soldiers are displayed in coffins. Civilians assumed the job of undertaking the tasks necessary to get the bodies to their families. (LOC.)

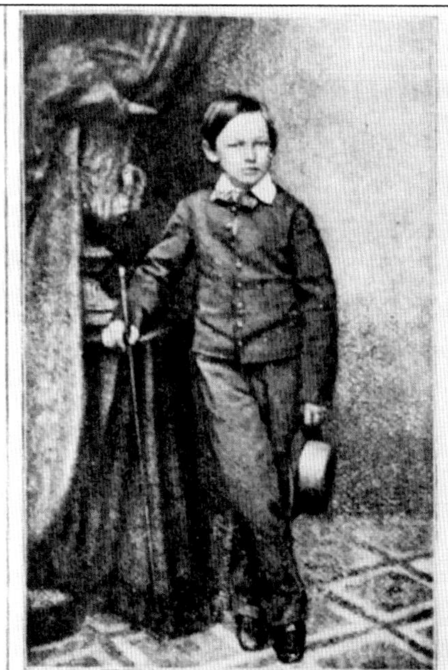

WILLIE LINCOLN, THIRD SON OF PRESIDENT LINCOLN, DIED FEBRUARY 20, 1862, AT THE AGE OF 12.

From a photograph taken by Brady at Washington, shortly before the death of Willie Lincoln.

When President Lincoln's beloved son Willie died, Abraham's wife, Mary Todd Lincoln, could not bear the thought of his death and insisted that he be embalmed by Dr. Thomas Holmes. The embalming technique involved filling the veins with zinc chloride, which resulted in a marble-like appearance. (LOC.)

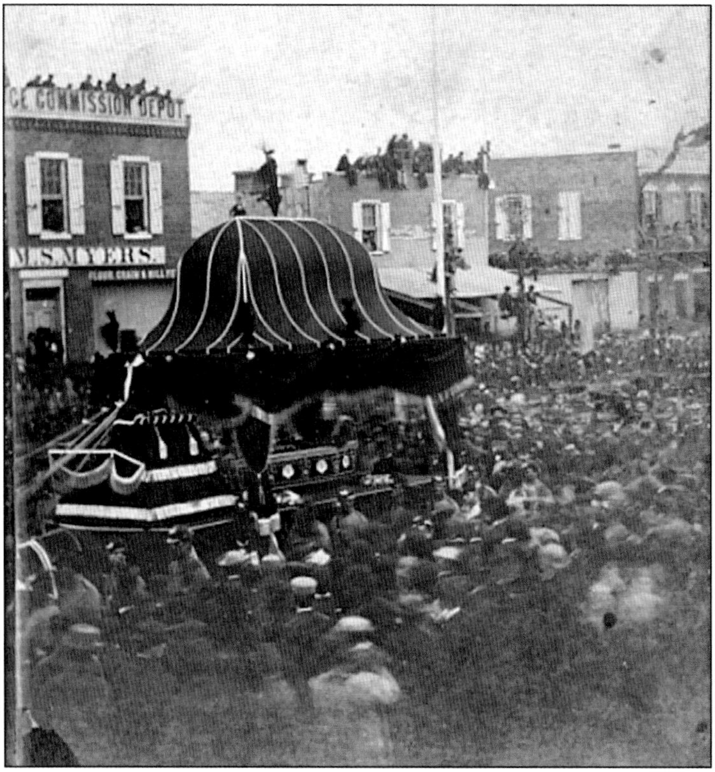

The assassinated President Lincoln was embalmed and his remains were taken on a 1,600-mile, 400-city train procession and then to a funeral car, as shown in this 1865 photograph. Embalmers accompanied the body in case additional embalming was needed. Lincoln's coffin was opened for public viewing and memorial services. The public was able to see firsthand the effects of embalming. (LOC.)

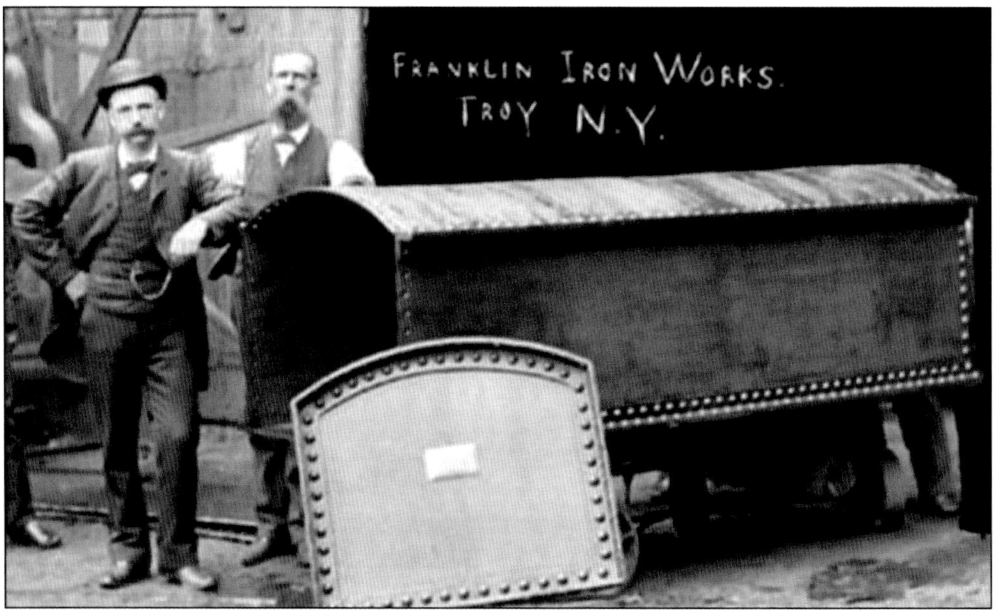

Coffins were mass produced in the Civil War to handle the volume of dead soldiers. Glass faceplates were installed in coffins to allow viewing. Iron caskets were first produced in 1850, and in 1871, the first steel casket was produced from a metal cook stove. Metal caskets deterred grave robbers. Pres. Ulysses Grant's iron casket is pictured here. (LOC.)

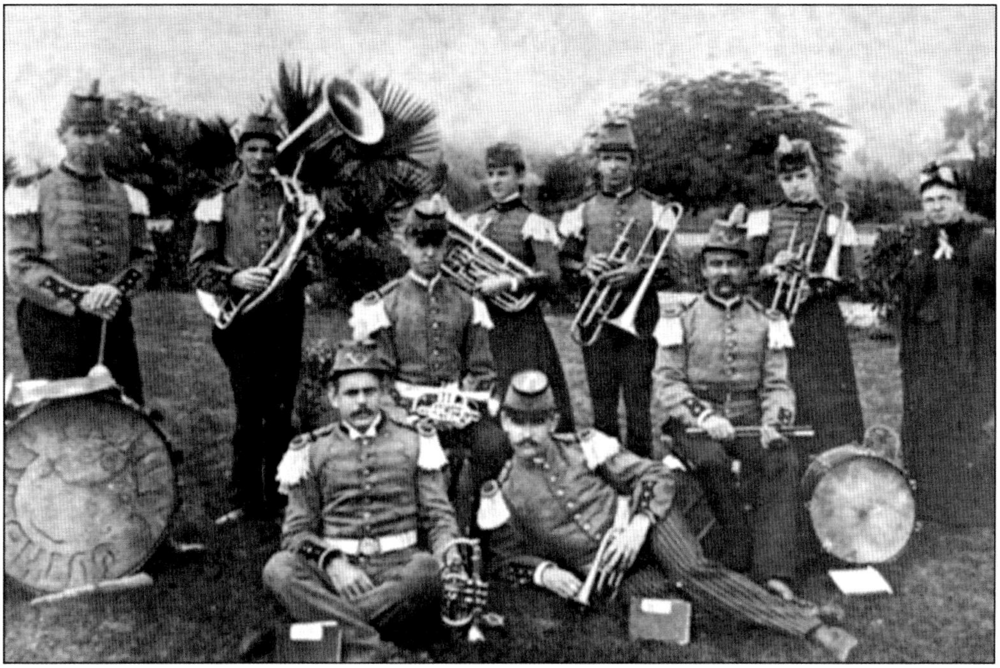

The design of coffins changed as more were transported by train. They were required to be lined with metal, sealed, and equipped with four handles. Local public health officers signed permits for transport and burial. Long Beach is one of three California cities to have a public health department and public health officer. Civil War surgeon Dr. William Lawrence Cuthbert served as public health officer in 1898. Cuthbert (pictured at left near the large drum) and his family formed the Cuthbert Family Band, playing locally. Cuthbert became the city's health officer in 1898. Born in 1831, he died in 1922 and is buried in the Long Beach Municipal Cemetery. (Below, City of Long Beach Public Works.)

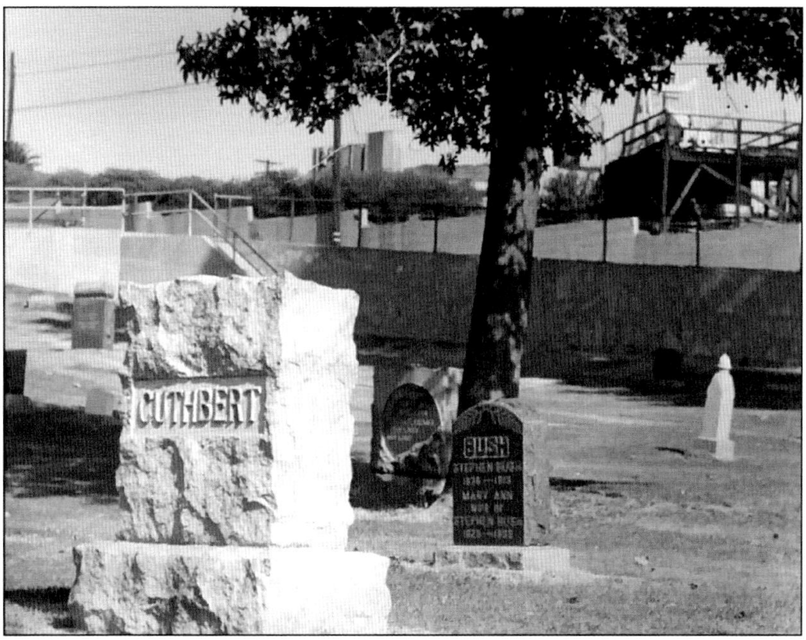

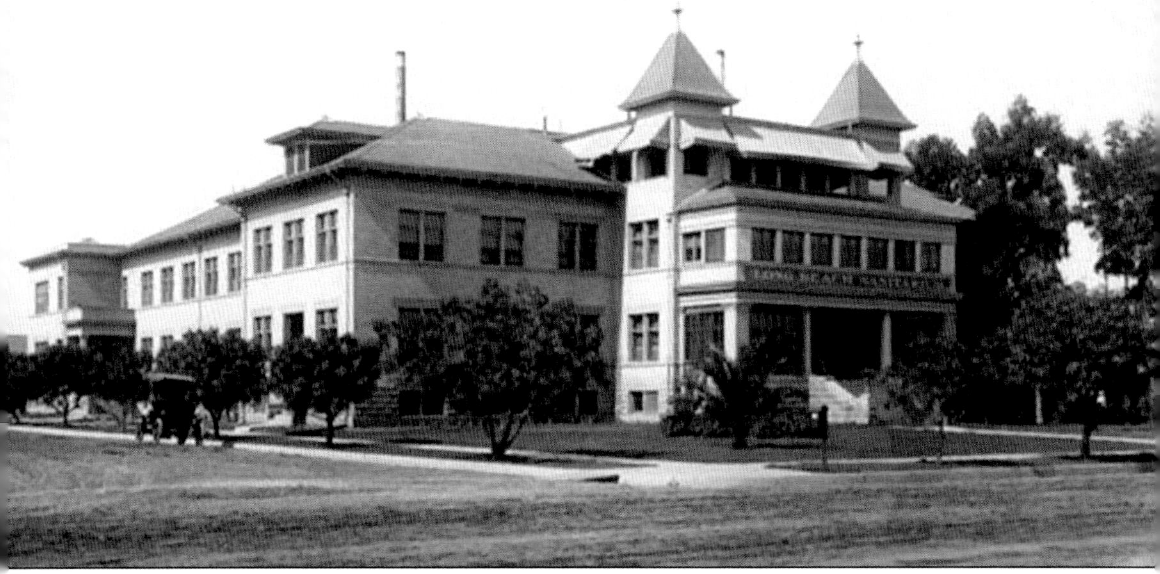

Harriman Jones came to Long Beach in 1903 and became its public health officer. Jones made headlines in 1908 when he ordered the Long Beach school board to set aside their personal feelings, follow the law, and require child vaccination. He served on a number of commissions, including the Long Beach Pure Food Commission. Jones also advocated for a municipal nurse to take care of schoolchildren and for the extension of sewers throughout the city. He was responsible for establishing several key medical organizations, including the Long Beach Sanitarium pictured here (now St. Mary Medical Center at Tenth Street and Linden Avenue), Seaside Hospital, and the Harriman Jones Clinic, located at Broadway and Cherry. The clinic was designated a historical site in 1989. Jones died in 1956 and is buried in Forest Lawn Glendale.

In 1907, state health officers asked Dr. W. Harriman Jones (pictured) to solve the mystery about a burial permit that had not been issued for George Layton, who died in May. Jones checked his records and contacted local undertakers Allen Walker and Eli Brown. They admitted handling a "William Layton" the past December, reporting that Layton "dropped dead at Sixteenth and American" waiting for a car to the county hospital. The undertakers buried Layton in the potter's field in the north end of the Municipal Cemetery. Jones issued many permits to Walker and Brown (as shown below), but none could be found for Layton. Walker and Brown dissolved their undertaking business later in 1907.

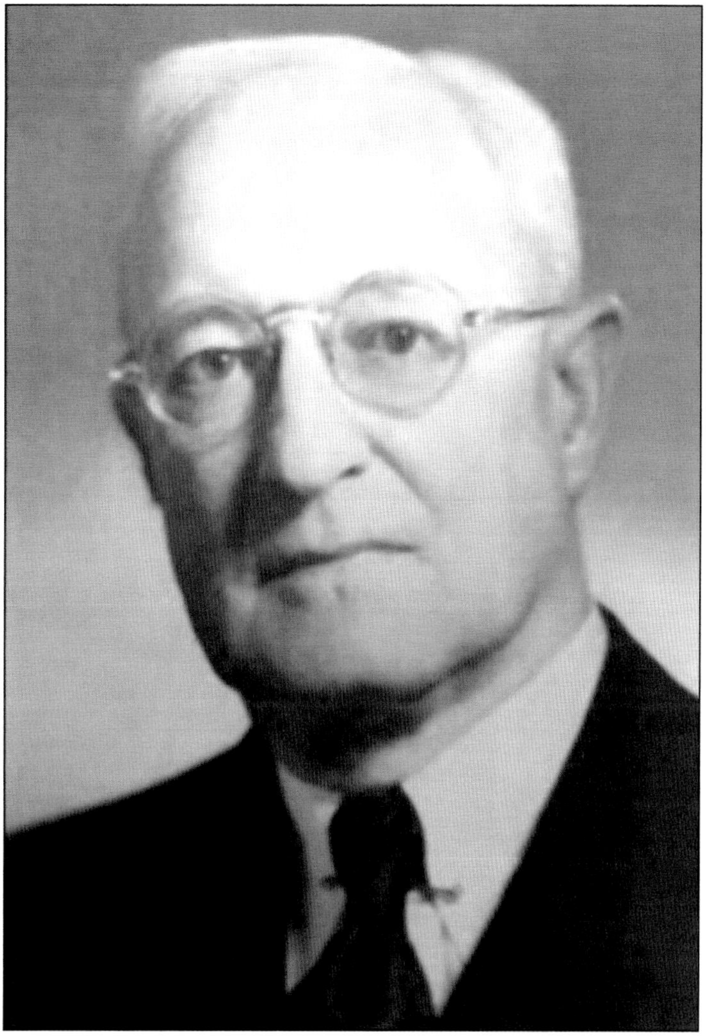

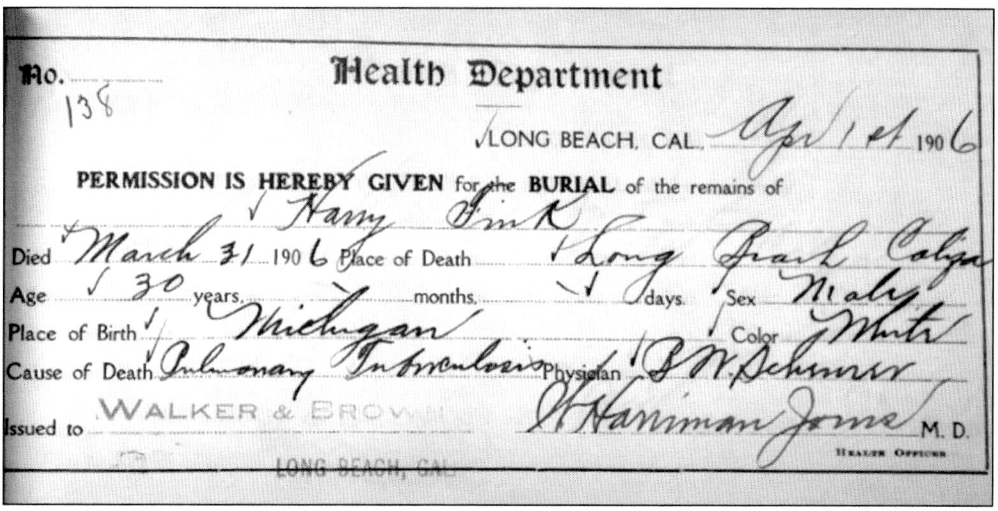

No. 138

Health Department

LONG BEACH, CAL., Apr 1st 1906

PERMISSION IS HEREBY GIVEN for the **BURIAL** of the remains of Harry Fink

Died March 31 1906 Place of Death Long Beach Calif

Age 30 years, 7 months, days. Sex Male

Place of Birth Michigan Color White

Cause of Death Pulmonary Tuberculosis Physician

Issued to WALKER & BROWN LONG BEACH, CAL. W. Harriman Jones M. D.

HEALTH OFFICER

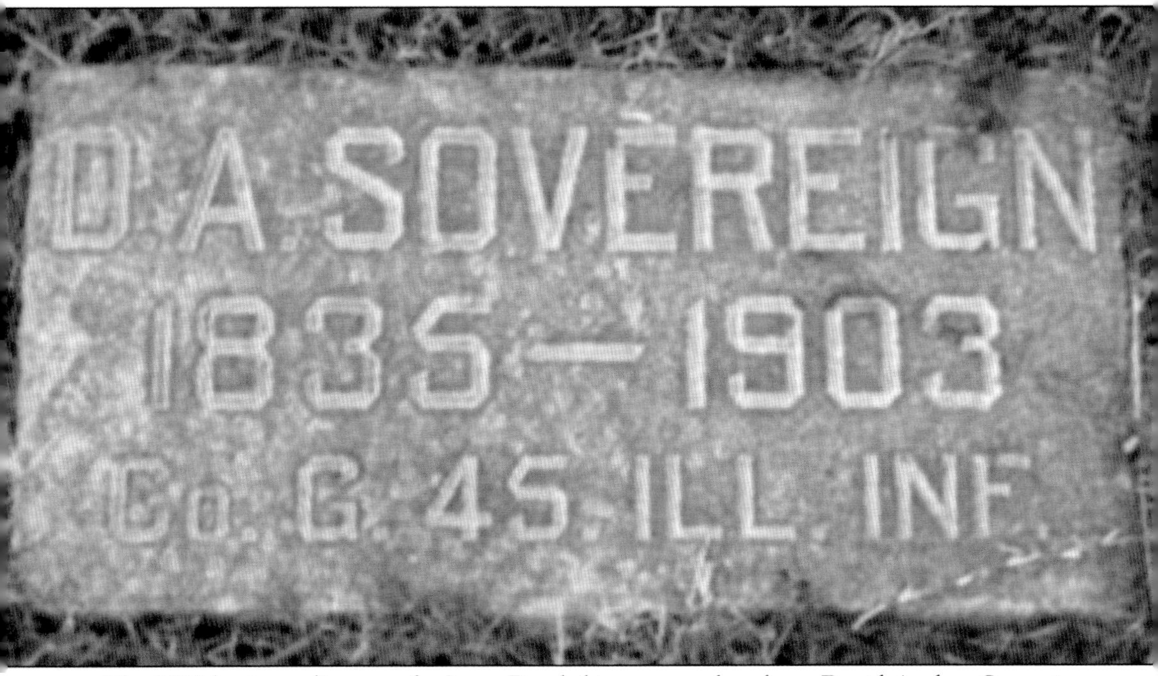

The 1899 business directory for Long Beach lists two undertakers: David Andrus Sovereign, located at 123 West First Street, and W.P. Wilson, located on Second Street between Pine and Pacific Avenues. Sovereign started his undertaking establishment in 1899 with wife Mary, Allan and Anna Walker, and G. Sandford. He served as superintendent of the Long Beach Signal Hill Cemetery (which became the Municipal Cemetery), earning one dollar per grave until 1901. A native of Canada, he enlisted in the Civil War as a private with Company G, 45th Regiment Illinois Infantry. Sovereign was very active in the local Grand Army of the Republic veterans' group. He died in 1903 after a three-month illness and is buried in the Sunnyside Cemetery, adjacent to the city cemetery. His wife, Mary, died in 1917 and is buried with him.

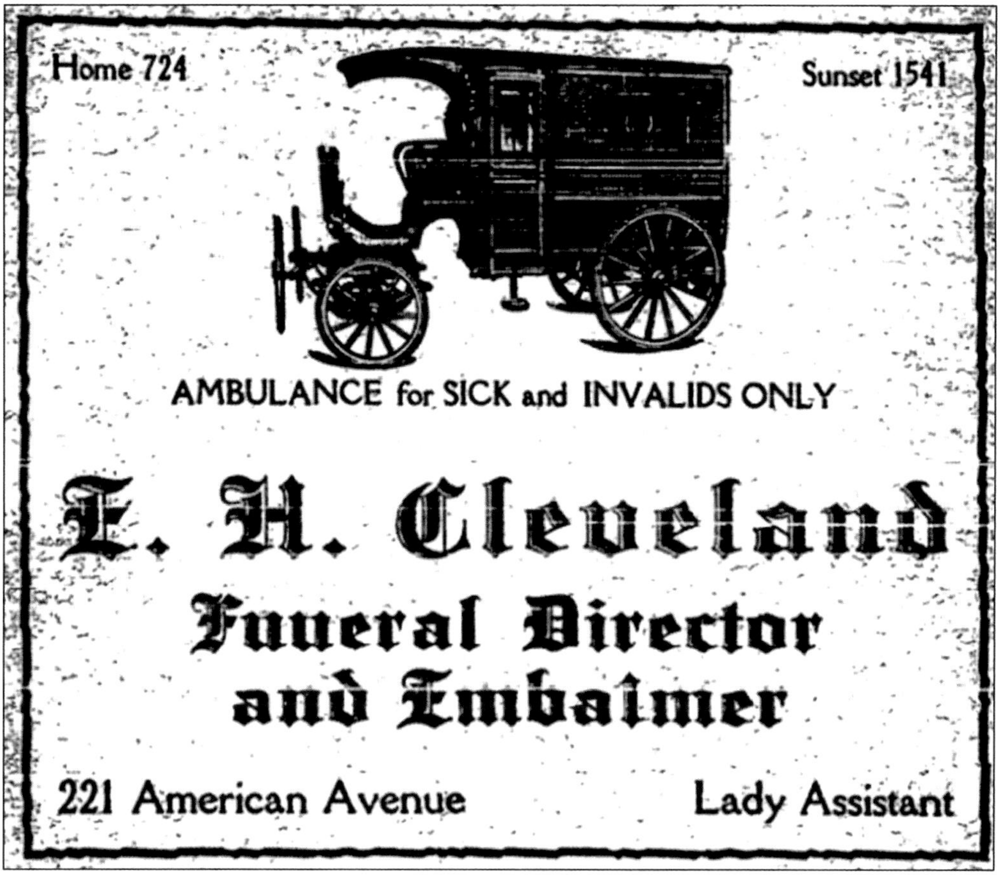

A need developed for funeral professionals as the handling of the dead became more detailed and commercial. Undertakers and embalmers soon became funeral directors. They conducted funeral services in funeral parlors or funeral homes and offered a variety of services. The first Funeral Directors Association was formed in 1881. By 1921, there were an estimated 23,000 funeral directors in the United States. They were either licensed embalmers or employed those who were. They also provided ambulance services to those who needed transport to local hospitals. Most were active members of the business community in their towns, as shown in these clippings from Long Beach directories.

Orelli, Abraham T., vice pres. Orelli-McFadyen Co., r. 115 E. Third.
Orelli, Augustine J., pres. Orelli-McFadyen Co., r. 115 E. Third.
Orelli, Mary, Miss, r. 115 E. Third.
Orelli-McFadyen Co., A. J. Orelli, pres.; A. T. Orelli, vice-pres.; Edgar McFadyen, sec., undertakers, 115 E. Third and livery 127 W. First.
Orelli, Rose, Miss, r. 115 E. Third.

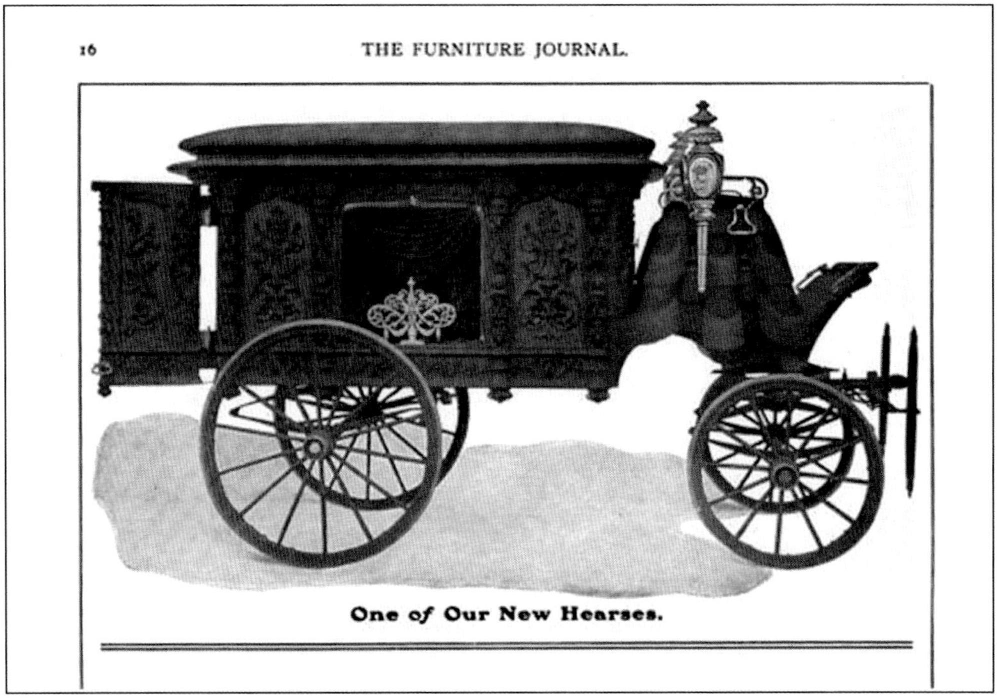

Early urbanization meant longer distances to a local cemetery. Embalmers, who often owned livery stables, offered horse-drawn wagons for the transport of the infirm with ambulances and the dead with hearses. Cities and towns had to create accessible roads from the urban areas to the rural cemeteries. The early Long Beach cemetery was located several miles from the city on a steep slope. As funerals became more elaborate, so did the vehicles that transported bodies, as shown in the advertisement above from a 1904 *Furniture Journal* and the photograph below of a 1910 Lincoln Ford hearse. (Below, LOC.)

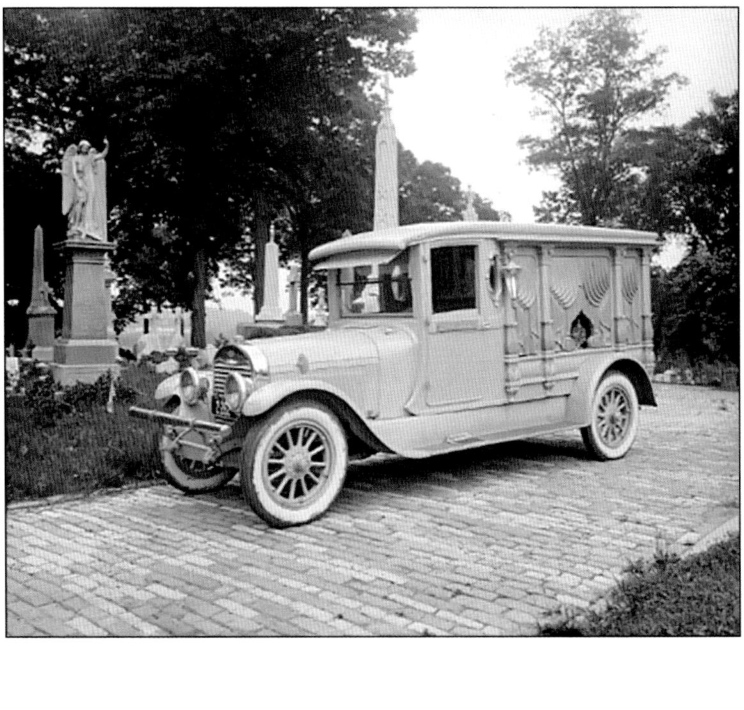

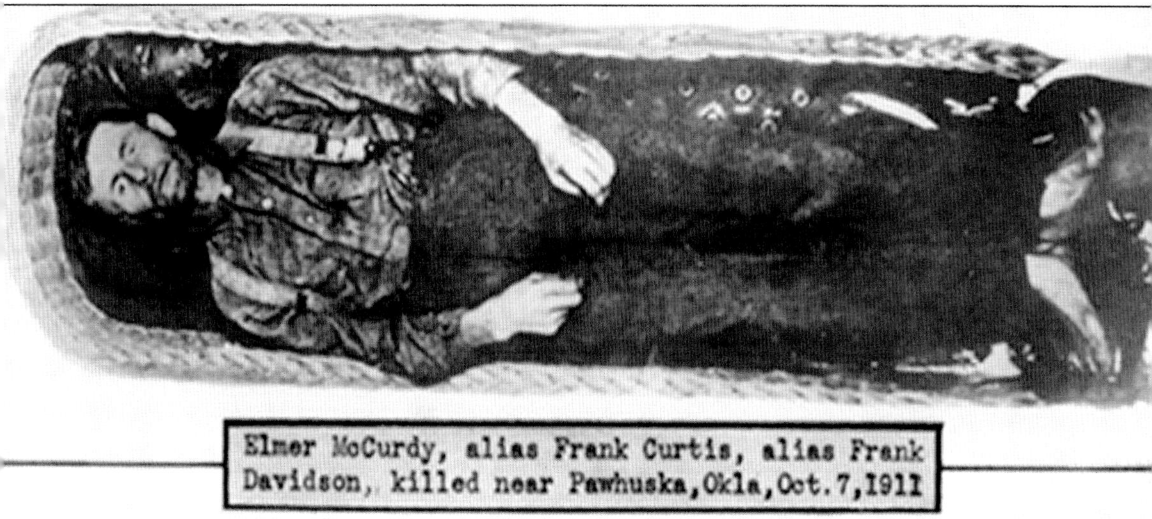

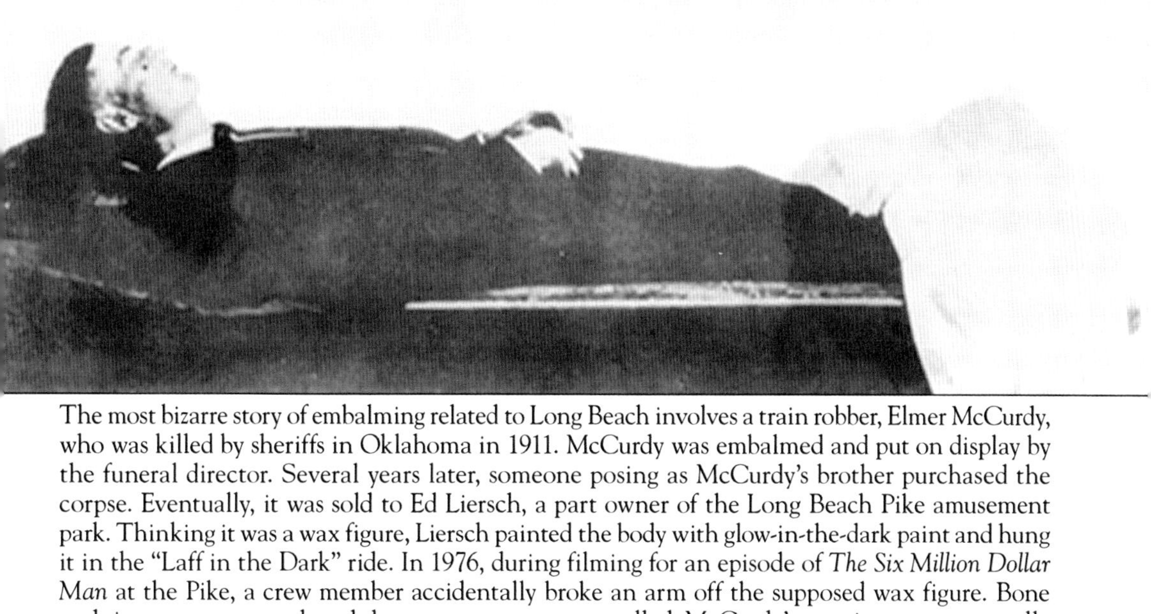

The most bizarre story of embalming related to Long Beach involves a train robber, Elmer McCurdy, who was killed by sheriffs in Oklahoma in 1911. McCurdy was embalmed and put on display by the funeral director. Several years later, someone posing as McCurdy's brother purchased the corpse. Eventually, it was sold to Ed Liersch, a part owner of the Long Beach Pike amusement park. Thinking it was a wax figure, Liersch painted the body with glow-in-the-dark paint and hung it in the "Laff in the Dark" ride. In 1976, during filming for an episode of *The Six Million Dollar Man* at the Pike, a crew member accidentally broke an arm off the supposed wax figure. Bone and tissue were exposed, and the county coroner was called. McCurdy's remains were eventually buried in Oklahoma in 1977. (Oklahoma Museum.)

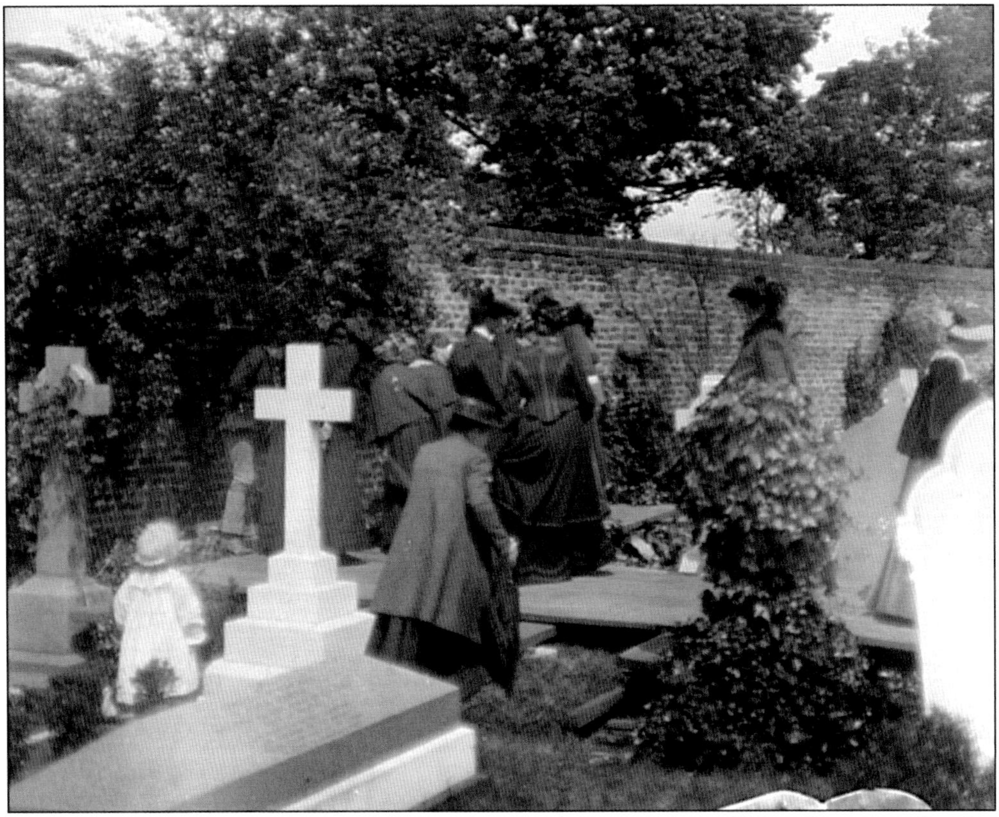

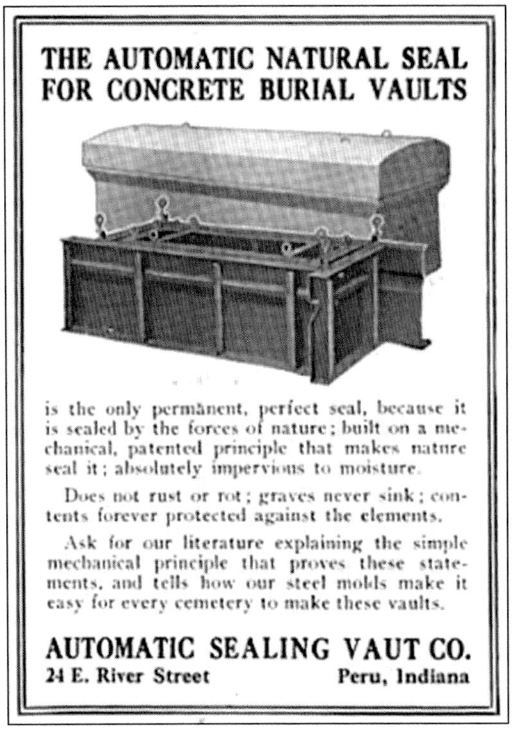

The Victorian-era Beautification of Death movement brought dramatic changes in funerals and burial places. Elaborate motifs on headstones with the words "not dead but sleeping" replaced the stark etchings of skull and crossbones. Mourning clothes became stylish, as shown in the 1900 photograph above. Post-mortem daguerreotypes were displayed at the viewing. Lockets of hair of the deceased were turned into mourning jewelry. Burial vaults of metal and concrete were marketed in the late 1800s as a way to keep the grave from collapsing as well as keeping water, germs, and rats out of the coffin. The vault advertisement at left is from a 1918 *Park and Cemetery* magazine. (Above, LOC.)

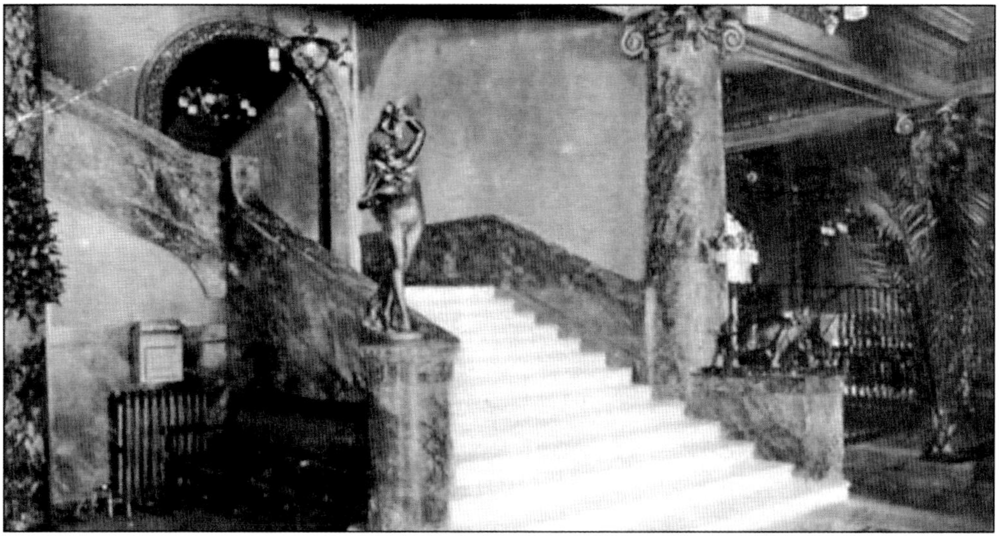

The elegant Long Beach Hotel Virginia was the site of a banquet for the Funeral Directors Association of Southern California in 1908. Over 100 men and their dates attended the lively dinner and dance. Hotel Virginia replaced Hotel Bixby, which collapsed in 1906, killing 11 workers and injuring many others.

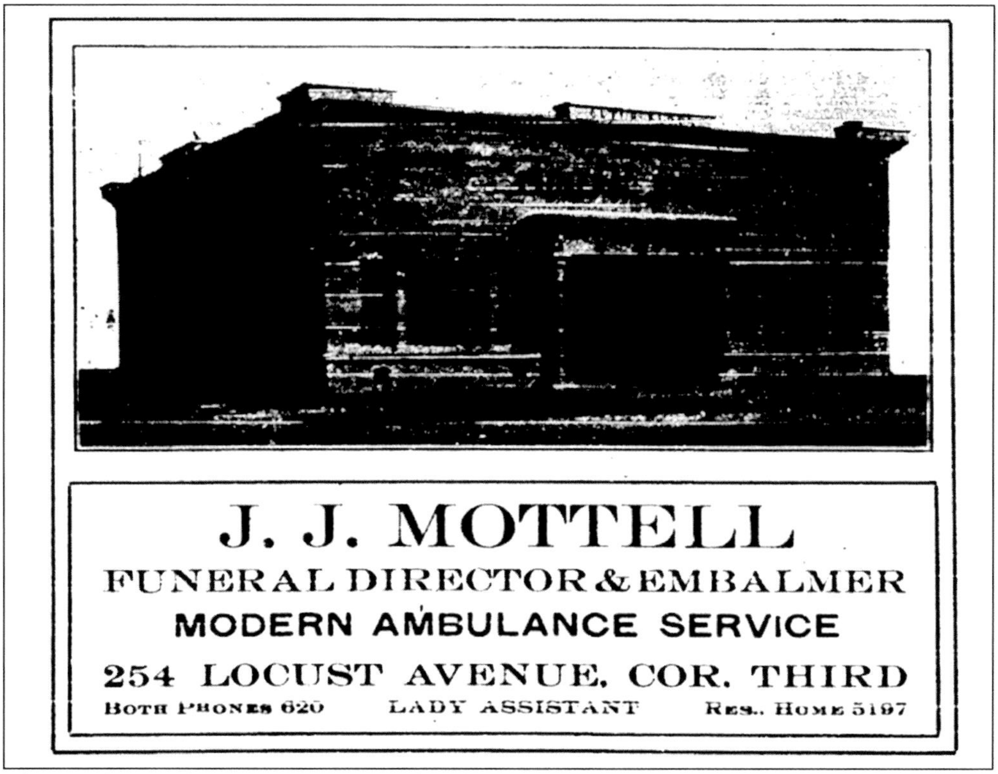

The population of Long Beach grew, and so did the funeral businesses. In the early 1900s, Joseph Jason "Uncle Joe" Mottell moved from Oakland, where he had served as funeral director with Brown Brothers. Mottell worked with Fred Pierce. Both made several real estate investments in Long Beach through their Seaside Development Company.

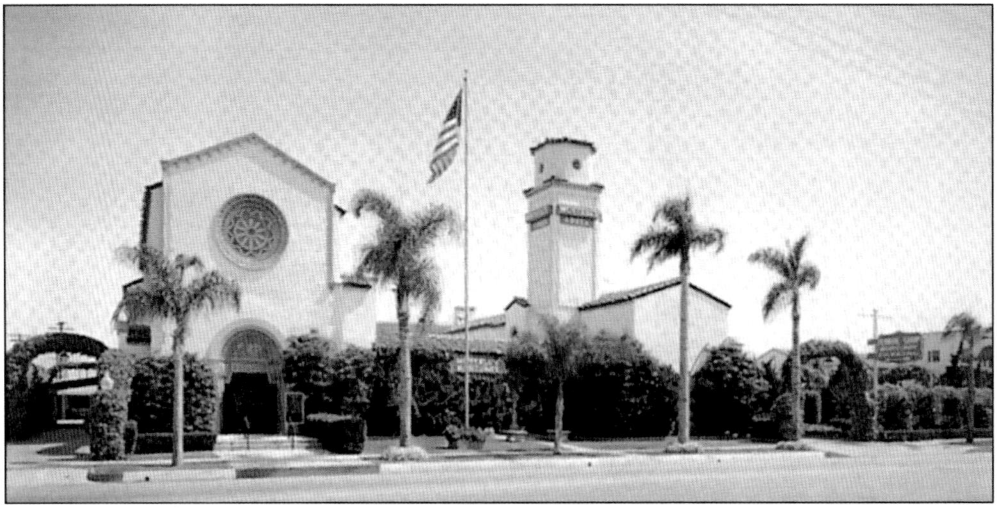

Mottell bought out Pierce and established J.J. Mottell Mortuary at Third Street and Alamitos Avenue. Known for its Spanish-style, park-like gardens and elegant chapel, Mottell's was used for funerals and weddings. Radio station KJLH-FM broadcast from the Mottell Mortuary. Mottell died in 1944 and is buried at Forest Lawn Long Beach.

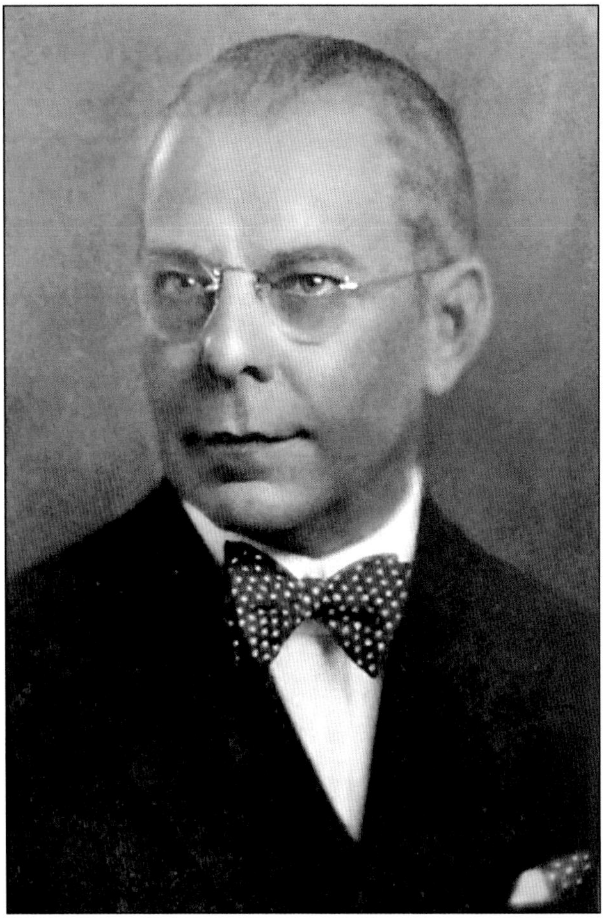

Uncle Joe Mottell held his birthday party for 30 years at the Long Beach Day Nursery to help raise funds. Over the years, Mottell merged with other funeral operators, such as Lon Peek. Today, the Mottell name has been merged with the Luyben Family-Dilday-Mottell Mortuary.

Three

The Long Beach Signal Hill Cemetery

After William Willmore relinquished his rights to the Willmore City/American Colony, the land was promptly renamed after its biggest asset: its eight-mile-long beach. The name suggested by Belle Lowe, the wife of local businessman William Lowe, won over "Crescent City," which was suggested by local businessmen.

The original American Colony map included a business sector near the oceanfront, parks, land for a college, residential lots, and farm lots to the north. The Long Beach Cemetery Company incorporated on March 18, 1893, and later became the Long Beach Cemetery Corporation. In 1893, D.P. Thayer, president of the Long Beach Cemetery Company and superintendent of the Long Beach Water Company, filed a plot map detailing the location of the Signal Hill Cemetery as the "East 5 acres of Farm Lot 68 of the American Colony Tract," which is three miles northeast of the business area.

The cemetery was named for its location on a slope of Signal Hill, which was the highest point adjacent to Long Beach. Early native settlers utilized the 365-foot-elevation to signal others, and so the Spanish named it Loma Sental. Several mansions were built atop the hill because of the view. Japanese farmers grew vegetables and collected garbage from the area to feed to their hogs. Signal Hill was included in the American Colony tract map but was not part of the newly incorporated city of Long Beach.

The "Signal Hill Cemetery" was deeded to the City of Long Beach in 1901 by the Long Beach Cemetery Corporation. It is not clear who operated the cemetery before it was given to the city or who exactly is buried there. The earliest burial is marked by a headstone with the date 1878.

In 1936, fire destroyed many of the burial records. Some of the founders of Long Beach are buried there, and many others are buried steps away in the adjacent Sunnyside Cemetery.

Today, Signal Hill Cemetery is known as the Municipal Cemetery of Long Beach and is operated by the Department of Parks, Recreation and Marine.

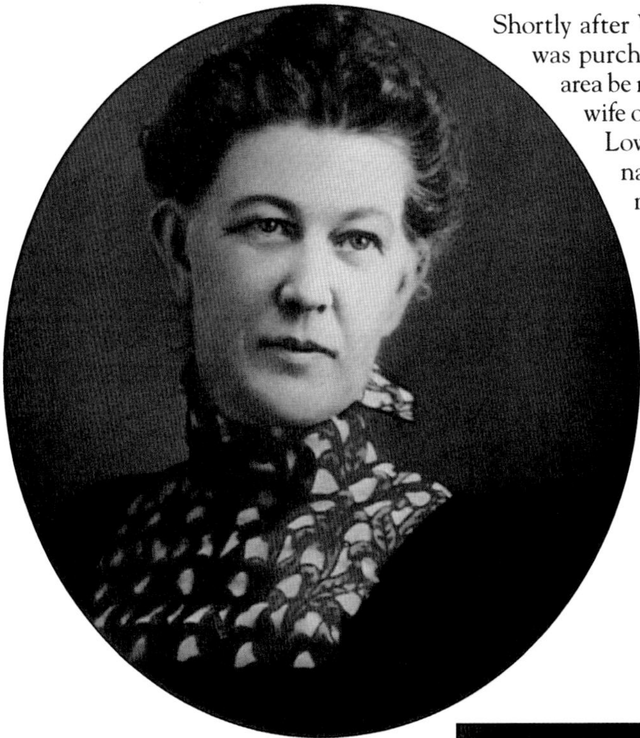

Shortly after Willmore City/American Colony was purchased, businessmen suggested the area be renamed Crescent City. Belle Lowe, wife of local general store owner William Lowe, argued the area needed to be named for its greatest asset, the eight-mile beach. Her suggestion won. William was later named the first postmaster of Long Beach.

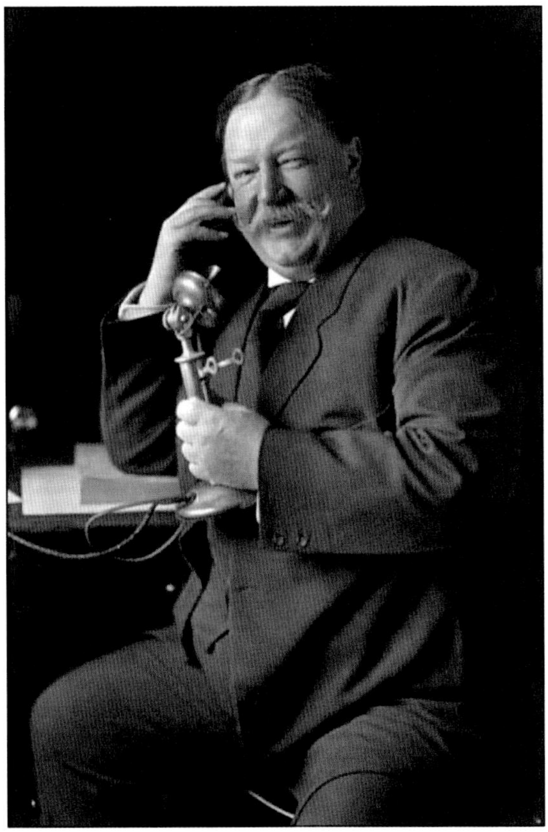

Long Beach's claim of population growth caught the attention of the federal government. US Treasury special agent E.M. Van Zant came to verify that census figures had not been "padded." Van Zant confirmed that the city grew from 2,252 in 1900 to 17,809 by 1910. In 1909, President Taft (pictured) visited Long Beach and publicly commended the rapid growth at a luncheon held at the Hotel Virginia. (LOC.)

Cemetary

Long Beach Cemetary—2 miles north of Long Beach, west of Signal Hill, near Terminal Railroad.
Under control of City Trustees.

The July 13, 1898, *Los Angeles Times* article "A Town Cemetery," announced that Long Beach would have a cemetery. The land was described as "East 5 acres of Farm Lot 68 of the American Colony Tract." It was quitclaimed by the Long Beach Cemetery Association along with $101 in outstanding accounts. The location was listed in the 1899 city directory.

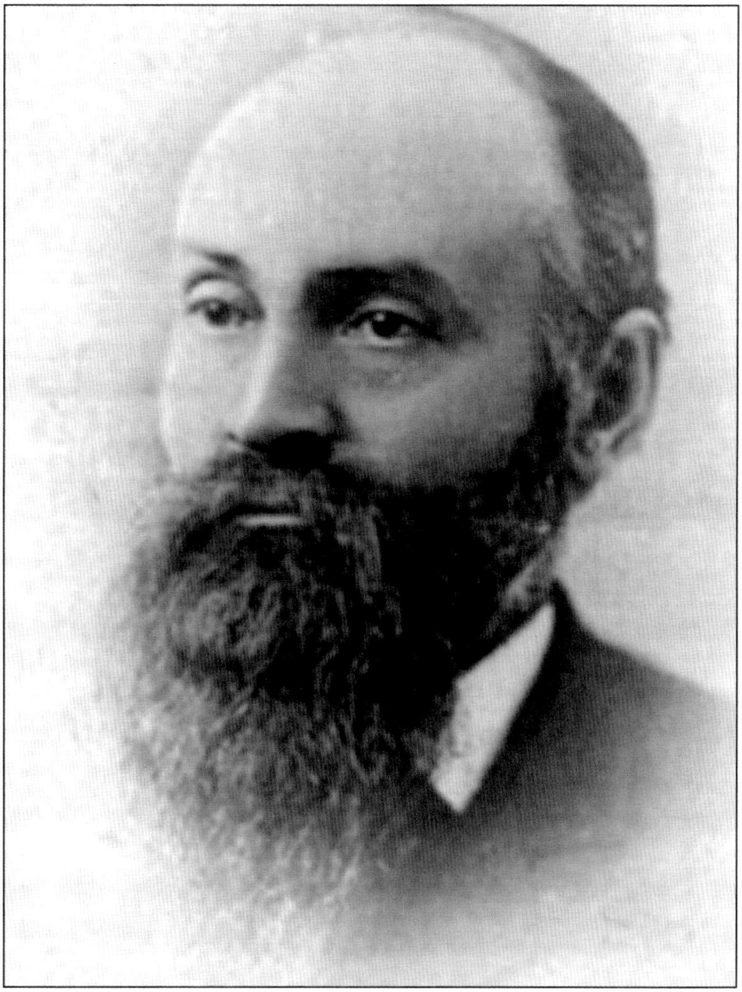

City trustees pledged that a 1,300-foot water pipeline would be connected by the Bouton Water Company, using an artesian spring immediately north of the cemetery property. Trustees gave Civil War general Edward Bouton (pictured) a franchise to provide water in exchange for three percent of gross receipts and free water for the city park and firefighting purposes.

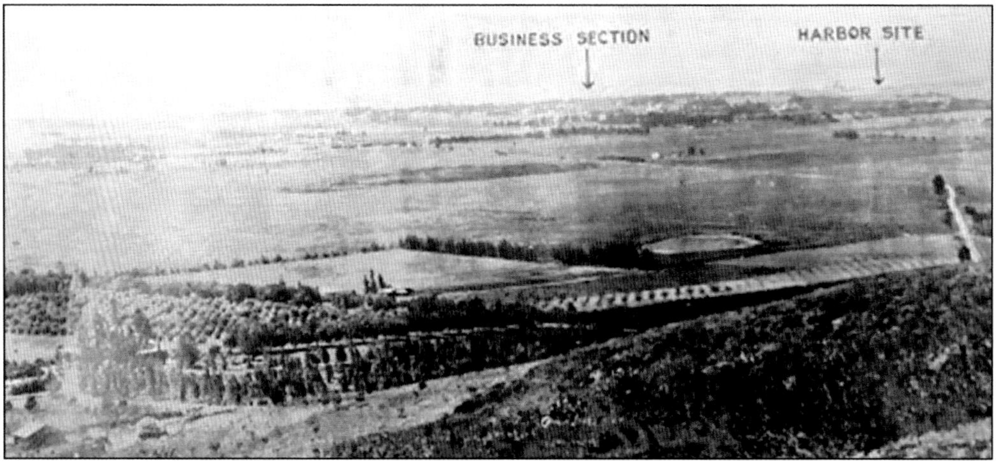

The trustees heatedly debated the use of public funds for improvements or to locate a city cemetery elsewhere. Officials worried that the hilly land flooded during rains. Gravel paths with curbing were laid. The road leading to the cemetery was lined with straw and a fence installed to keep out "roving animals." This photograph shows an early view of Long Beach from a sloping Signal Hill.

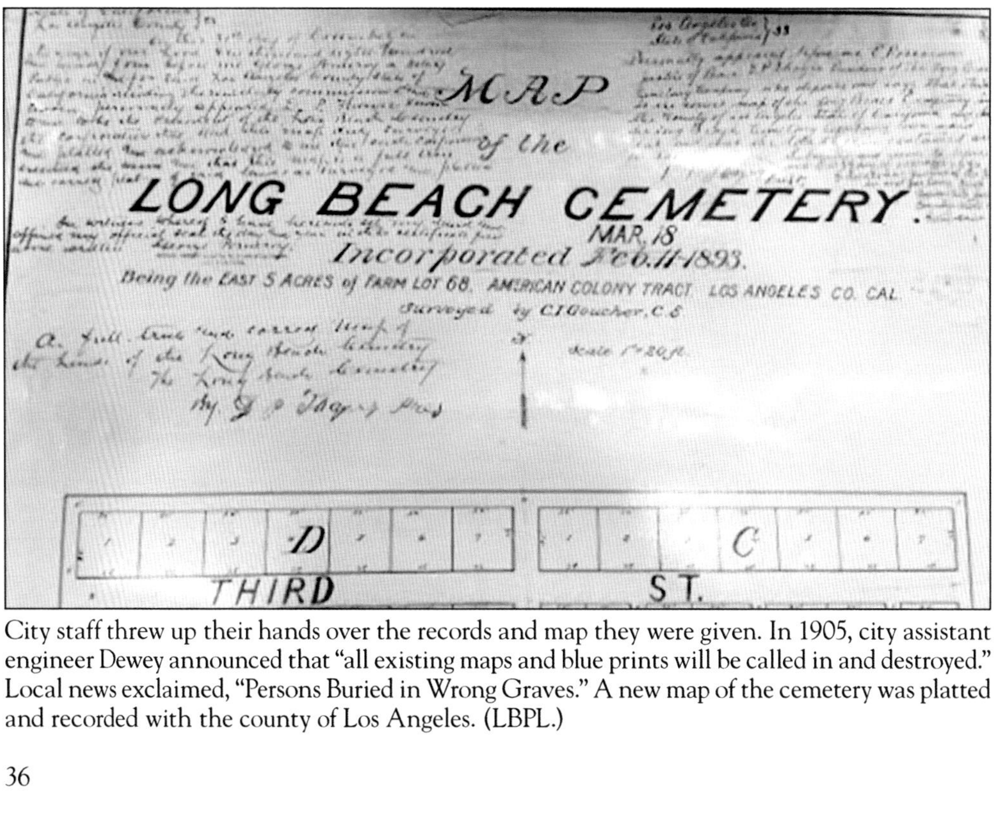

City staff threw up their hands over the records and map they were given. In 1905, city assistant engineer Dewey announced that "all existing maps and blue prints will be called in and destroyed." Local news exclaimed, "Persons Buried in Wrong Graves." A new map of the cemetery was platted and recorded with the county of Los Angeles. (LBPL.)

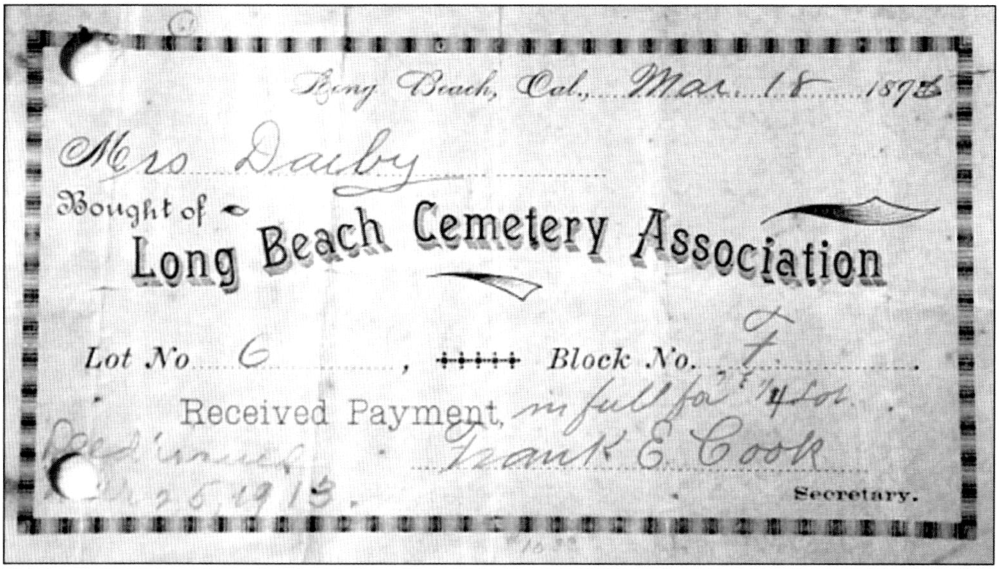
Long Beach, Cal., Mar. 18 189

Mrs Darby

Bought of

Long Beach Cemetery Association

Lot No 6, Block No. 7

Received Payment, in full for 1/4 lot.

Frank E. Cook

Secretary.

Cemeteries were not required to record burials until 1905. A fire in 1936 destroyed much of the city records. Some handwritten receipts for burials and other correspondence remain in six boxes. One letter is from a grieving father during the Great Depression promising to pay the $5 "open and close" gravesite fee once he found work. Records do not indicate whether his infant was ever buried. (City of Long Beach Public Works.)

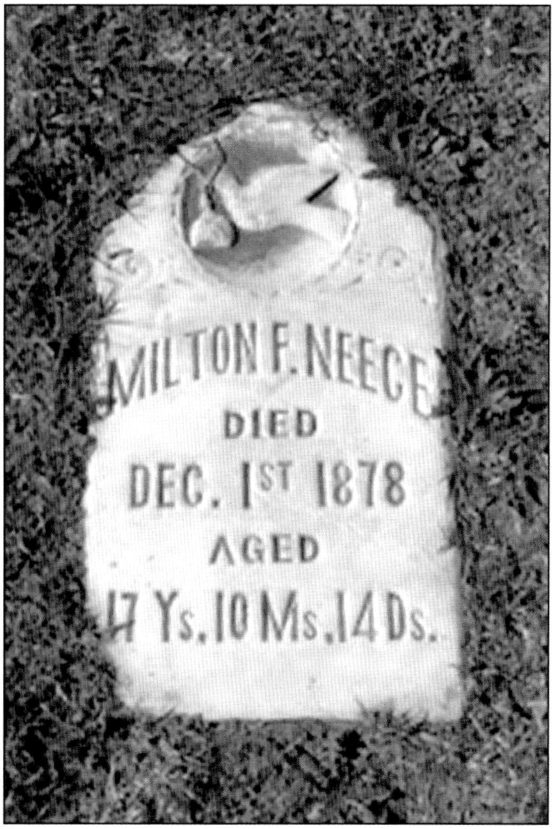

The headstone marked with the earliest burial in the Municipal Cemetery is 17-year-old Milton Neece, son of Adam M. and Amanda O. Neece, who died in 1878. Milton is buried next to his mother, who died in 1903. Amanda Neece's headstone is inscribed, "She did what she could." Adam was elected judge in Compton in 1892 and served as one of Long Beach's first marshals in 1905.

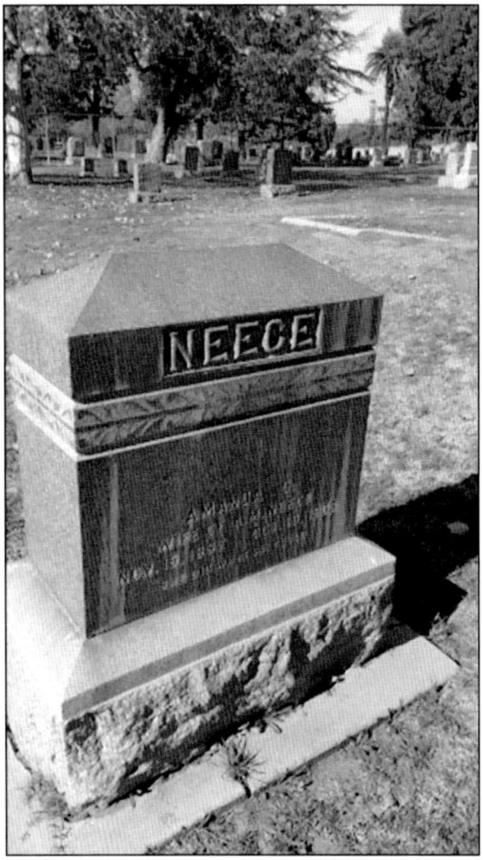

Adam Neece remarried Alma K., who quickly sued her stepsons George and Thomas in 1905 for $50,000, claiming they enticed Adam to stay away from their house shortly after marriage. Adam married again at age 74 to Mary J. Patterson, who is buried in the Long Beach Cemetery with Mabel Nixon and Karl Morgan.

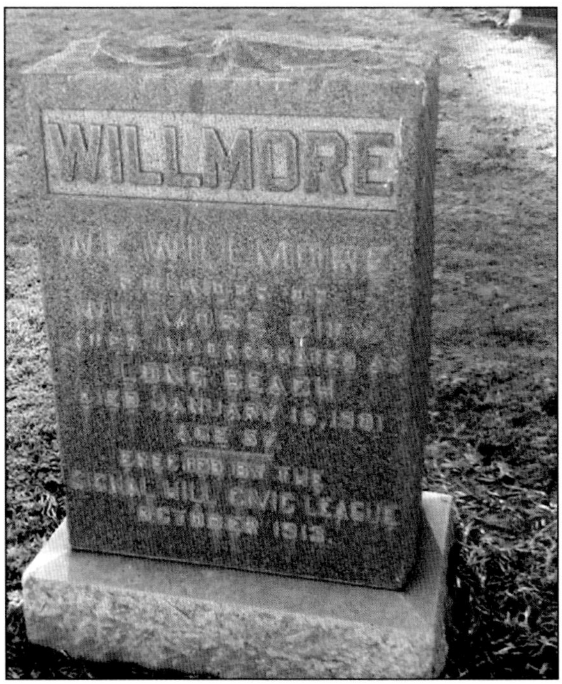

William E. Willmore left the American Colony in 1884 and tried to develop land in Texas. That venture also failed. He returned to Long Beach and died in the county "poor house" in 1901. His grave in the Municipal Cemetery remained unmarked until a group of women of the Signal Hill Civic Alliance raised funds in 1912 for this headstone.

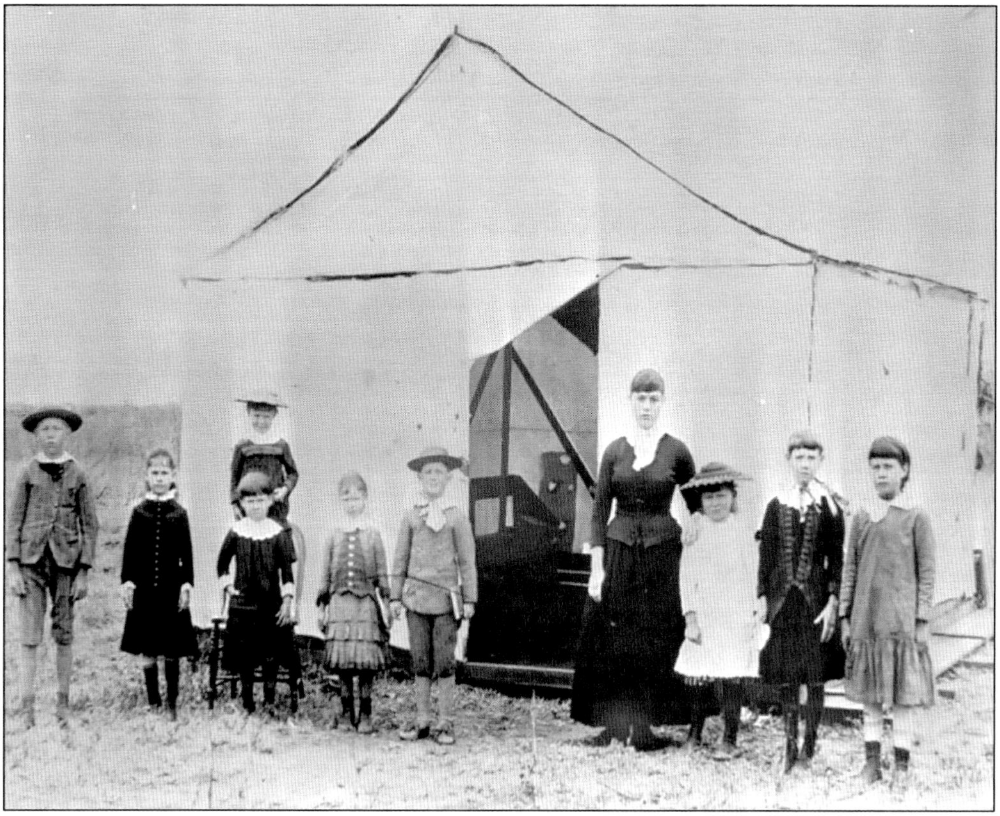

Long Beach founders strongly supported public education. In 1885, seventeen-year-old Grace Eugenia Bush was hired as the first teacher. She is pictured in front of the school tent with her students at Sixth Street and Pine Avenue. Bush came to Long Beach with her family, who were related to the city's first public health officer, Dr. William Cuthbert.

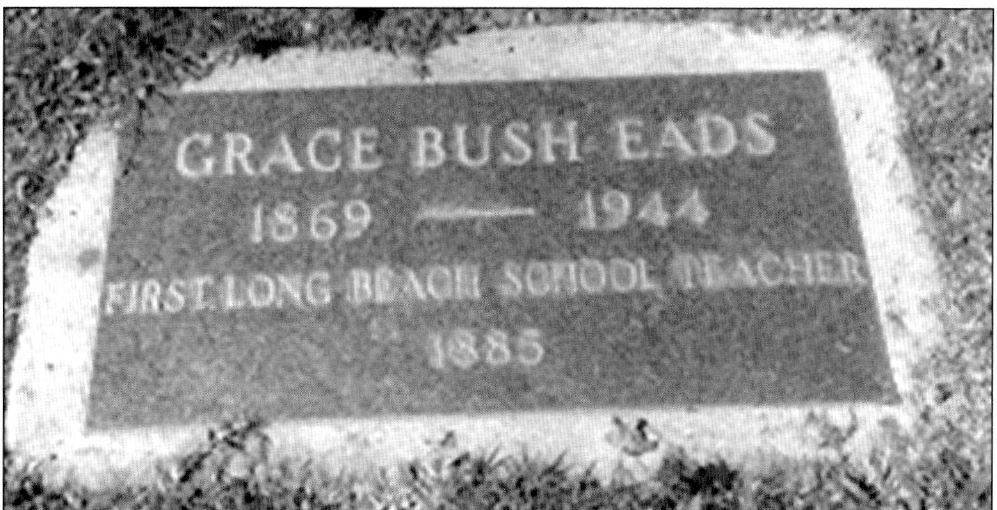

Grace Bush was paid $25 a month to teach. Her father, Stephen Bush, helped establish the horse car line that helped connect early Long Beach to the railroad. Grace married Jefferson Eads and lived in Culver City at the time of her death in 1944. She is buried near her family.

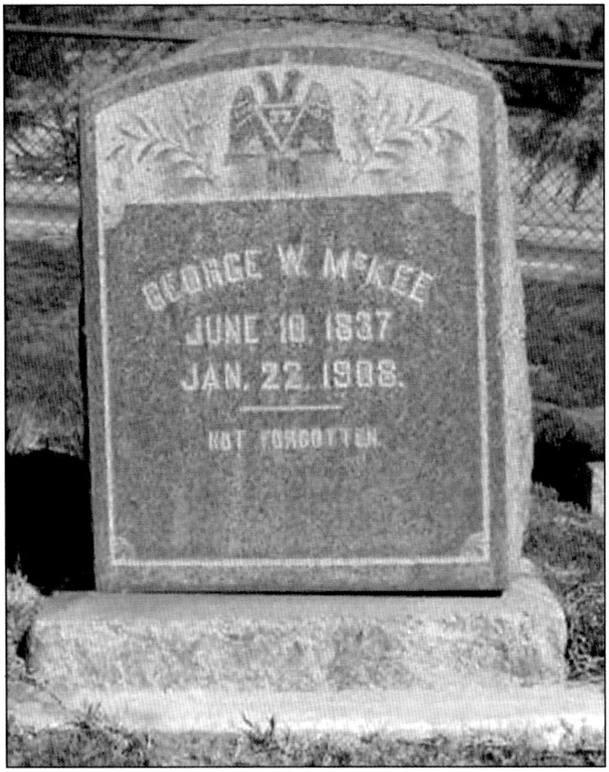

An estimated 1,800 are buried in the Municipal Cemetery. However, the families of many prominent citizens of early Long Beach chose to bury their relatives elsewhere. In 1908, Belle Lowe, the woman who named the city, buried her brother George McKee, a Civil War veteran, in the city cemetery. Belle buried her husband in Angelus Rosedale Cemetery, where she later joined him.

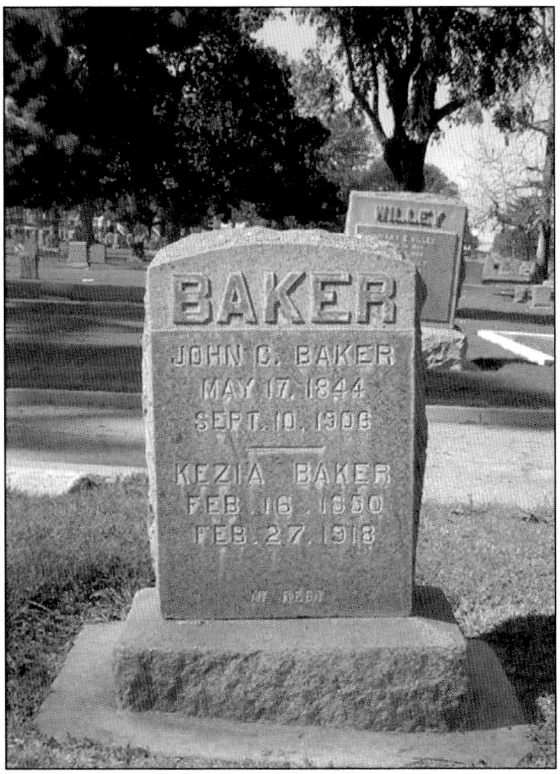

J.C. Baker, a veteran of the Civil War, was elected constable in 1893 and then as marshal in 1895. Baker also served as commander of the Great Army of the Republic veterans' group. He is buried with his wife, Kezia.

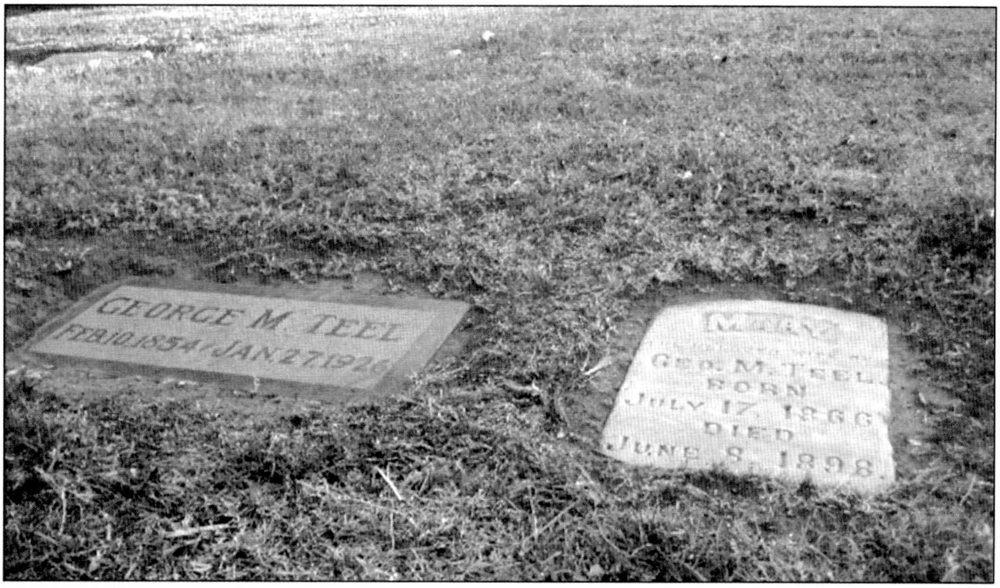

The Teel plot is one of the largest in the cemetery. The deeply religious Teels traveled by wagon train from Denton County, Texas, after the Civil War. George Marion Teel was a preacher in the Nazarene Church. He married Mary McCoy in 1895, who bore five children before she died. His second wife had one child. He married his third wife in 1919, and he died in 1926.

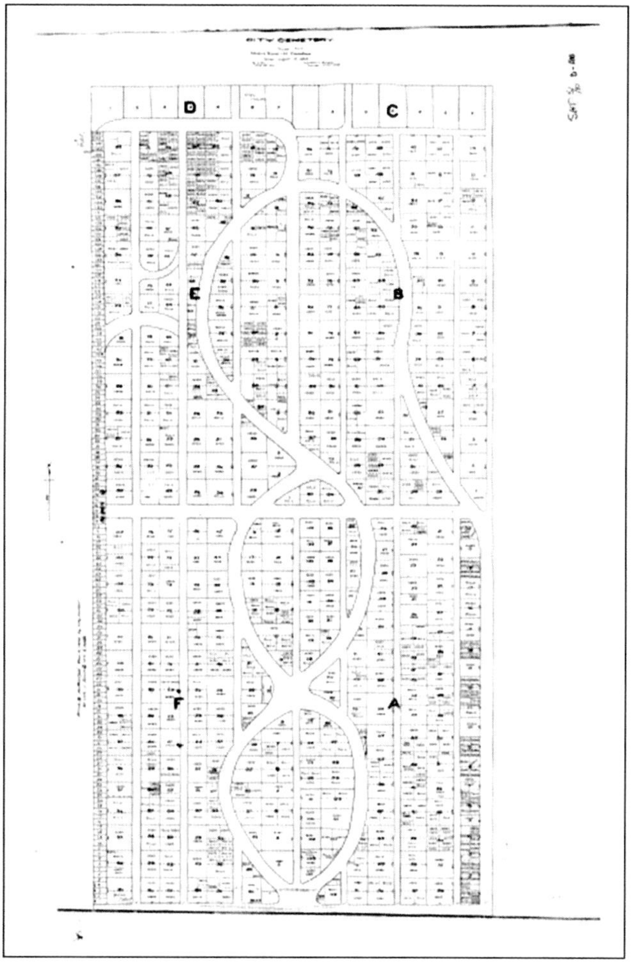

The cemetery map shows the land divided into sections and lots. Because it was not exactly clear who had been buried on the grounds, the grounds had to be "sounded" to find out if a lot was empty. Identification of graves has become even more difficult as grass has been allowed to grow over the grave markers that at some point were laid flat.

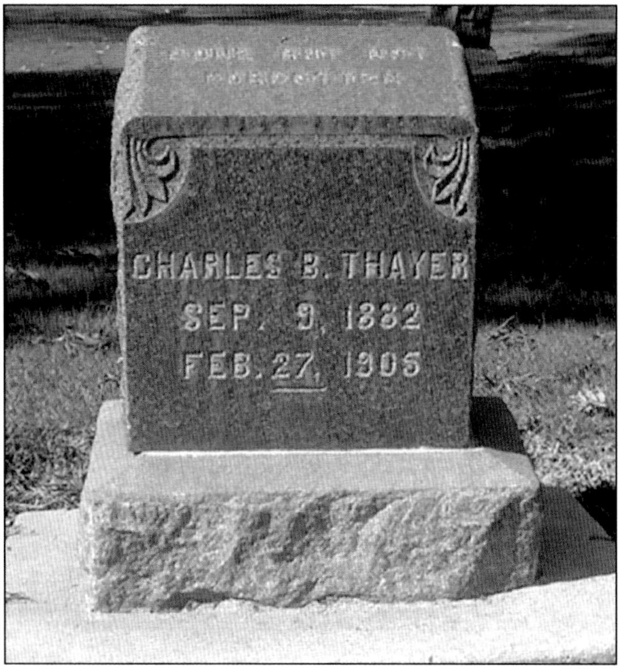

The early founders of the cemetery included Deloss Potter "D.P." Thayer, who in 1894 was listed as president of the Long Beach Cemetery Company. Thayer, a Civil War veteran, served as the superintendent of the Citizens Water Company and then later as a debt collector for the Land Development Company. In 1892, he ran unsuccessfully as a Republican candidate for constable. He married three times. One son, Charles B. "C.B." Thayer, was 22 when he was electrocuted working on the Pacific Electric trolley system in Long Beach. It is not clear where D.P. is buried. Both his son, C.B., and daughter, Lydia "Nellie" Saunders, are buried in this cemetery.

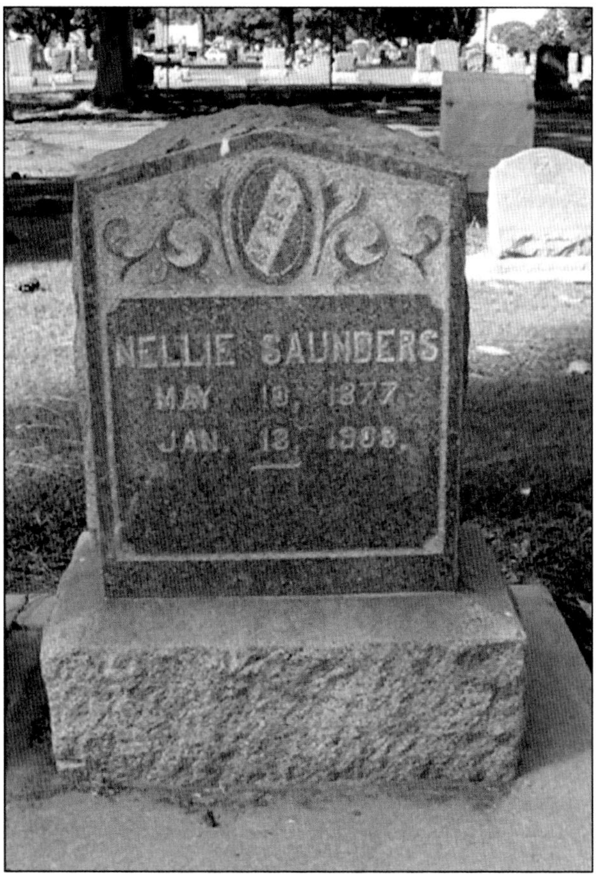

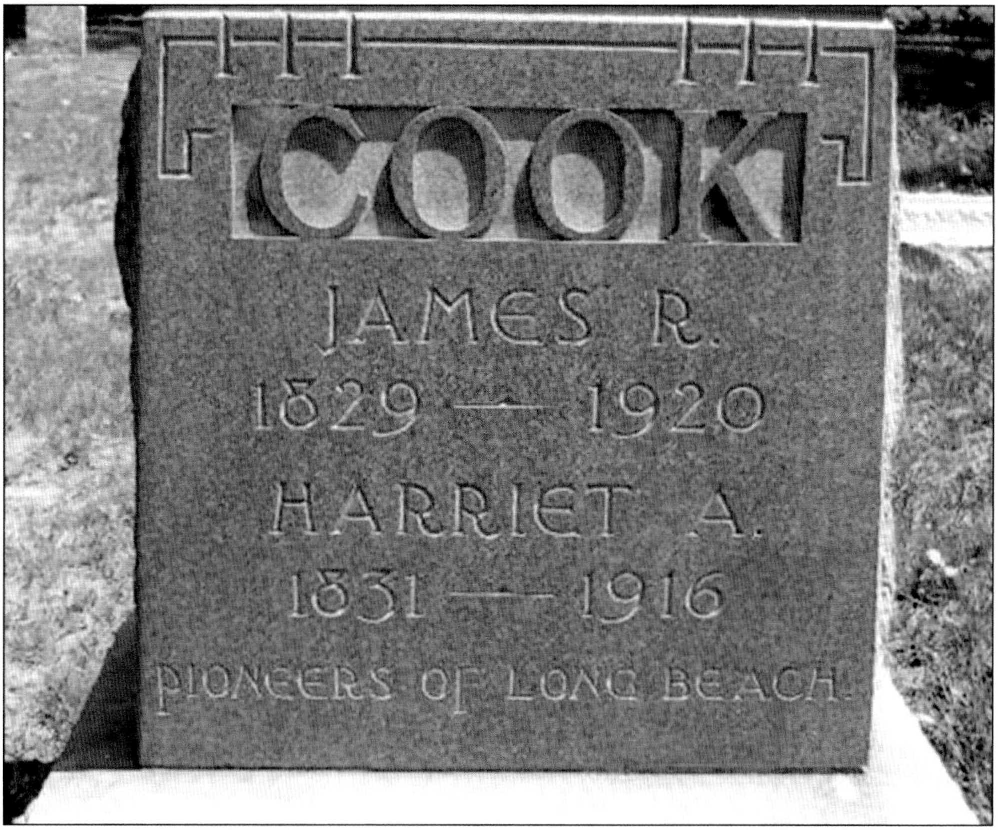

James and Harriet Cook were the first to build in Willmore City at 327 Pine Avenue, which is why their headstone proclaims them "Pioneers of Long Beach." Cook bought two 25-foot lots from William Willmore. His daughter Dr. Amy Rowse was an osteopathic doctor in the 1890s. Cook was cremated at Rosedale and buried in 1920 next door in Sunnyside.

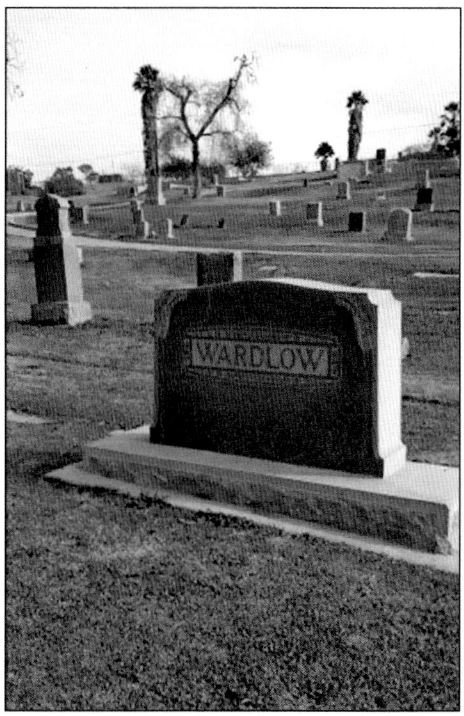

Traditionally, graves were placed facing east to greet the rising sun, or for Christians, in the direction anticipated for the second coming of Jesus. Because of the hilly nature of some cemeteries, bodies were buried in all directions. Until the early 1900s, graves had both headstones and foot stones. Gravesite edifices were constructed to reflect the economic status of those buried.

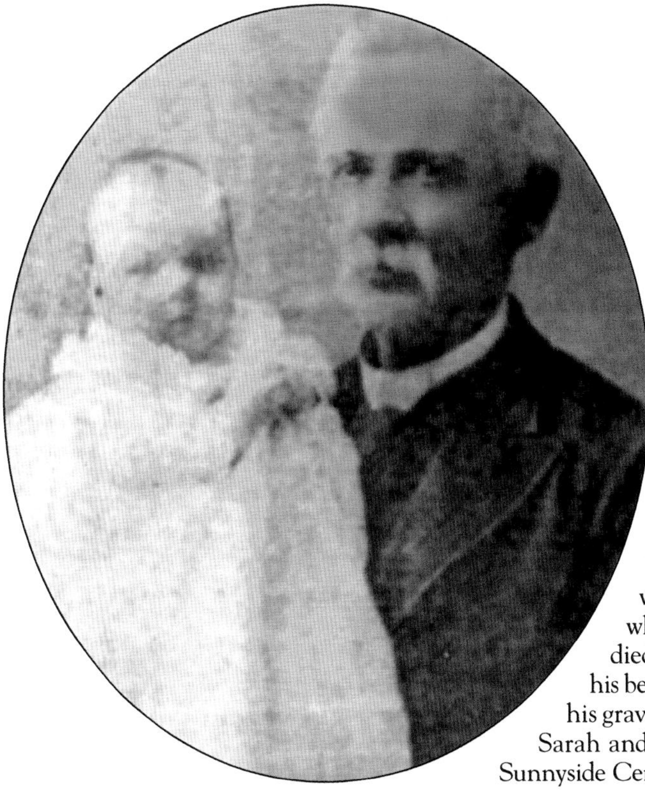

John Roberts was elected by his fellow trustees as the first president (mayor) of Long Beach. He came here in 1884 and started the San Pedro Lumber Company. Through his efforts, the Salt Lake Railroad was extended to Long Beach. He had several children with his third wife, including a daughter, Sarah, who married Dr. Joseph Steers. John died in 1907, and while records show his being buried in the plot with his wife, his grave cannot be located. His daughter Sarah and her husband are both buried in Sunnyside Cemetery. (Left, LBPL.)

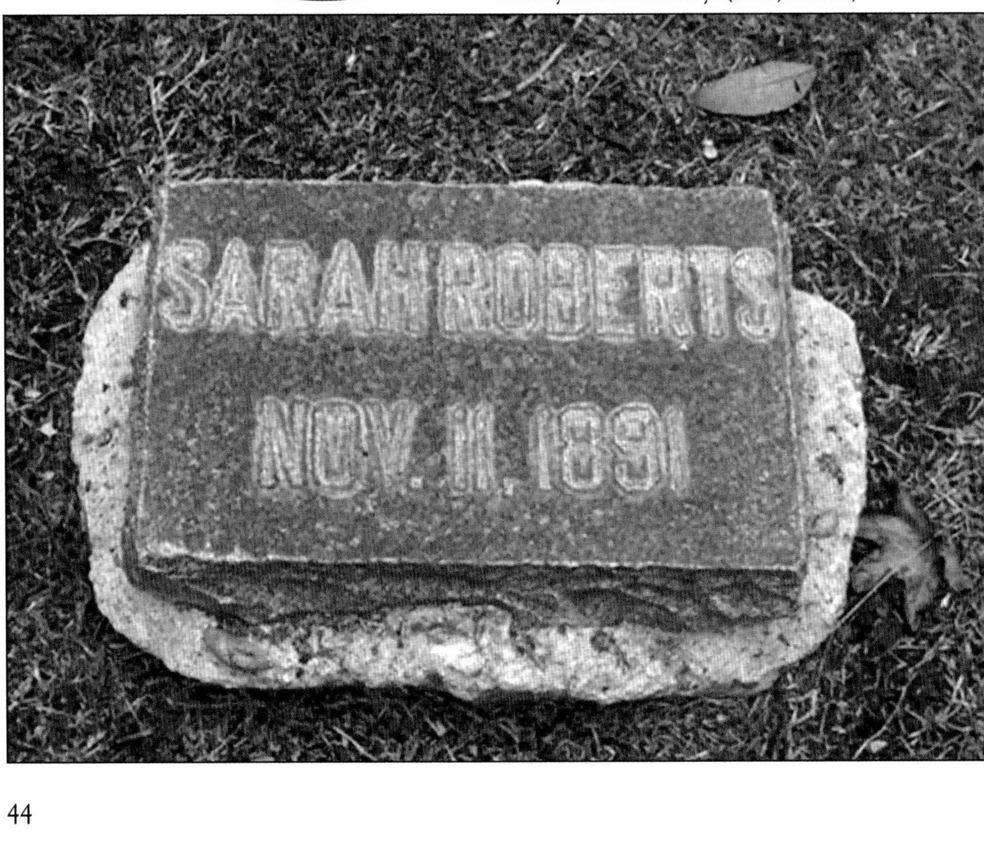

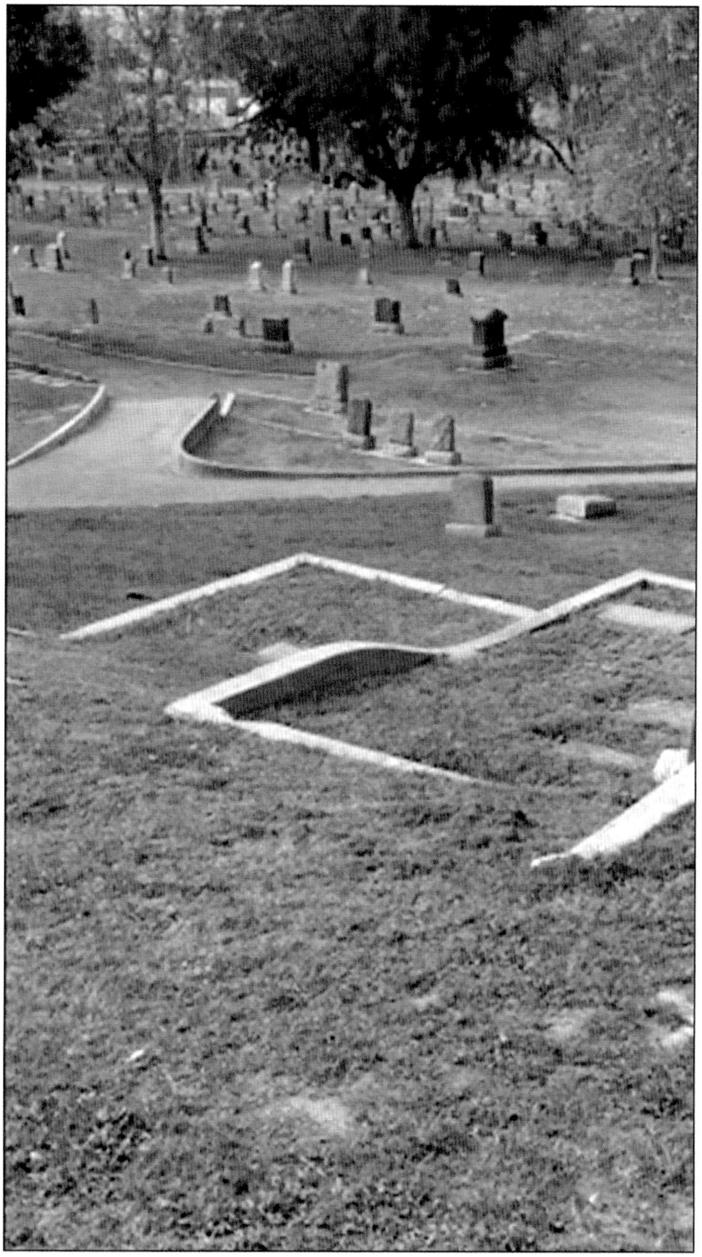

The city trustees were petitioned by residents who were concerned about the poor condition of the cemetery. Fewer and fewer people were visiting cemeteries and attending their relatives' burial sites. Privately owned cemeteries were funded by perpetual care endowments. The city enacted a monthly charge for upkeep of the grounds. Urbanization sparked the idea that a graveyard should be in a more rural or park-like environment and no more than four miles from the city and available by road. Long Beach hired Arthur Falkenhayn as superintendent of parks in the early 1900s, who supported the German-inspired park cemetery and proposed removing moss that had grown through years of neglect and to plant a "uniform lawn scheme, leaving trees, shrubbery and rose bushes wherever the landscape effect would artistically permit." The current cemetery has little landscaping.

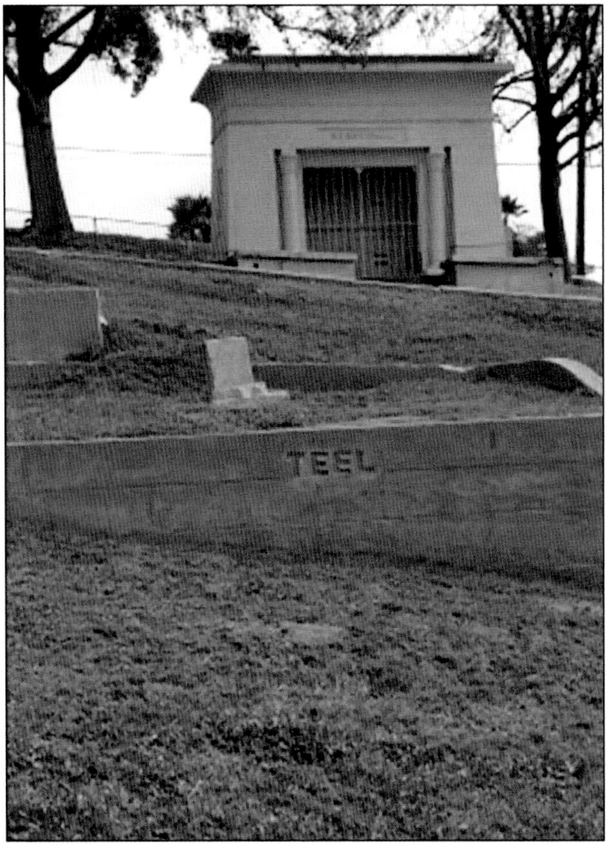

The only mausoleum standing in the Long Beach Cemetery is situated above the Teel plot and was built for Oscar Fitzwilliam Heartwell, who died in 1913 at the age of 96. Heartwell was the oldest living Odd Fellow in California. His banking and real estate development family included his son J.F. Heartwell and grandson Col. Charles Heartwell. The structure contains Oscar, J.F., Cora (J.F.'s wife), his son James, and James's wife, Erlene, who was interred in 2002.

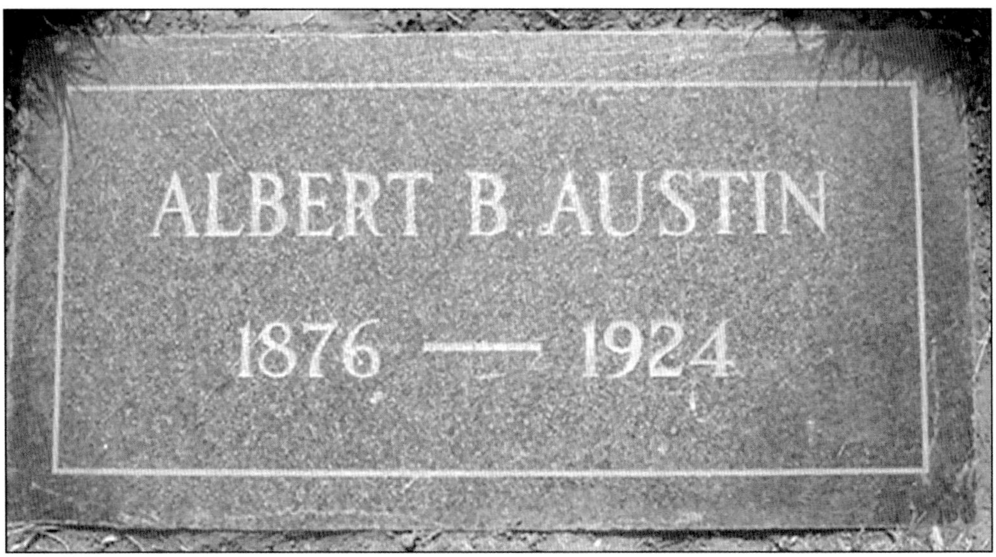

Dr. William Hanna Austin died in 1910. Newspaper stories in 1911 describe a "pure white manufactured stone" mausoleum built with six vaults in "Egyptian style" by William's son, local architect Horace Austin. Around 1955, the mausoleum disappeared without explanation. Cemetery records indicate Austin, his son Albert, and wife Florence were all reburied in the ground. Albert served as chief of police.

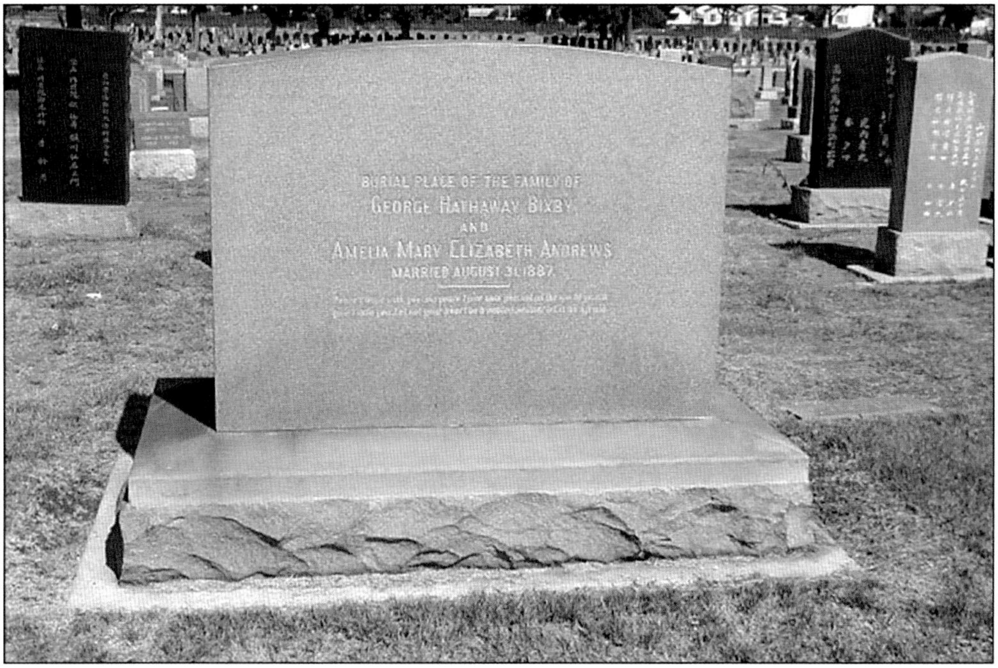

Records show that the Bixby family own a plot, which is empty. The bodies of George Hathaway Bixby and his wife, Amelia Bixby, were exhumed and reburied in Evergreen Cemetery in 1923. Several Bixby family members are buried at the adjacent Sunnyside Cemetery and a few miles away at Forest Lawn Long Beach.

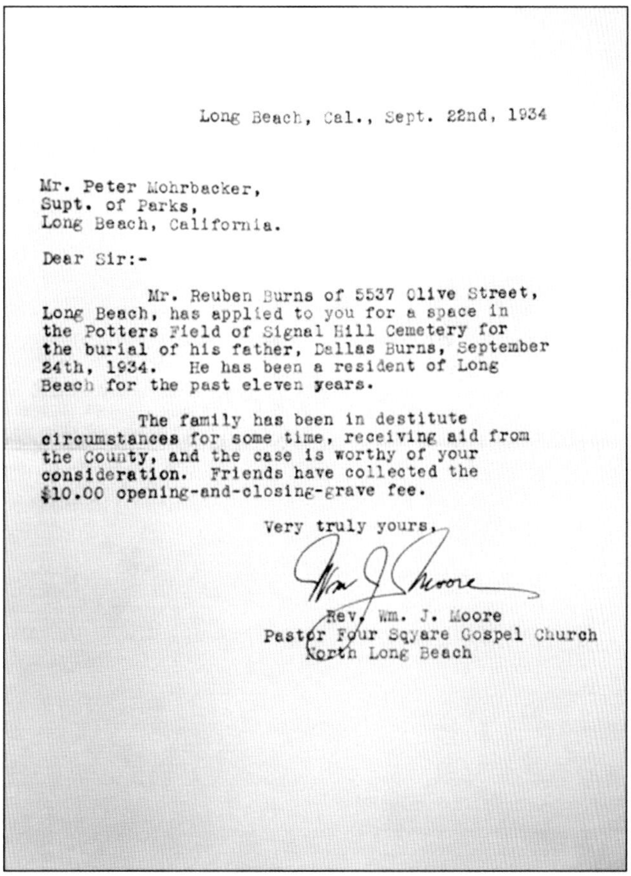

Long Beach, Cal., Sept. 22nd, 1934

Mr. Peter Mohrbacker,
Supt. of Parks,
Long Beach, California.

Dear Sir:-

Mr. Reuben Burns of 5537 Olive Street, Long Beach, has applied to you for a space in the Potters Field of Signal Hill Cemetery for the burial of his father, Dallas Burns, September 24th, 1934. He has been a resident of Long Beach for the past eleven years.

The family has been in destitute circumstances for some time, receiving aid from the County, and the case is worthy of your consideration. Friends have collected the $10.00 opening-and-closing-grave fee.

Very truly yours,

Wm J Moore

Rev. Wm. J. Moore
Pastor Four Sqyare Gospel Church
North Long Beach

Poor and nonwhites were buried in the least desirable parts of the cemeteries, called "potter's field," without headstone or marker. "Potter's field" is a biblical reference for a graveyard for strangers on land whose soil is only good for potting clay. Records show numerous locations of unmarked graves and graves designated "Mexican" in Lot C. During the Depression, even the $10 fee for burial was too much for some. (City of Long Beach Public Works Department.)

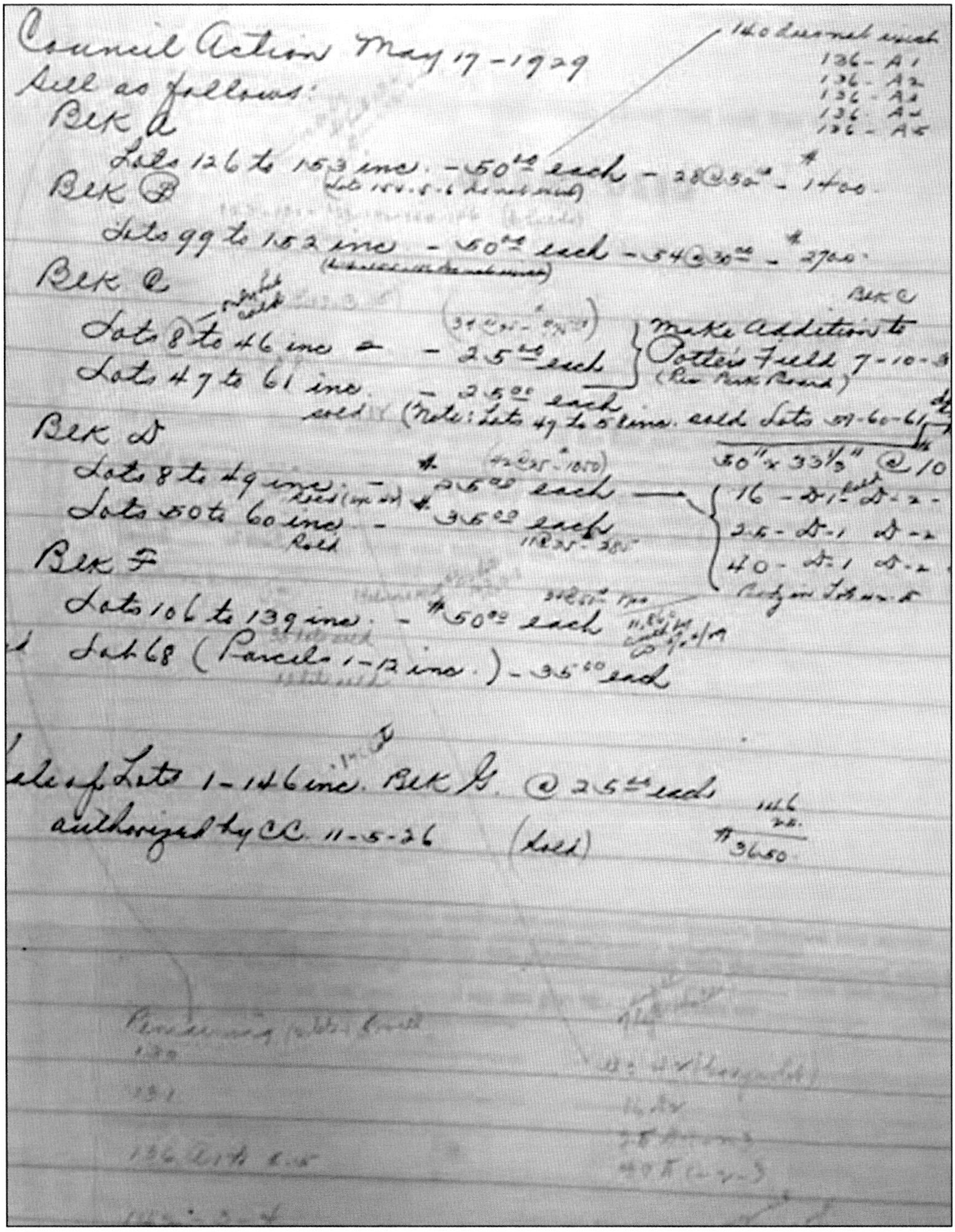

Council Action May 17-1929
Sell as follows:
Blk A
Lots 126 to 153 inc. - 50.00 each - 28 @ 50.00 - $1400
Blk B
Lots 99 to 152 inc - 50.00 each - 54 @ 50.00 - $2700
Blk C
Lots 8 to 46 inc - 25.00 each } Make Addition to Potter's Field
Lots 47 to 61 inc. - 25.00 each
Blk D
Lots 8 to 49 inc. - 25.00 each
Lots 50 to 60 inc - 35.00 each
Blk F
Lots 106 to 139 inc. - $50.00 each
Lot 68 (Parcels 1-12 inc.) - 35.00 each

Sale of Lots 1-146 inc. Blk G. @ 25.00 each
authorized by CC 11-5-26 (sold) $3650

The city mismanaged the cemetery for many years. In 1905, city trustees discovered that the deed to the cemetery had never been recorded, and instead, part of the property was sold for taxes. Often, the wrong person was buried in the potter's field. In 1907, a body was found floating near the pier. It was identified by a laundry marker. A man stated he had given a shirt with that mark to a "James Gallagher." The coroner declared the body as Gallagher and ruled death by suicide, because of the sand in his pockets used to weigh him down. He was buried the same day. Gallagher read his obituary and came into town, explaining he had been in Riverside and was not dead. As the notes on city files above indicate, in 1929, the city added more area to potter's field. (City of Long Beach Public Works Department.)

In 1914, eighteen-year-old Delbert D. Wardlow was shot after riding his horse out to Talbert in Orange County to get beer. Wardlow got into an argument and was shot several times. He mounted his horse to get away, but bled to death. The owner of the property, Epitacio Valenzuela, who did not shoot Wardlow, was nonetheless convicted of manslaughter with a 10-year prison sentence.

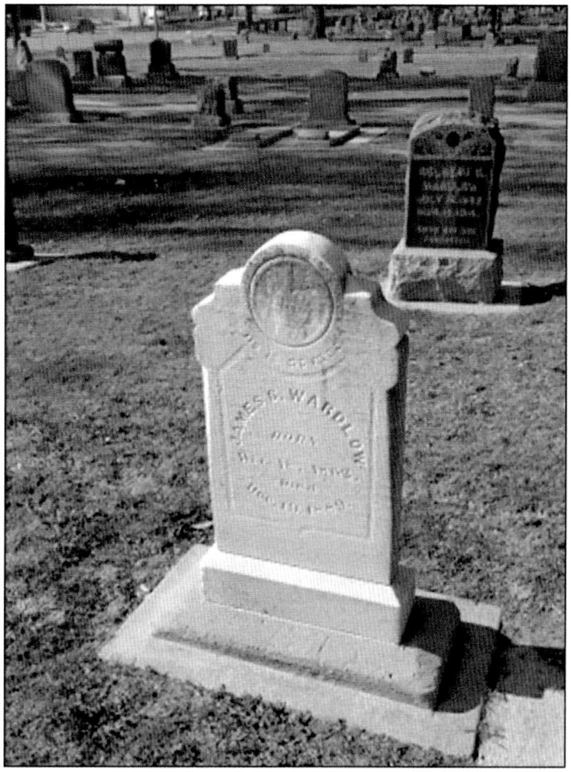

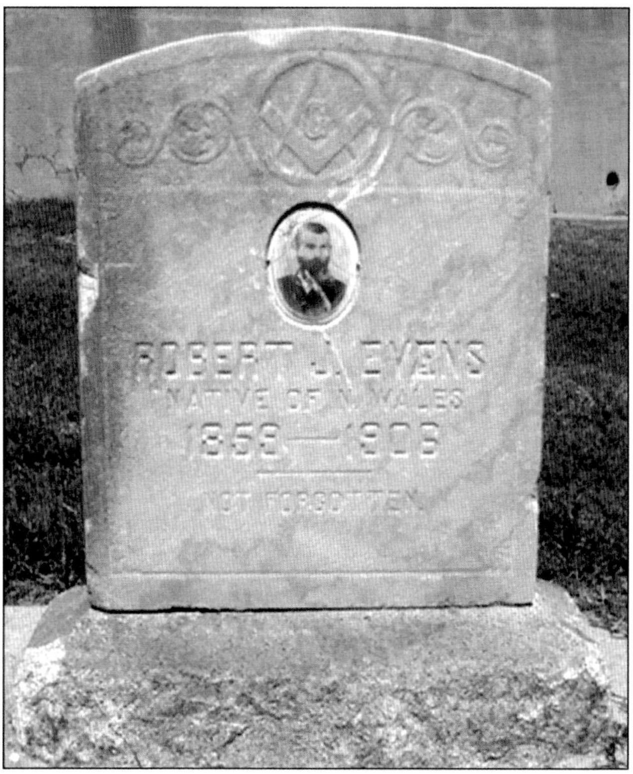

Robert J. Evans's headstone is one of few in the Municipal Cemetery that includes a photograph. Evans, a native of Wales, died in 1906 after being in Long Beach for only three months. His brother W.H. Evans developed commercial buildings and was very active in the Sons of St. George, an English fraternal organization that started in Pennsylvania to counter Irish workers in the coal mines.

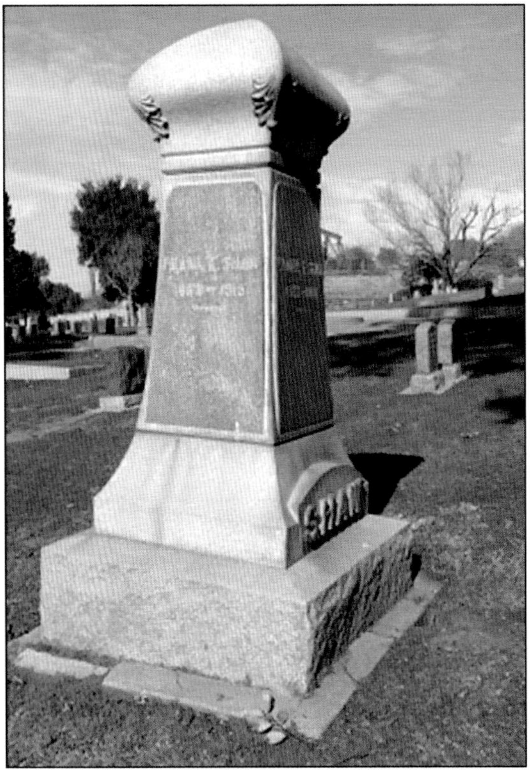

The Shaw family was prominent in Long Beach. In 1906, Daniel Sydney Shaw, a city pioneer and the vice president of the First National Bank of Long Beach, died in his home at Seventh Street and Junipero Avenue due to complications from pneumonia. Shaw was born in 1822 and came to Long Beach from Maine in 1854. He and his wife, Louise Grimnell Shaw, had seven children, several of whom met tragic endings.

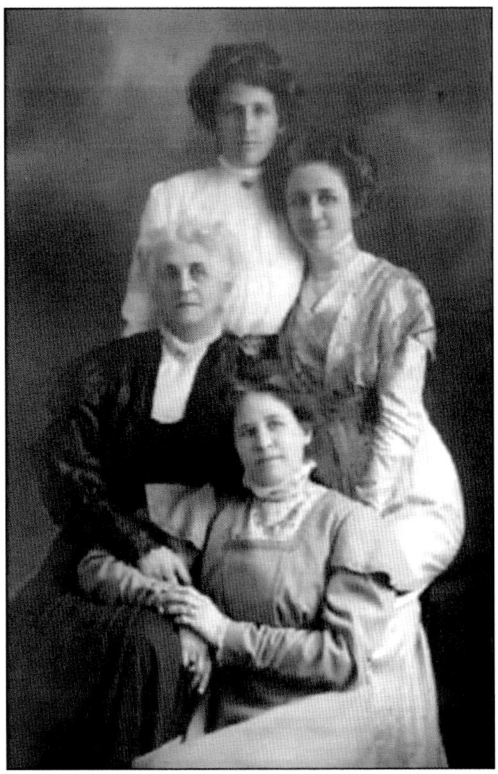

In 1912, Daniel and Louise Shaw's 36-year-old daughter Helene Edith Shaw Cleaver (pictured at bottom) shot herself in the mouth because of chronic pain. In 1915, son Frank E. Shaw committed suicide by placing a hose into his mouth and connecting it to a stove. Frank was despondent because of serious financial losses, including repossession of his automobile just a few days prior to his suicide. (Janice Buchanan.)

The *Coshocton Tribune* in Ohio reported that Silas Moore, a former resident, had died of "paralysis" on his fruit farm in Long Beach on September 27, 1895. His marker is inscribed, "His life was like an even spun thread." Moore began teaching at age 19. He later became a farmer and founder of Monroe Township in Ohio. Moore married twice and fathered eight children. In 1888, he moved to Long Beach.

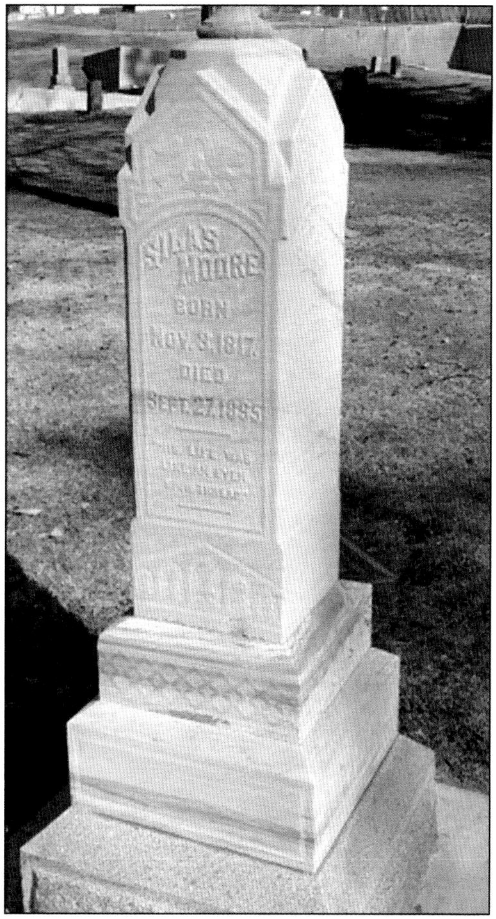

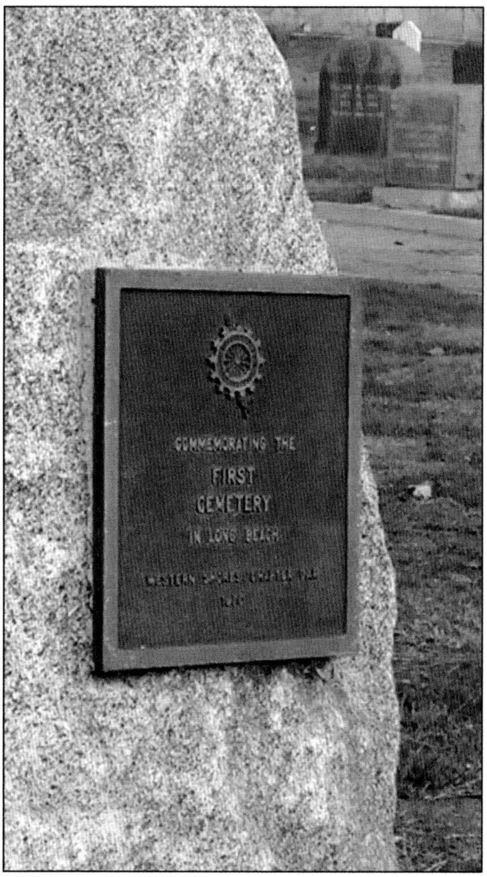

In 1970, the Western Shores Chapter of the Daughters of the American Revolution dedicated a plaque naming the Municipal Cemetery as the first in Long Beach. There are early newspaper articles mentioning a "Palm Cemetery," which some think is located underneath Forest Lawn Long Beach. However, an 1893 article in the *Record-Union* and *Los Angeles Herald* discusses a "Palm Cemetery Association" formed in Clearwater, which is now the city of Paramount.

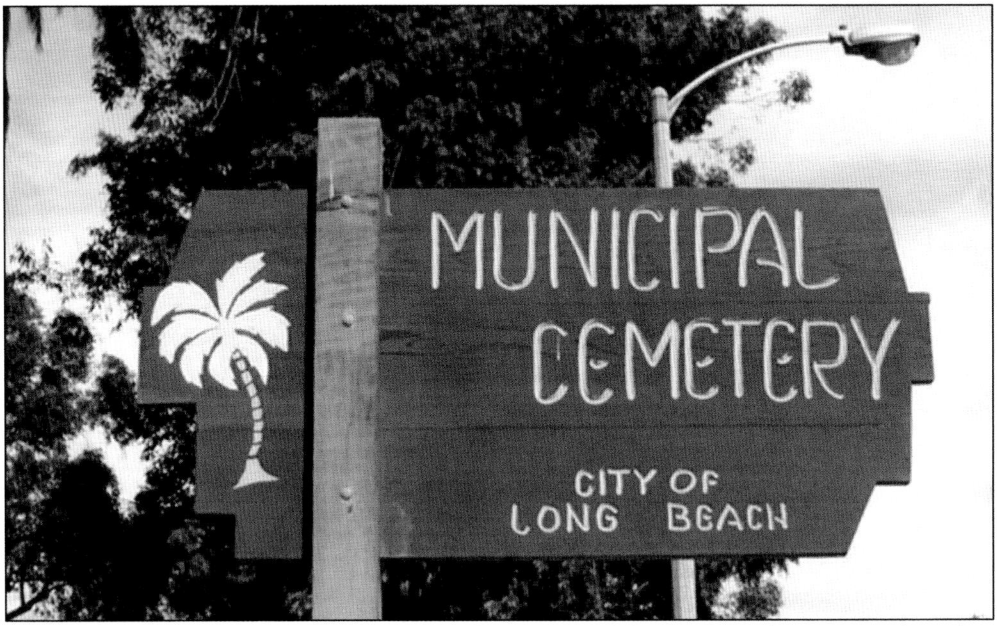

Today, the Municipal Cemetery of Long Beach is separated from Sunnyside Cemetery by only a chain link fence. In earlier days, a high hedge separated the two "cities of the dead," as pictured below. Operation of the cemetery is the responsibility of the city's superintendent of parks, although landscaping is contracted out. Burials are still allowed. The cemetery is located at 1051 Willow Street at the corner of Orange Avenue and is open every day until dark. Many of the roads of the cemetery were removed, so parking is limited. The one building on the premises is a locked utility shed. (Below, City of Long Beach Public Works Department.)

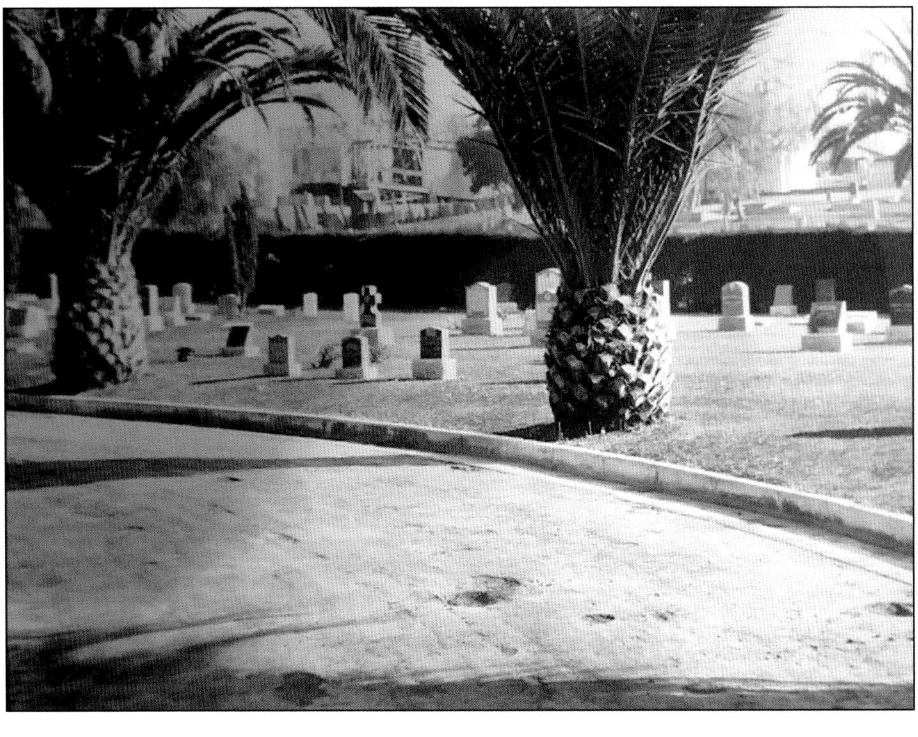

Four

The Most Valuable Cemetery in the United States

In 1904, a local newspaper announced, "The Long Beach Cemetery Association has secured an eighty-acre tract west of American Avenue and just north of the Willows. It is broken enough to make easy work for a landscape gardener to make it a beauty spot." The 80-acre tract was never used for a cemetery, but a 15-acre plot adjacent to the Signal Hill Cemetery was used for Sunnyside Cemetery.

Sunnyside offered a park-like setting and promised perpetual care through endowment assessments. Many prominent Long Beach families are buried there: Walker, Stearns, Harnett, Buffum, Woodruff, and dozens of others. Sunnyside has a specific area for Civil War veterans and contains many headstones with embedded pictures of the deceased.

In 1915, the owners announced the sale of a lot in the northwest corner for the building of a mausoleum. The new owner had other plans and wanted to lease the lot to an oil company for drilling.

The cemetery became a battleground in 1921 with the discovery of what would be the world's richest oilfield on Signal Hill. At once, cemetery land became the most valuable property in the area, as relatives fought for mineral rights and cemetery owners planned to sell off lots for drilling.

A cemetery protective association formed to urge the city council to prevent drilling in the cemetery. The city council offered to purchase 100 to 200 acres away from Sunnyside so that the buried could be relocated.

A permit to drill in the cemetery was not issued; however, the oil company was able to slant-drill (also called "whip-stocking") from the Jergins Lease north of Sunnyside Cemetery. Several families sued for oil rights. In 1937, the court ruled that families had only an easement for burial and did not have rights to the minerals below.

The scene of oil derricks surrounding cemeteries brought Ansel Adams, famed photographer, to Long Beach in 1939 to capture what he called "the strange juxtaposition" of a cemetery surrounded by oil derricks. His photograph of the Rhea gravesite with the "Angel of Sorrows" sculpture atop was featured in *Life* magazine and was acquired by the Huntington Museum.

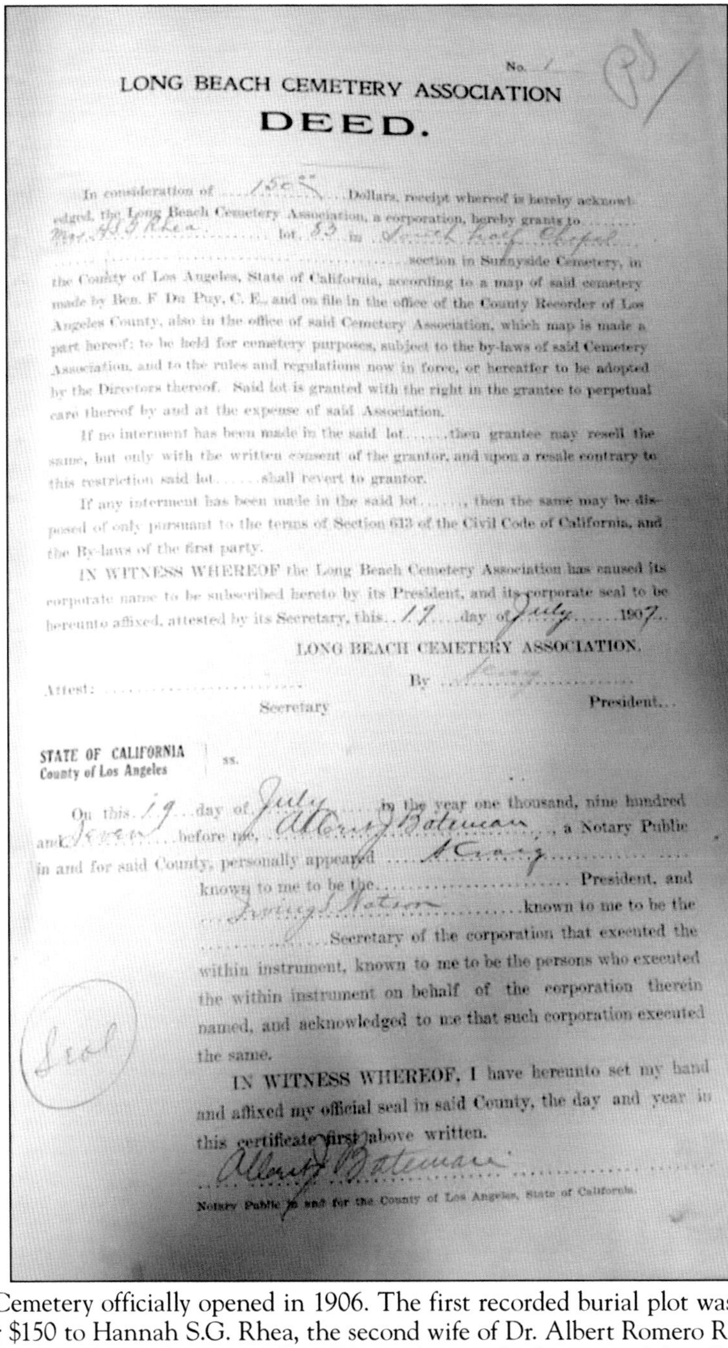
No. 1

LONG BEACH CEMETERY ASSOCIATION

DEED.

In consideration of 150.00 Dollars, receipt whereof is hereby acknowledged, the Long Beach Cemetery Association, a corporation, hereby grants to Mrs. H S G Rhea lot 83 in South half Chapel section in Sunnyside Cemetery, in the County of Los Angeles, State of California, according to a map of said cemetery made by Ben. F Du Puy, C. E., and on file in the office of the County Recorder of Los Angeles County, also in the office of said Cemetery Association, which map is made a part hereof; to be held for cemetery purposes, subject to the by-laws of said Cemetery Association, and to the rules and regulations now in force, or hereafter to be adopted by the Directors thereof. Said lot is granted with the right in the grantee to perpetual care thereof by and at the expense of said Association.

If no interment has been made in the said lot...... then grantee may resell the same, but only with the written consent of the grantor, and upon a resale contrary to this restriction said lot...... shall revert to grantor.

If any interment has been made in the said lot......, then the same may be disposed of only pursuant to the terms of Section 613 of the Civil Code of California, and the By-laws of the first party.

IN WITNESS WHEREOF the Long Beach Cemetery Association has caused its corporate name to be subscribed hereto by its President, and its corporate seal to be hereunto affixed, attested by its Secretary, this 19 day of July 1907.

LONG BEACH CEMETERY ASSOCIATION.

Attest: .... Secretary

By .... President.

STATE OF CALIFORNIA
County of Los Angeles } ss.

On this 19 day of July in the year one thousand, nine hundred and seven before me, Albert J Bateman, a Notary Public in and for said County, personally appeared .... known to me to be the .... President, and Irving J Watson .... known to me to be the .... Secretary of the corporation that executed the within instrument, known to me to be the persons who executed the within instrument on behalf of the corporation therein named, and acknowledged to me that such corporation executed the same.

IN WITNESS WHEREOF, I have hereunto set my hand and affixed my official seal in said County, the day and year in this certificate first above written.

Albert J Bateman

Notary Public in and for the County of Los Angeles, State of California.

Seal

Sunnyside Cemetery officially opened in 1906. The first recorded burial plot was sold on July 19, 1907, for $150 to Hannah S.G. Rhea, the second wife of Dr. Albert Romero Rhea. On May 10, 1907, retired Civil War physician Albert Rhea, who was deaf, was struck by a Pacific Electric trolley while bicycling along Third Street. He crossed the track and was hit by the train, which dragged him several feet. He died later that day. Rhea's gravesite and the marble sculpture atop are perhaps the most photographed in the cemetery. In 1939, Ansel Adams was so taken by the contrast of oil derricks and headstones that he stopped and photographed both the gravesite and the cemetery. In 2007, vandals knocked the angel off the pedestal. The city provided a crane, which put her back in place.

Tragedy continued to strike the Rhea family. Nine members of the funeral party were seriously injured when their carriages collided and they were thrown to the ground. The hackman claimed the steep grade caused him to lose control of the horses as they went down the hill. Dr. Rhea's wife, Hannah, is buried without any marker. Her sister Elizabeth Covert is also buried in the plot.

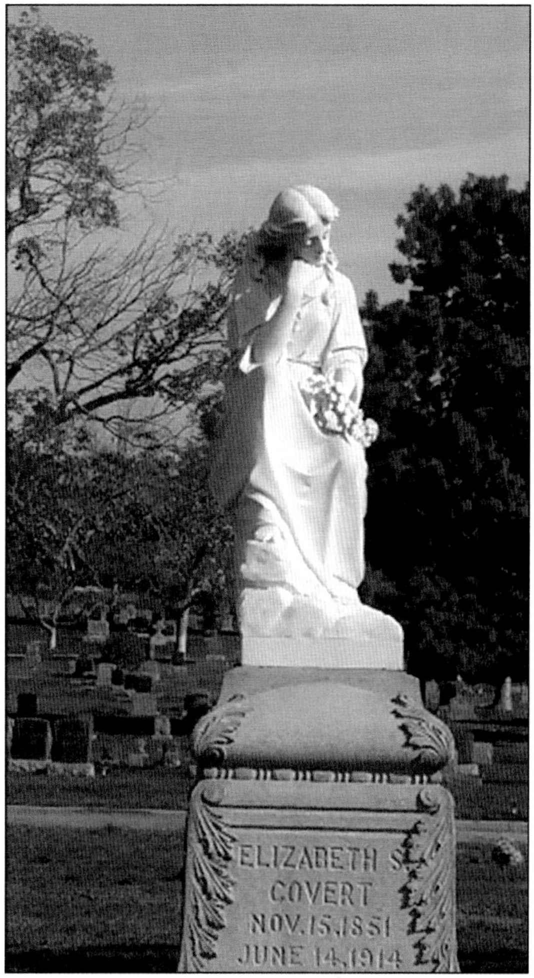

Rev. Frank W. Johnson was among the first burials. The remnants of his plain marker reflect his old New England Puritan background. Born in 1851, he began preaching in Vermont at 24. He and his wife, Katherine, moved to Phoenix because of his health. They moved to Boyle Heights. When his wife was killed in a "run-away accident" in Santa Barbara, he moved to Long Beach.

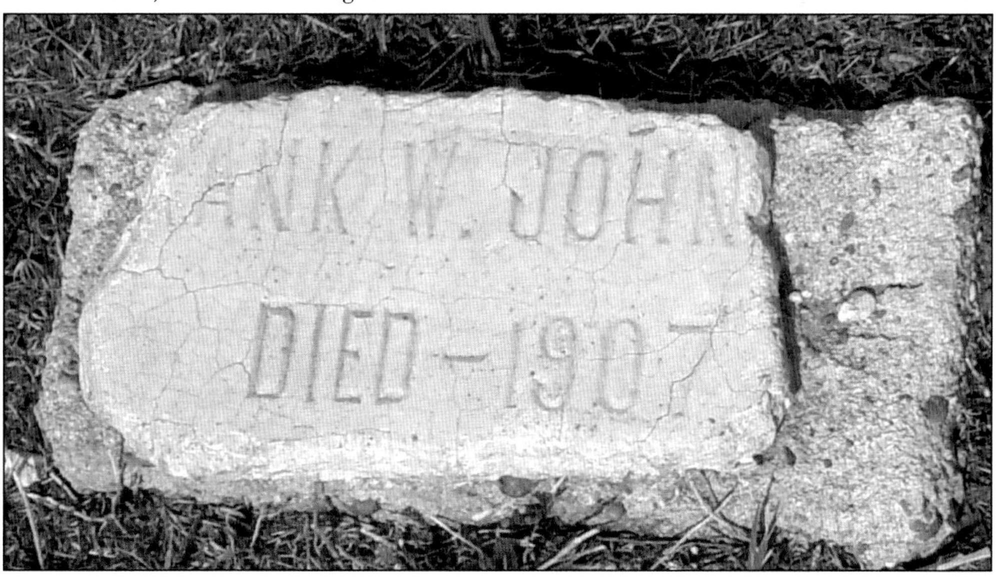

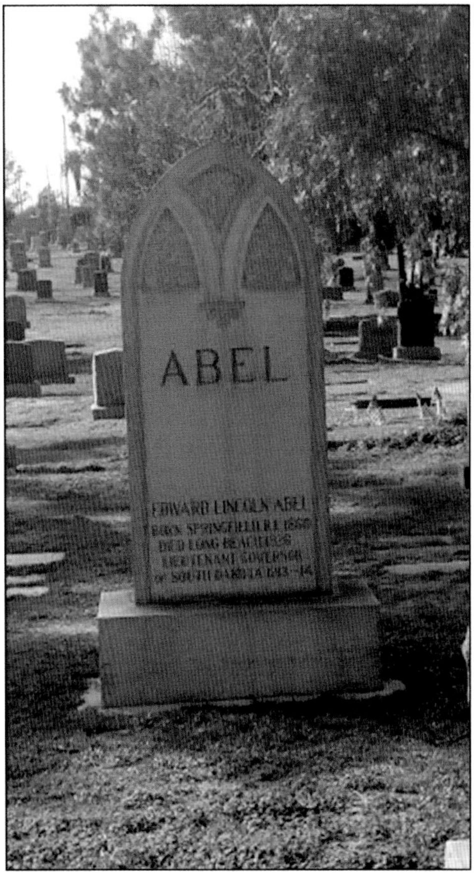

Edward Lincoln Abel was born in Springfield, Illinois, in 1860. He was a lawyer, farmer, and banker in South Dakota. He served as mayor, alderman, city attorney, and president of the local board of education. He was elected South Dakota lieutenant governor in 1912 for two years. He moved to Long Beach and died here in 1926.

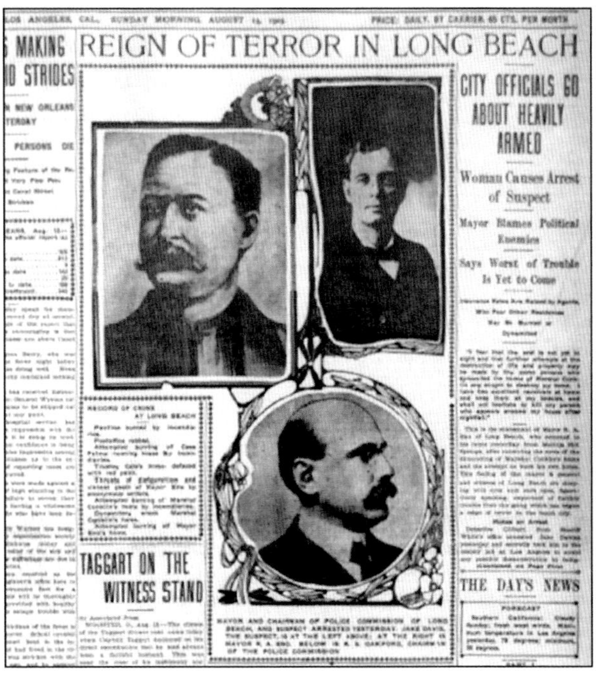

REIGN OF TERROR IN LONG BEACH

CITY OFFICIALS GO ABOUT HEAVILY ARMED

Woman Causes Arrest of Suspect

Mayor Blames Political Enemies

Says Worst of Trouble Is Yet to Come

TAGGART ON THE WITNESS STAND

THE DAY'S NEWS

In 1905, the local press reported that there was a series of attacks on the homes of elected officials and public buildings by anonymous individuals and dubbed it the "Reign of Terror in Long Beach." Mayor Rufus Eno claimed to have received a note threatening him with "disfigurement." Someone doused Eno's house in oil so it could be set on fire. Other homes were dynamited. Eno resigned in 1906 after being arrested for taking a $350 bribe from an architect who wanted the contract to design the city's "pleasure pier and sun parlor." Eno died in 1925 in San Bernardino.

Robert Banta observed in *Park and Cemetery* magazine in 1921 that Sunnyside Cemetery was "full of good monuments, close together" because Long Beach is a "two grave town" due to more than one half of the population being elderly retired couples who moved to Long Beach to live the remainder of their lives.

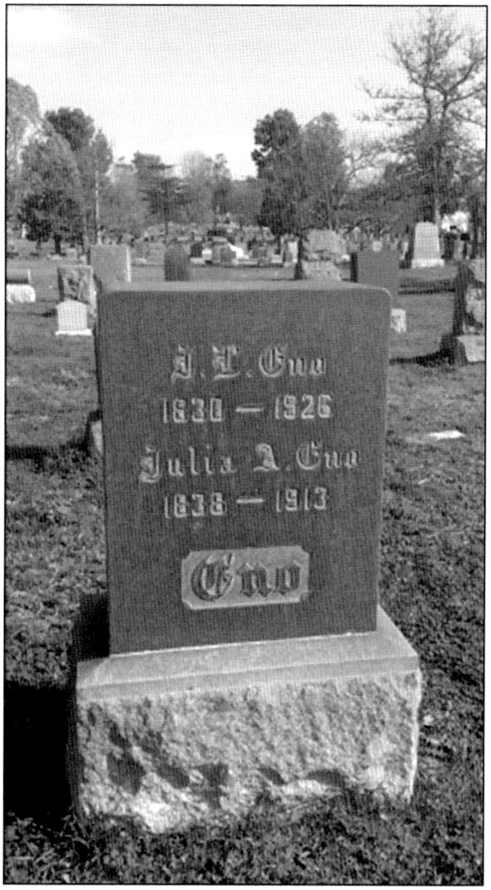

Real estate promoter Frank W. Stearns was born in 1862 on the farm owned by his Civil War veteran father, T.P. Stearns. He began teaching at 18 but moved to Long Beach in 1888 because of his poor health. He later established a large real estate business, F.W. Stearns and Company. He also served on the city council.

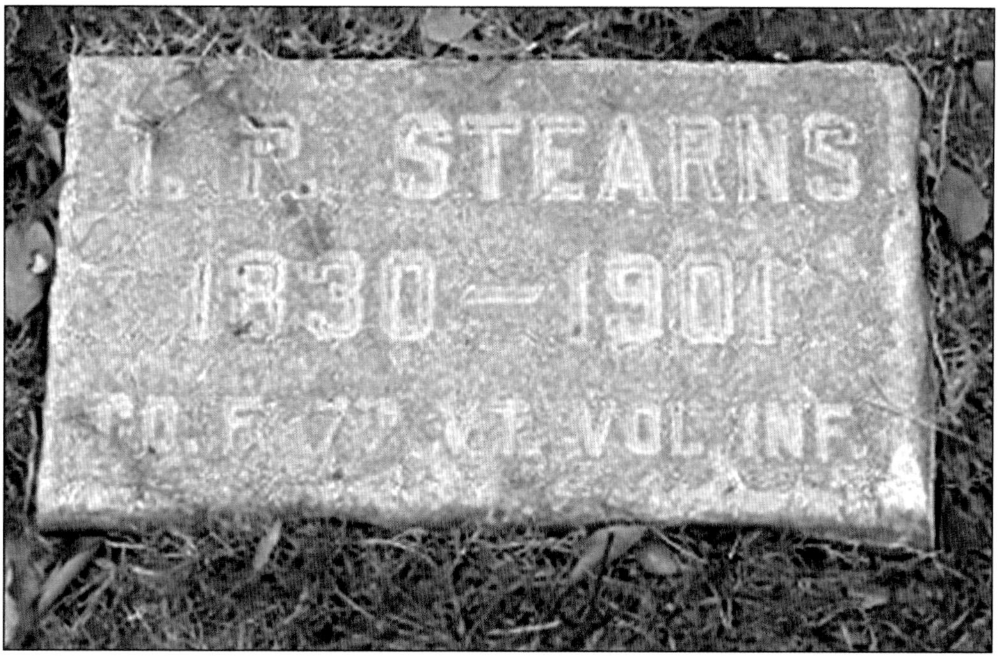

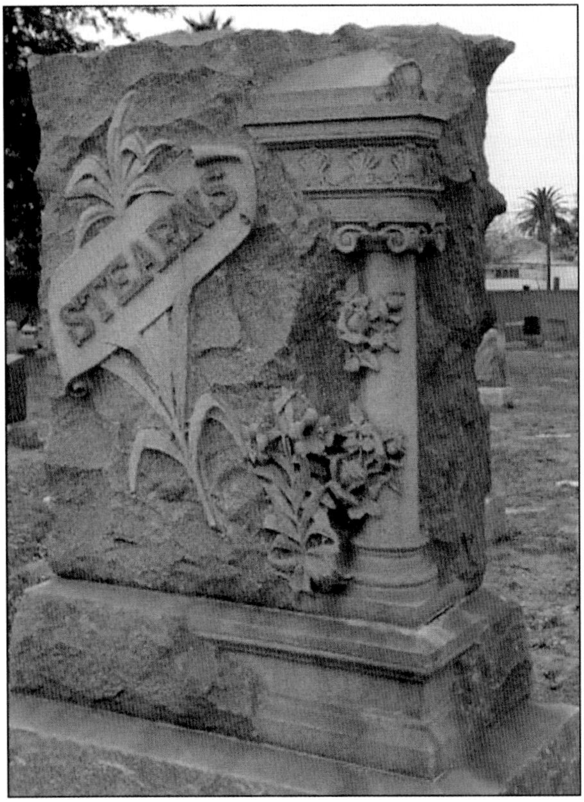

Frank Stearns was involved in establishing numerous residential tracts and the Inner Harbor Gas and Electric Company, which provided gas and electricity to homes. He served on the Long Beach City Council and was very active in the presidential campaign of Grover Cleveland. Stearns died in 1911. Long Beach named a major street and park for the Stearns family.

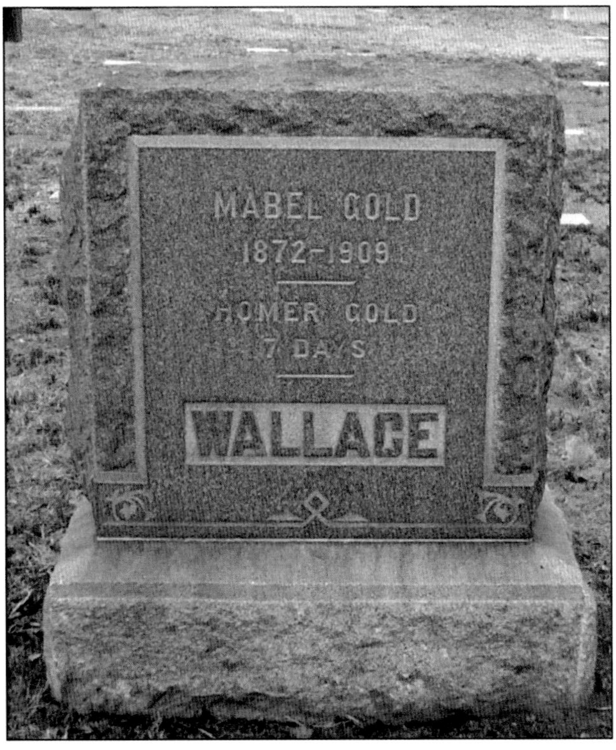

Mabel Gold Wallace was a bright 37 year old involved in the local Ebell Club and known throughout Southern California for her work with First Methodist Episcopal Church. Her husband, William, was the cashier of the Exchange National Bank. Mabel died suddenly in 1909, leaving a daughter and two sons, one of whom was an infant, Homer, who died later at seven days old.

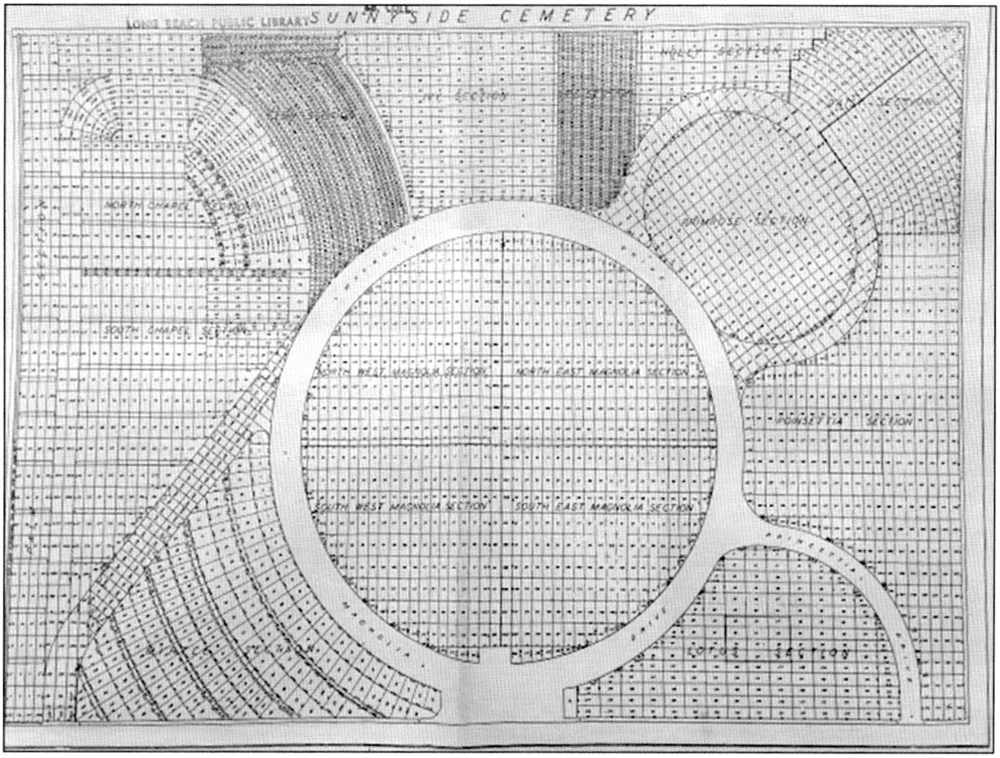

In 1910, owners of Sunnyside Cemetery finally agreed to the demands of the veterans to provide burial space and allow government-provided headstones to be erected. Veteran families were offered an opportunity to move the graves of those buried in other parts of the cemetery to the new space at no cost. A portion of the "Palm" section was designated for veteran burials. (LBPL.)

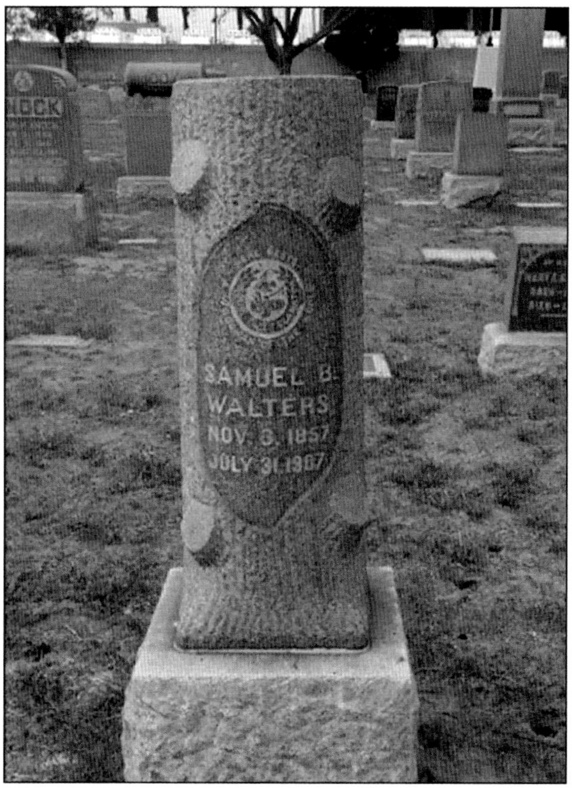

Secret fraternal organizations (and their female auxiliaries) such as the Sovereign Camp of the Woodmen of the World provided funeral benefits and arranged funerals. The Woodmen, founded in Nebraska in 1890, also sold life insurance and provided headstones in the shapes of tree logs with the inscription "Here rests a Woodman of the World," as shown here.

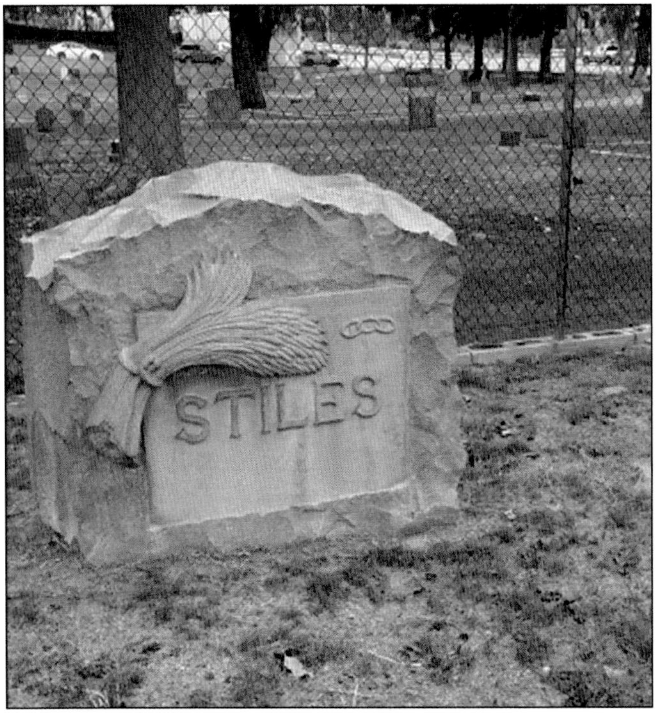

The Independent Order of Odd Fellows, started in England in the 17th century as the "odd laborers" in worker guilds, is a religious, fraternal organization. Odd Fellow members have symbols inscribed on their headstones showing the three chain links of friendship, love, and truth. A.M. Stiles was a former Minnesota legislator who died in Long Beach in 1928. He is buried in the family plot.

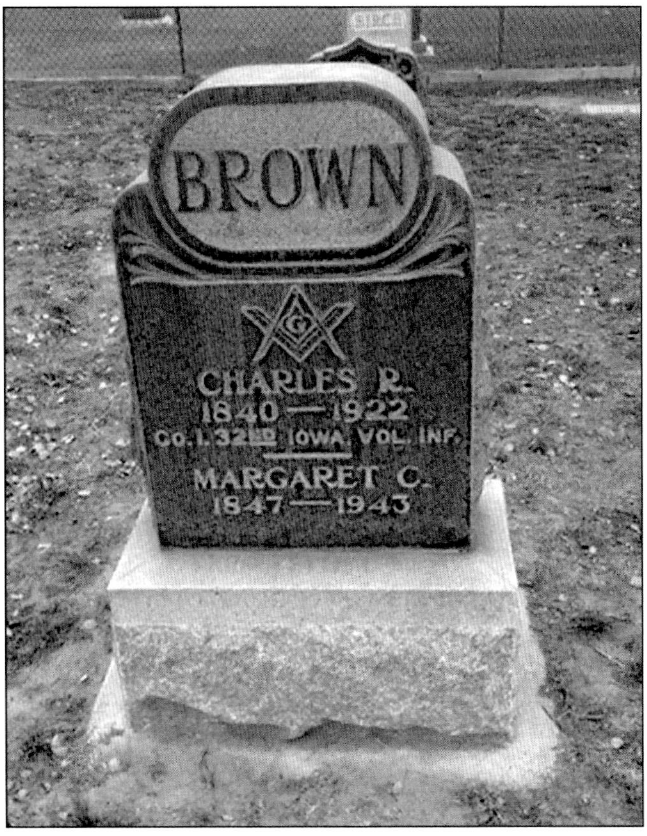

Fraternal organizations were very popular in the 1920s. By 1930, Freemasons claimed two million members in the United States. A square and compass surrounding a "G" for God are the symbols of the Freemasons inscribed on this headstone. Freemasons trace their origins to the stonemasons of the 14th century.

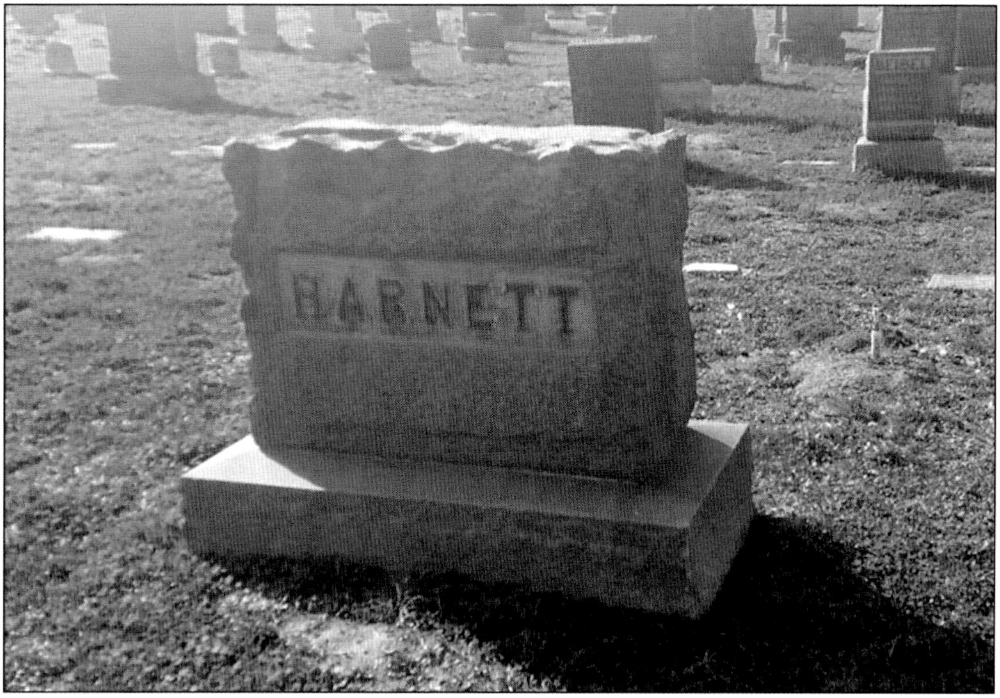

Jane Elizabeth Harnett, born in 1873, was the first history teacher at Long Beach High School. Her history of Long Beach was used in its entirety by Walter Case in his popular History of Long Beach and Vicinity book series. Harnett developed the first student body commission in California. She died suddenly in 1918 of pneumonia and her father, Ernest, died days later in an automobile accident.

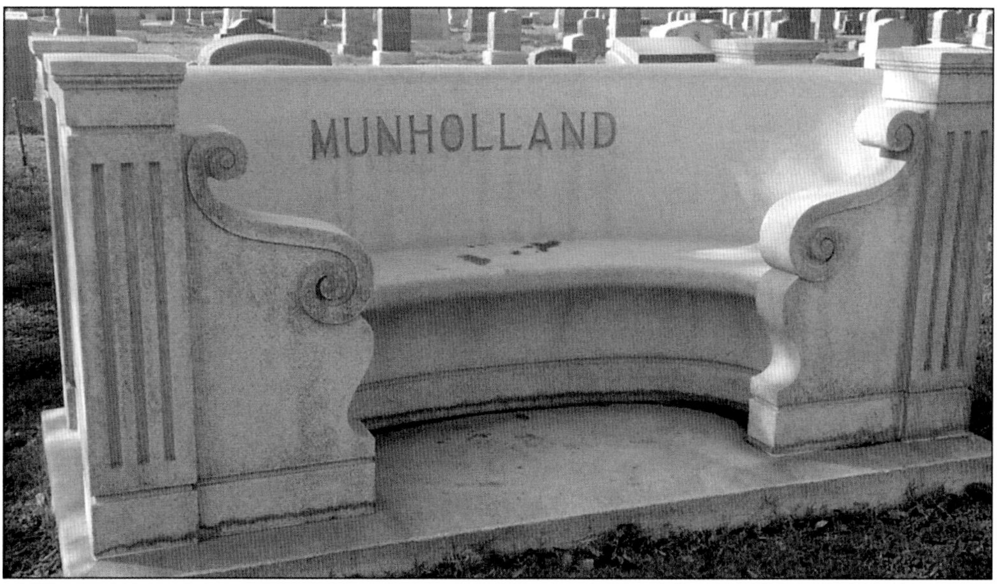

The large cement bench-like structure for the Munholland family is unique. John G. Munholland and his wife, Lulu McDuff, were transplants from Iowa. He was a successful realtor and served on the park commission. He constructed the Munholland and Mun apartments on Ocean Boulevard and Elm Avenue, where he died in 1917. Munholland's son James served as city prosecutor.

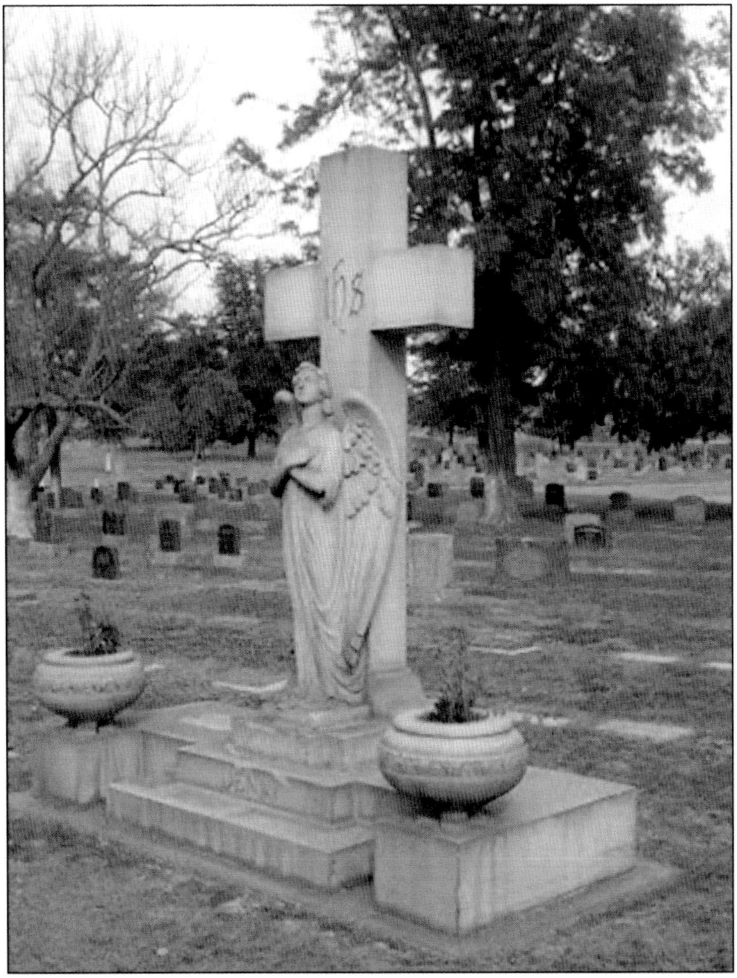

One of the more religious-looking statutes in the cemetery is the marker for the Denni family. Alois Louis Denni migrated from Switzerland in the 1880s and worked at the Bixby dairy ranch on Rancho Los Alamitos. Later, he opened his own dairy ranch on Signal Hill and another one where Los Alamitos High School is now located. When oil was struck on Signal Hill, he moved his family to Wilmington, where he became active in banking and served as president of the Wilmington Mutual Building and Loan Association. Denni died in 1933. He is buried with his wife and children.

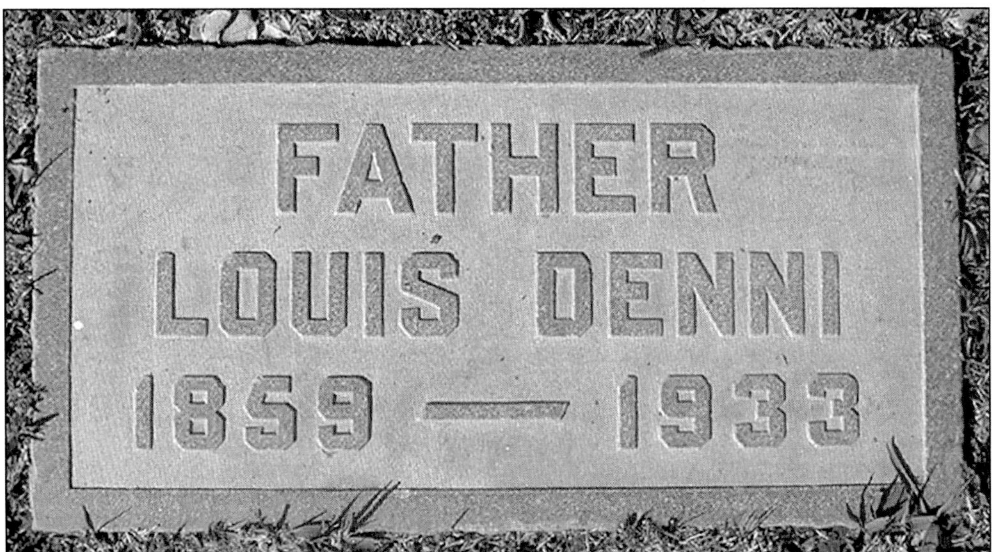

Mayor Ray Clark's funeral in 1926 was reported as the largest attended. Clark died suddenly at the newly opened Community Hospital Long Beach following tonsil surgery. He was mourned by over 400 Masons and others at the First Presbyterian Church. He came to Long Beach in 1908 and started Clark Drug Company in 1910. Clark was mayor from 1923. His wife, Mayme, who remarried, is buried with him.

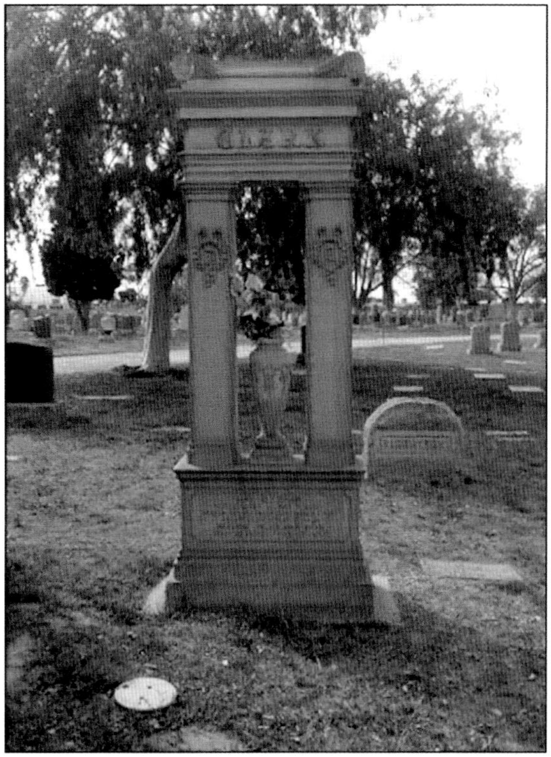

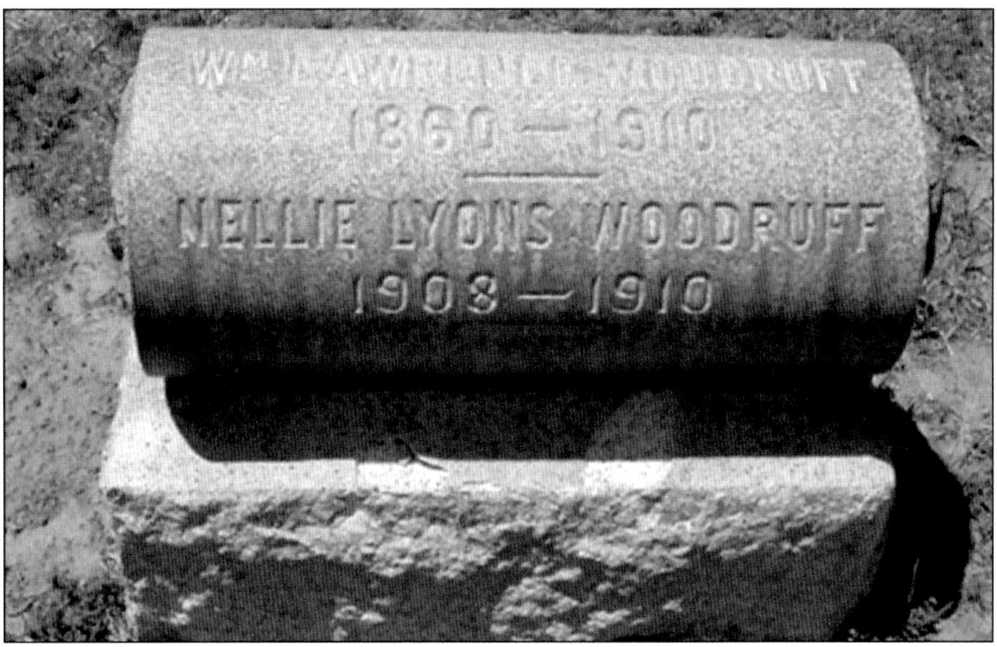

New Jersey native Dr. William Lawrence Woodruff came to Long Beach in 1905, married Mary Ellen Lyons, and opened the Woodruff Sanitarium at 137 Cedar Avenue. During surgery, a 250-pound patient fell on Woodruff, causing a pulmonary embolism and his death. Woodruff's 22-month-old daughter Nellie died a few days later following adenoid surgery. Woodruff was known for his theory of using vibration to treat patients.

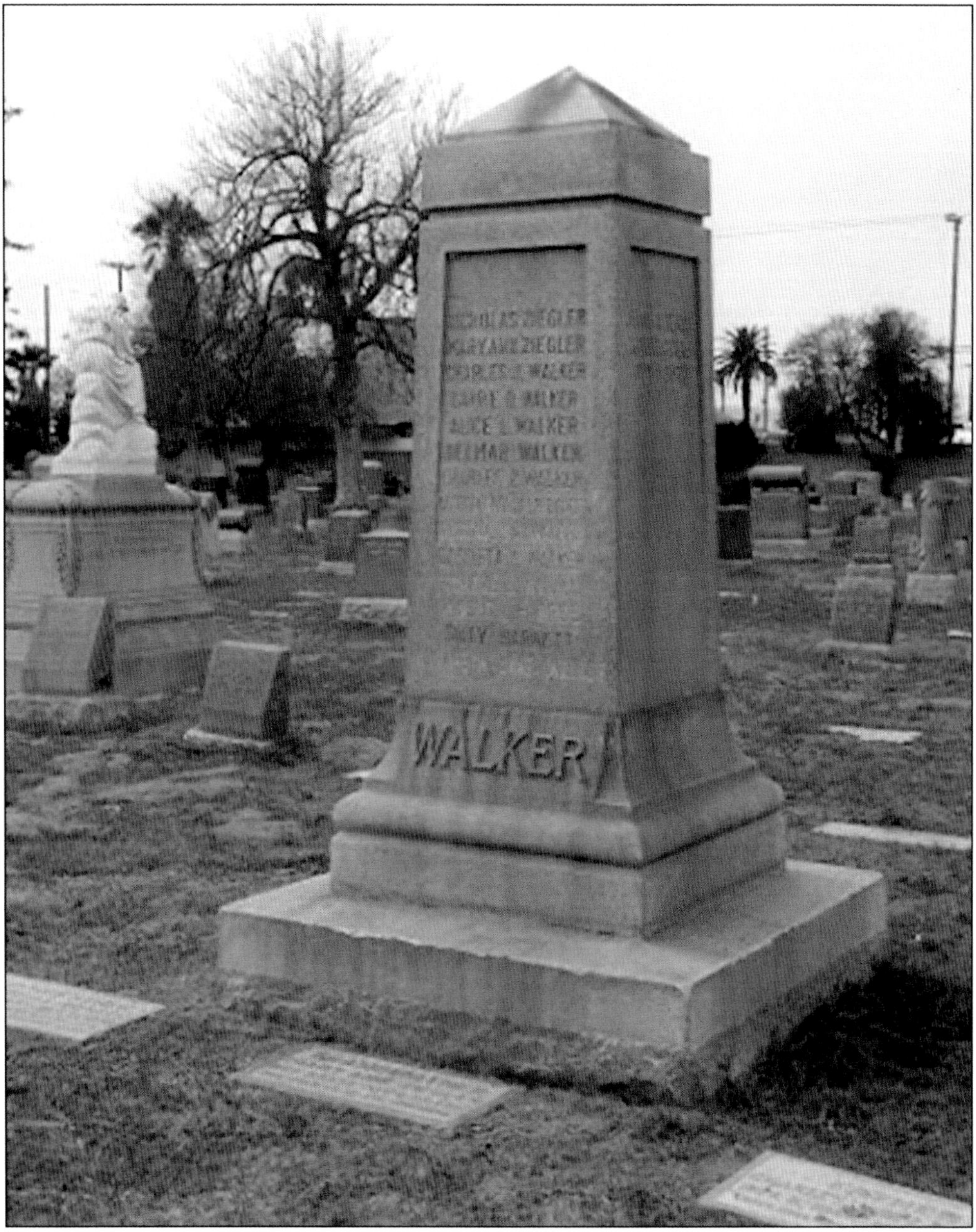

The Walker family is considered among the most prominent in Long Beach. Charles J. "C.J." Walker married Carrie Ziegler in 1895. C.J. was one of the original incorporators of the Long Beach Cemetery Association in 1906, which established Sunnyside. Elected to the city board of trustees, he was selected as mayor. In 1904, he ran unsuccessfully for the 69th Assembly District. Walker resigned as mayor, citing "poor health and business demands" and wrote the city a check for $1,000 to defray the costs of a special election to fill his vacancy. He was involved in the Bixby Hotel, Pine Avenue Pier, Southwestern Transportation and Steamship Company, Inner Harbor Gas and Electric Company, and the First National Bank of Long Beach. In 1907, Walker established Farmers and Merchants Bank. That same year, his 10-year-old daughter Alice died of appendicitis.

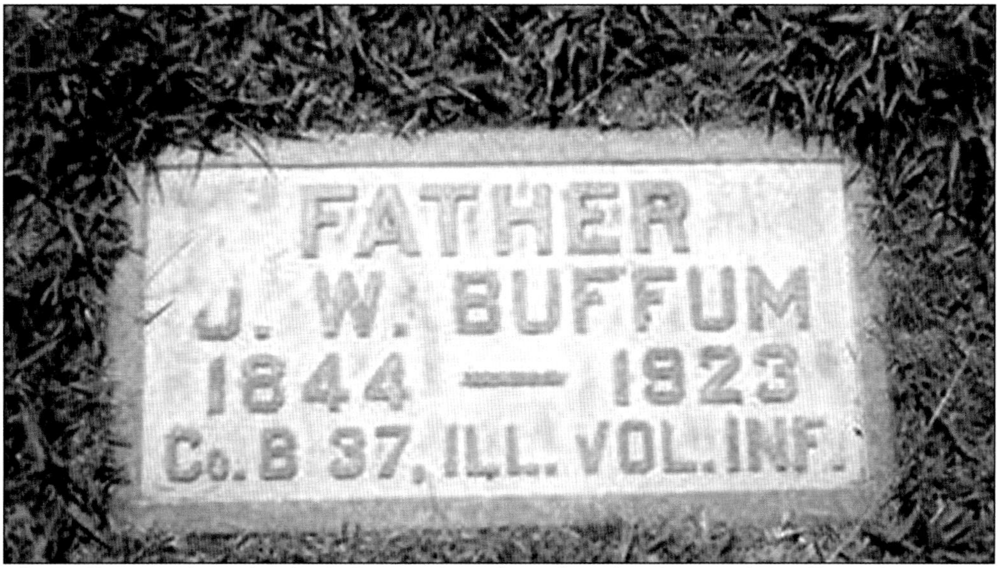

The Buffums are buried in both Sunnyside and in "the other Sunnyside" at Forest Lawn Long Beach. In Sunnyside, Civil War veteran John W. Buffum is buried in the same plot with his daughter Clara Ziegler, whose husband, Frank, worked in the Walker-owned Farmers and Merchants Bank. Both John and Clara are buried in the Walker plot.

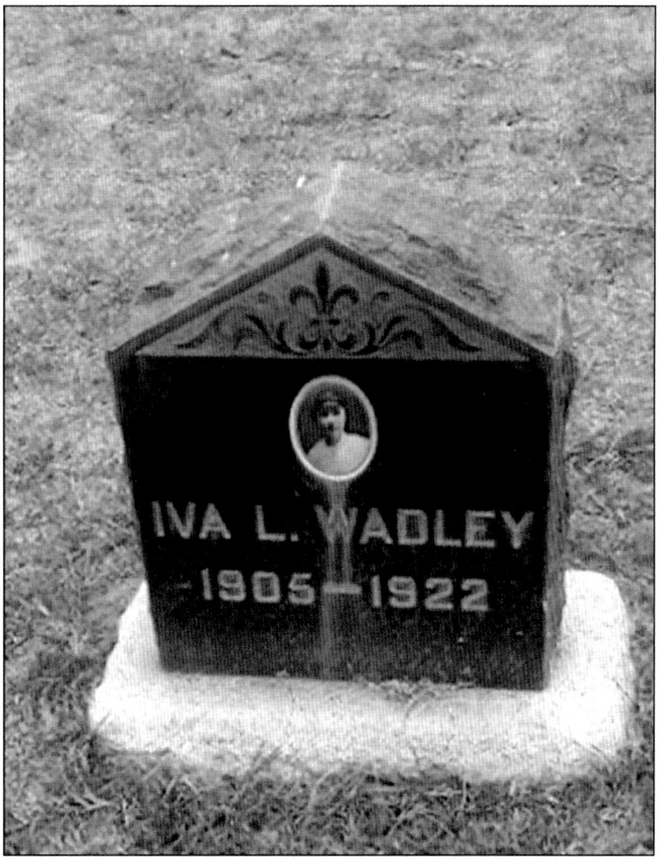

Embedding non-film, non-paper photographs into headstones started with the popularity of daguerreotypes in the 1830s. Sunnyside has many headstones with pictures of those buried. Seventeen-year-old Iva Lee Wadley, a native of Arkansas, died of tuberculosis. Her parents, Ed and Ida, returned to Arkansas, where they are buried.

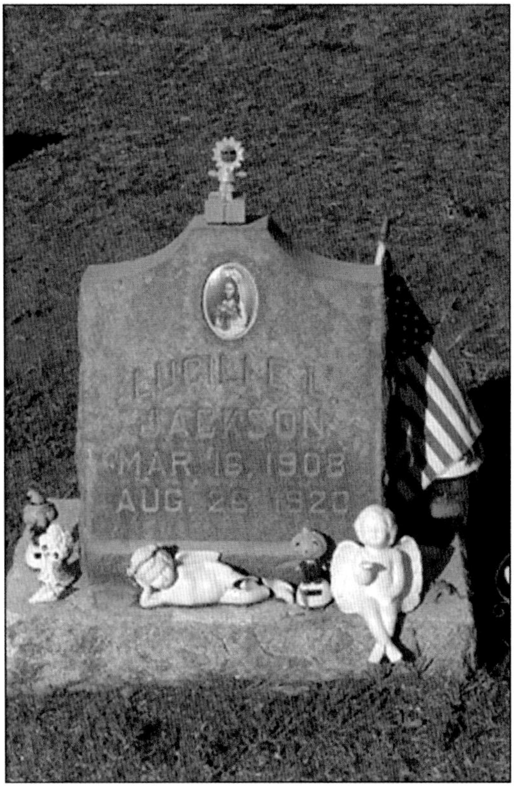

By 1893, J.A. Dedouch Company of Oak Park, Illinois, began producing memorial portraits. Montgomery Ward sold the memorial portraits through their catalog for $6.50 to $13.50. In the 1920s, the embedded pictures of the deceased were colorized, as is the marker for 12-year-old Lucille L. Jackson. Jackson's gravesite often has objects left behind by visitors. The largest display of embedded pictures is found on the Christensen and Beck headstone. Martin Christensen was a native of Denmark and died in 1933, as did his wife, Marie. Their daughter Julia Marie Beck died in 1952 and is buried nearby.

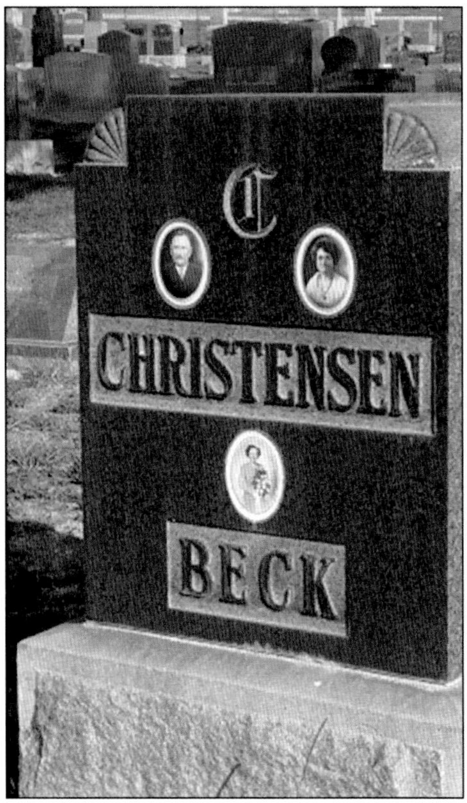

Carlos Alberto Jose de Jesus De Ruiz y Berault de St. Maurice, better known as Captain De Ruiz, a native of Havana, Cuba, entered the US Naval Academy in 1871 as an appointee of President Ulysses S. Grant. He served as city engineer for 12 years and was responsible for completing the tidelands survey in 1916, which determined the area the city could claim. He died of a heart attack at 69.

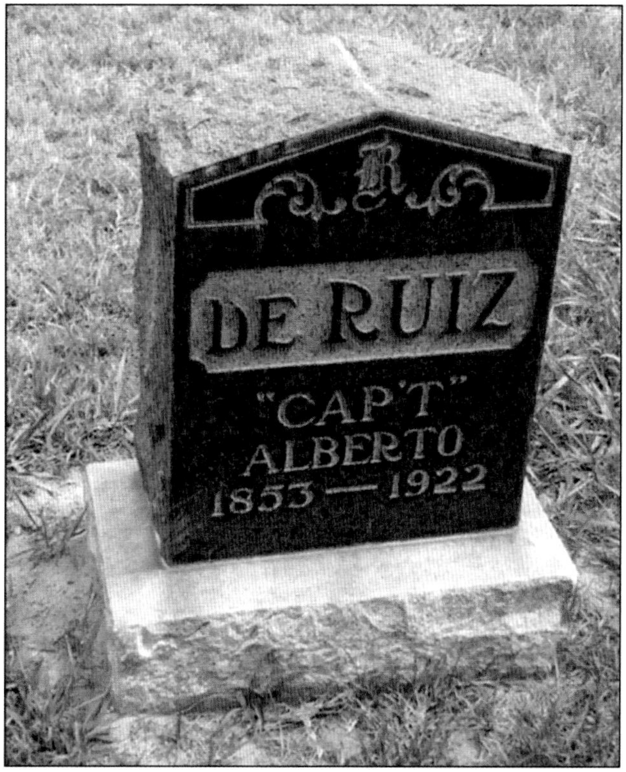

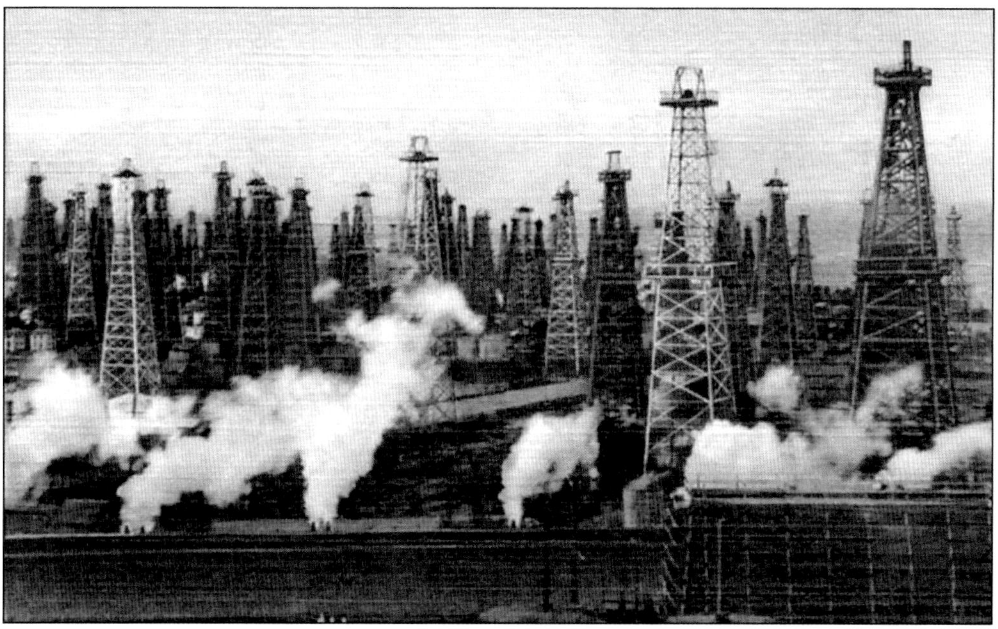

Businessmen from Santa Ana and Long Beach announced plans to build a memorial park and cemetery on the north slope of Signal Hill in 1918. Both the city and Los Angeles County commissioners blocked the plan, stating that a cemetery was prohibited in unincorporated areas. Many large homes had been built on Signal Hill. Just three years later, Signal Hill would be the site of the world's richest oil field.

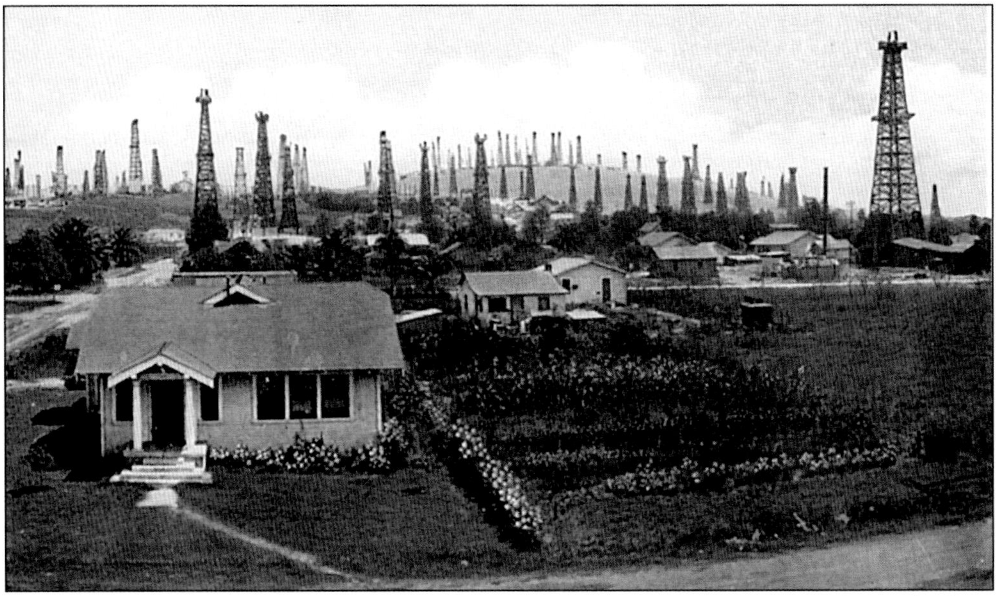

Before oil was discovered on Signal Hill in 1921, it was the site of large homes with breathtaking views and Japanese hog farms and gardens. In 1921, the farms and gardens were seized. There were no public restrictions on where Japanese could be buried, and Japanese graves are located in the northern part of Sunnyside. By 1923, more than 259,000 barrels of oil a day were being taken from 300 wells.

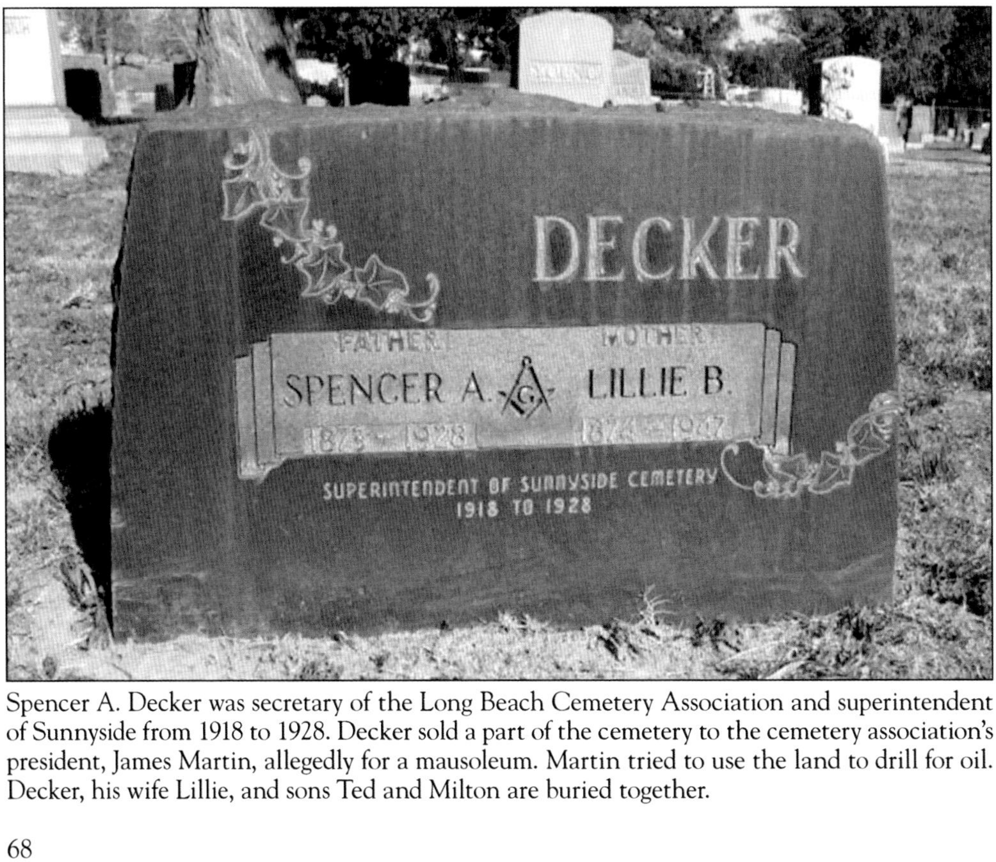

Spencer A. Decker was secretary of the Long Beach Cemetery Association and superintendent of Sunnyside from 1918 to 1928. Decker sold a part of the cemetery to the cemetery association's president, James Martin, allegedly for a mausoleum. Martin tried to use the land to drill for oil. Decker, his wife Lillie, and sons Ted and Milton are buried together.

The city received numerous protests against drilling for oil in Sunnyside Cemetery and proposed establishing a 100- to 200-acre new cemetery away from oil drilling, where bodies could be moved. A Cemetery Protection Association formed to fight the drilling. Eventually, the landowners were allowed to slant drill from the adjacent property. This US Army aerial view shows the cemetery (circles) at lower right. (LOC.)

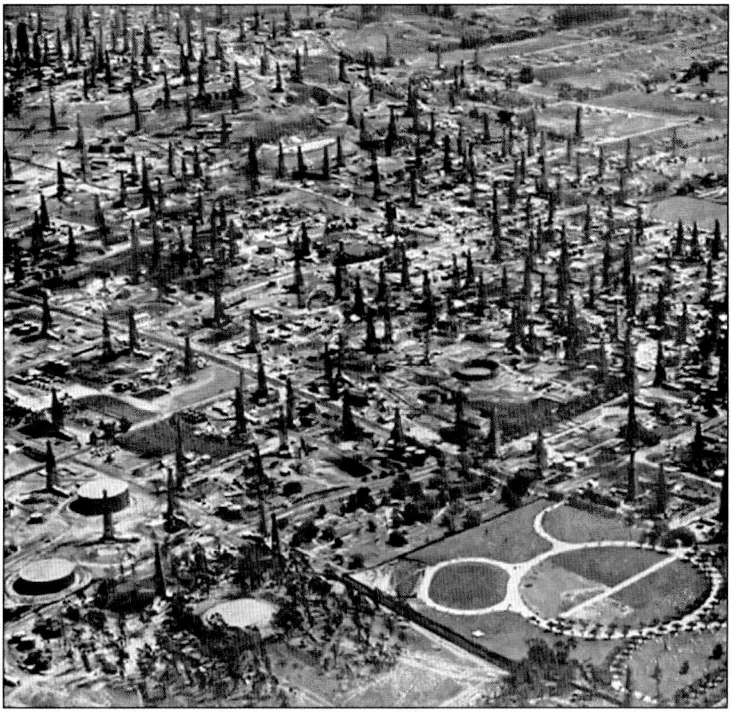

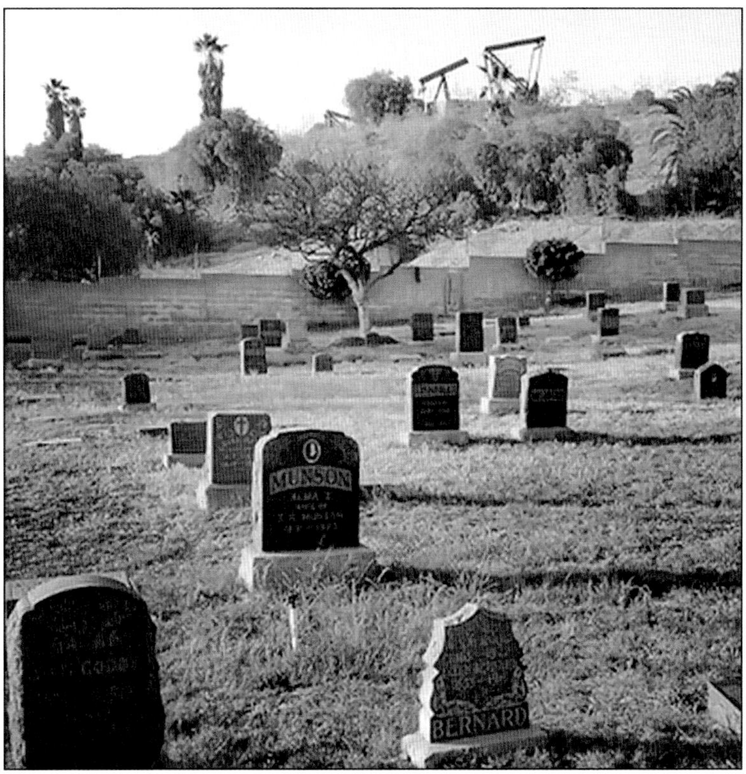

Eleven families of those buried in Sunnyside sued the operators, contending that the slant drilling for oil underneath the cemetery desecrated the graves, and they were entitled to the oil that was drilled. In 1937, the court ruled "not one leaf has been stirred or a flower uprooted," and the descendants only had claim to an easement for a burial plot and nothing else. Drilling continued adjacent to the cemetery.

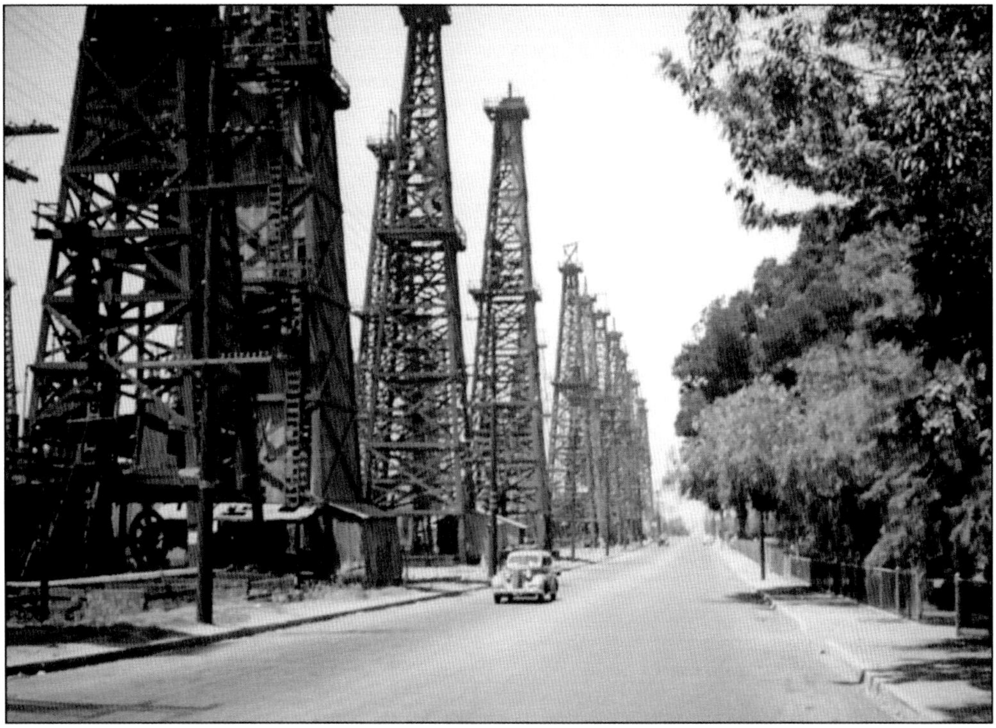

The fight for oil underneath Sunnyside Cemetery attracted national news. Numerous photographers, including Herman Schultheis (above) and Ansel Adams (below), found it surreal to see headstones surrounded on three sides by hundreds of oil derricks. Schultheis photographed the Municipal and Sunnyside Cemeteries, which are pictured above to the right of the derricks on Willow Street. Adams told reporters that he drove by Sunnyside Cemetery in 1939 and saw "a marble angel of death behind oil derricks." The photographs show the early cemeteries with oaks and willows as well as palm trees. After the battle for oil ended, public interest in Sunnyside Cemetery faded. (Above, Herman J. Schultheis Collection, LAPL; below, Ansel Adams Collection, LAPL.)

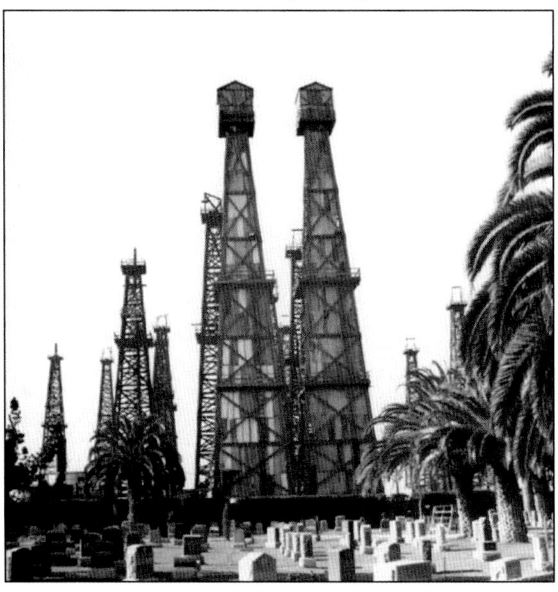

While most oil derricks have been removed or made smaller, active oil drilling can still be seen around both Sunnyside and Municipal Cemeteries. Immediately north of both cemeteries is city-owned property that will become the Willow Springs Regional Park. The city recently relocated the last remaining Pacific Electric trolley station and placed it right behind Sunnyside.

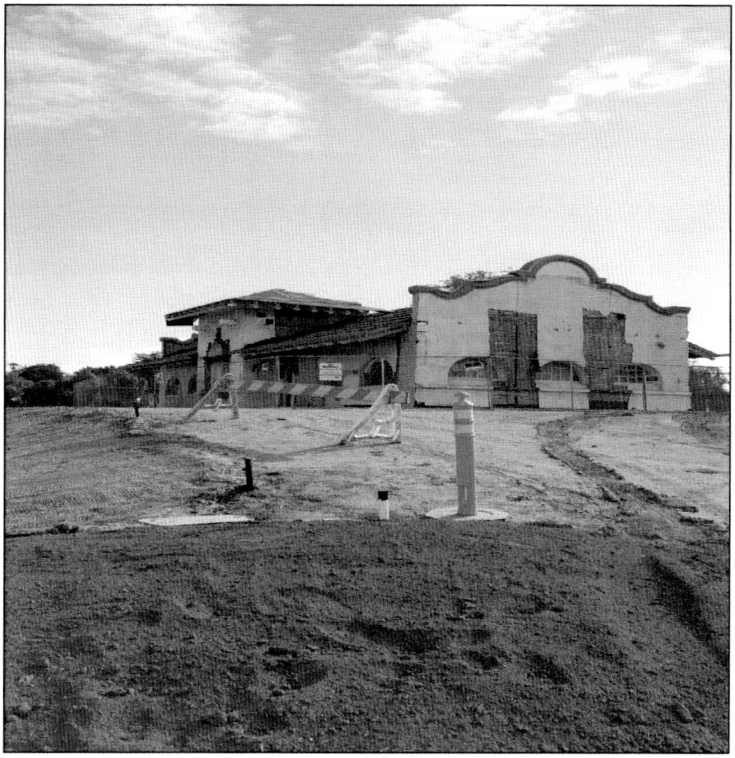

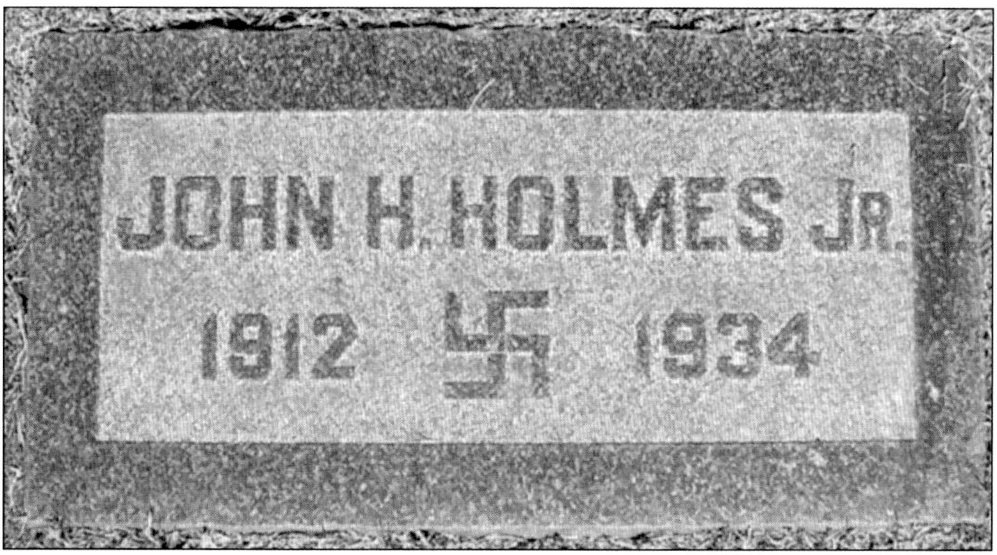

It is not clear if the inscription on the headstone for John H. Holmes Jr. is a Nazi swastika or the native symbol for good luck, which was in common usage before the Nazis adopted it. Holmes died in 1934. His father, John, was a shipbuilder. There are 19 Holmeses buried in Sunnyside.

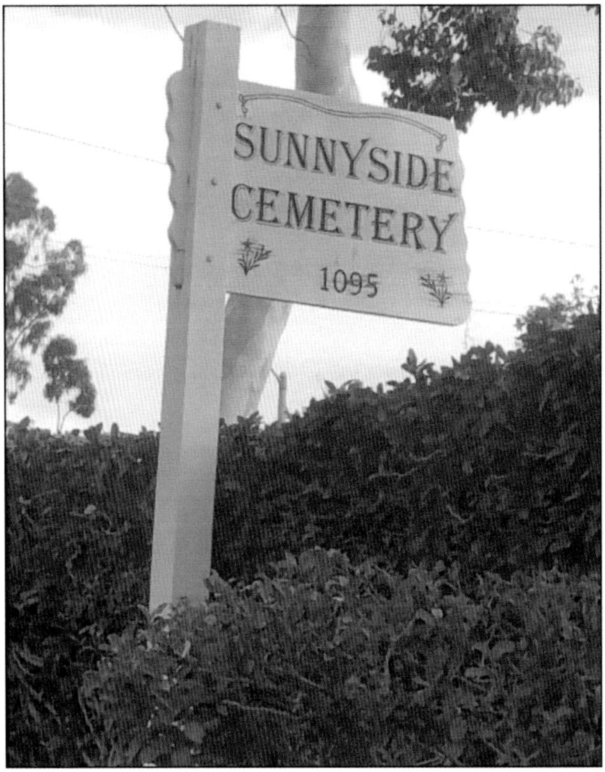

Eventually, the cemetery fell into neglect and mismanagement. It changed hands several times, finally winding up under oversight of the state cemetery board due to embezzlement of endowment funds and neglect of graves. Today, Friends of Sunnyside Cemetery, a nonprofit whose board members have family buried in Sunnyside, oversees operations for the 16,236 buried. In 2000, the City of Long Beach designated Sunnyside Cemetery a historic landmark.

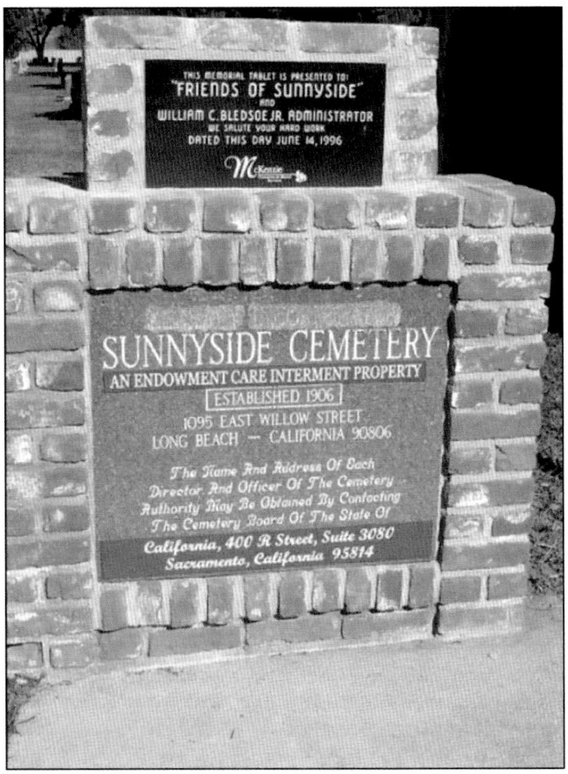

Since 1995, Sunnyside Cemetery is the primary site for the annual Historical Cemetery Tour, sponsored by the Historical Society of Long Beach. Specific gravesites are selected, and professional and volunteer actors in period costumes provide a narrative of the lives of those buried at the sites. The tour is held on the Saturday before (or on) Halloween.

Five

The Other Sunnyside Cemetery

Often people will contact the manager of Sunnyside Cemetery on Willow Street, inquiring about the location of a grave, only to be told the relative is buried in "the other Sunnyside Cemetery" in northern Long Beach.

Tucked into a large residential area on Cherry Avenue and San Antonio Drive stands Sunnyside Memorial Park and Mausoleum.

Operators of the first Sunnyside promised a mausoleum in 1915 and retained the design services of Sidney Lovell, who had designed the Rose Hills mausoleum in Chicago. Once oil was discovered on Signal Hill in 1921, a "cemetery war" broke out when it was discovered that the land for the mausoleum was sold for oil drilling.

Families pressured Long Beach to stop the drilling. City manager Windham announced that Sidney Lovell, president of the American Association of Cemeteries, had been looking for "his final and greatest effort in constructing an artistic burial ground." Windham remarked that if Lovell did not use the design for another site, the city could retain him as a consultant. He also added that with a new cemetery, graves could be removed from Sunnyside and reburied "without expense to the families concerned."

Southwest Builder and Contractor magazine announced that in 1922, Cecil E. Bryan and Company was hired by the Pacific Builders Company doing business as the Sunnyside Mausoleum Association to design a "$300,000 concrete Spanish mausoleum structure on a 5-acre site at Cherry Avenue and Downey-Whittier Blvd." It would include "200x102 ft., 1000 crypts, 1000 sarcophagi niches, 25x70 foot pipe organ, chimes tower, rest rooms, offices, art glass windows, marble inter., bronze trim, and ventilating system." The mausoleum and grounds were designed by Clarence Jay. Cecil Bryan not only built over 80 mausoleums, but also invented the noiseless coffin elevator for mausoleums.

It opened in 1923 with a receiving vault that the held bodies awaiting final entombment. An east wing was added in 1925. In 1933, approximately 6,000 more marble crypts were added, and in 1940, a chapel next to the crematorium was completed.

The 38-acre cemetery, mausoleum, and mortuary were bought in 1960 by Forest Lawn. It took a number of improvements before Forest Lawn would rename the site Forest Lawn Memorial Park Sunnyside. Today, it is known as Forest Lawn Long Beach.

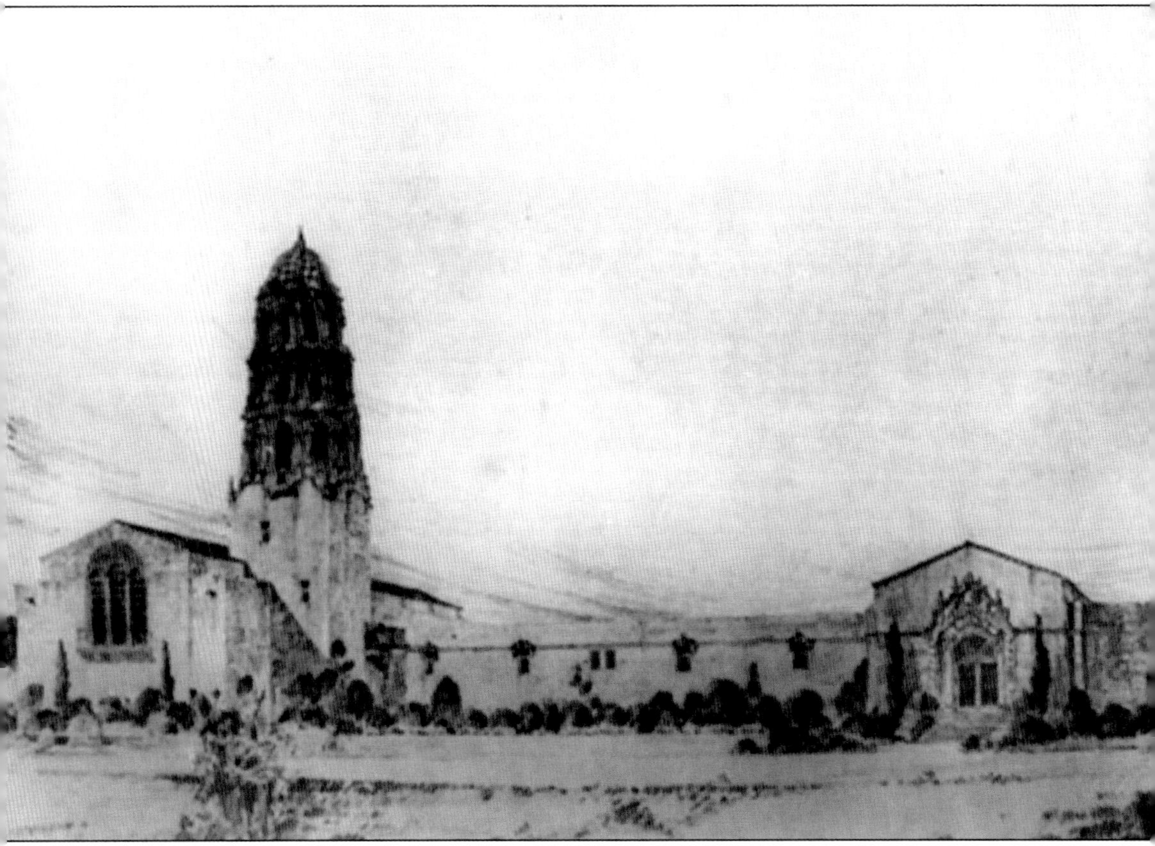

When the city of Lompoc, California, was considering a mausoleum in its local cemetery in 1915, the Long Beach Public Health officer, Dr. Ralph Taylor, wrote: "I consider the Mausoleum of the unit type where each crypt is separate and so constructed that any gases which might be formed must pass through an antiseptic fluid before reaching the outside air to be the most modern, scientific, sanitary method of burial." Sunnyside Mausoleum was advertised as being the "largest in the country" and an alternative to the "unkempt and unwholesome graveyard." Families could place their relatives in lavish marble crypts, surrounded by elaborate stained-glass windows and artwork and sculptures. If families preferred, they could utilize crypts in the outside gardens. Pictured is the earliest photograph available of the mausoleum. (Mrs. Cecil E. Bryan III.)

Community mausoleums became popular around the time the new Sunnyside was designed. The style of architecture is similar to the Spanish Mission cloister design and has many religious themes throughout. An east wing was added in 1925. Over the years, more marble crypts were added as well as a Cathedral Tower and Memorial Chapel. (Mrs. Cecil E. Bryan III.)

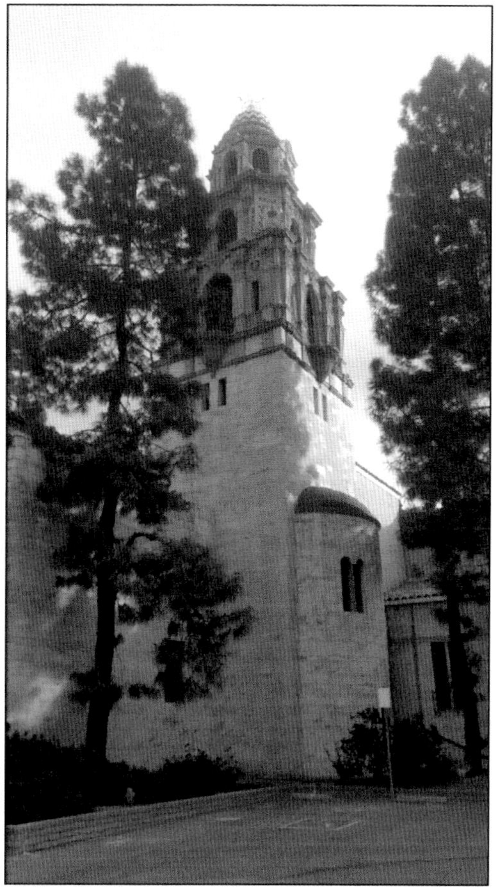

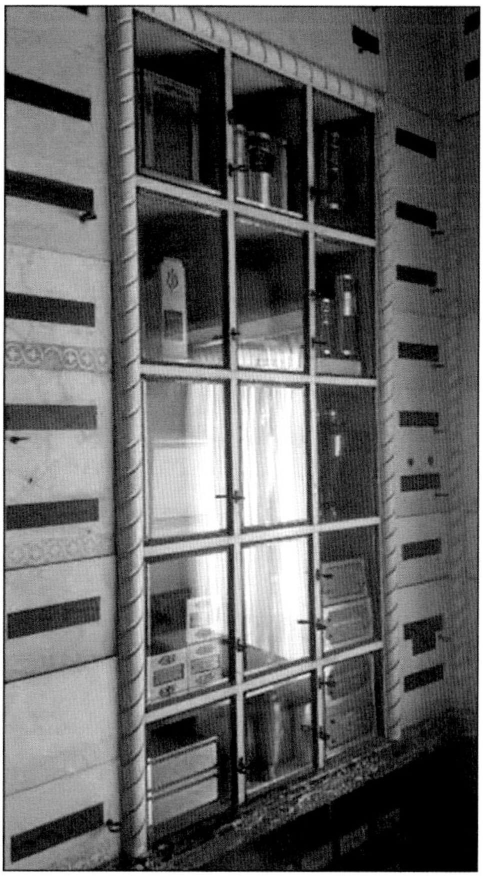

Cremation services on the premises made it easy for families. Cremation reduces a body to bone fragments, which are placed in an urn. The innovative columbarium provides glass plate–enclosed shelves that give the appearance of being inside an expensive home library. There are also outside columbaria throughout the grounds.

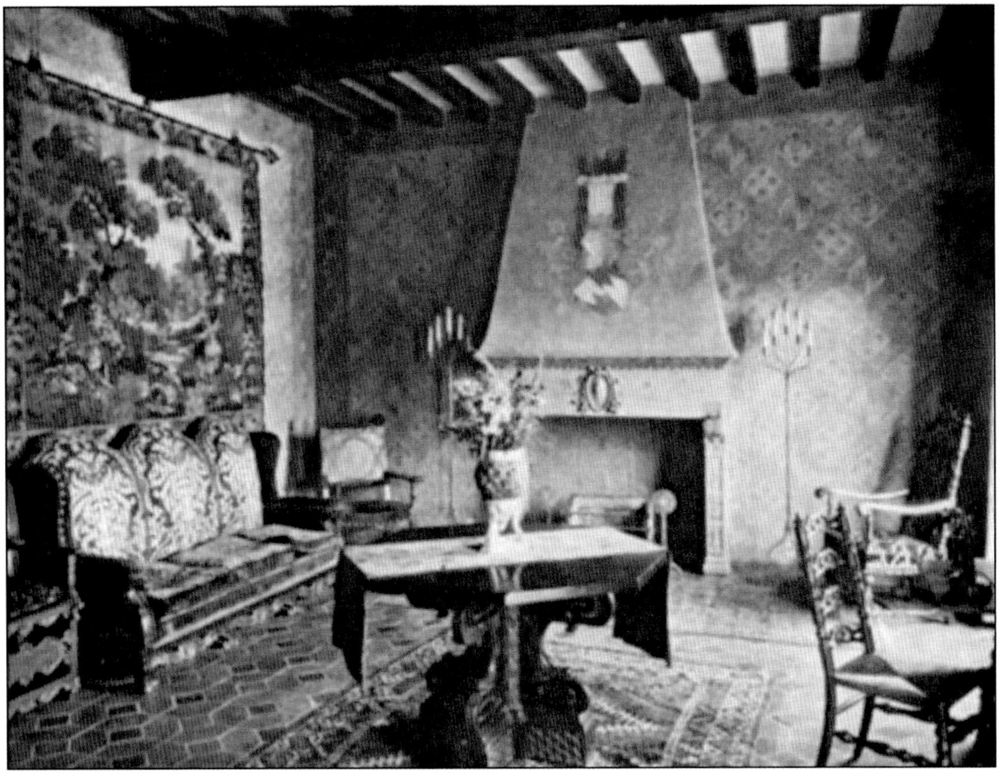

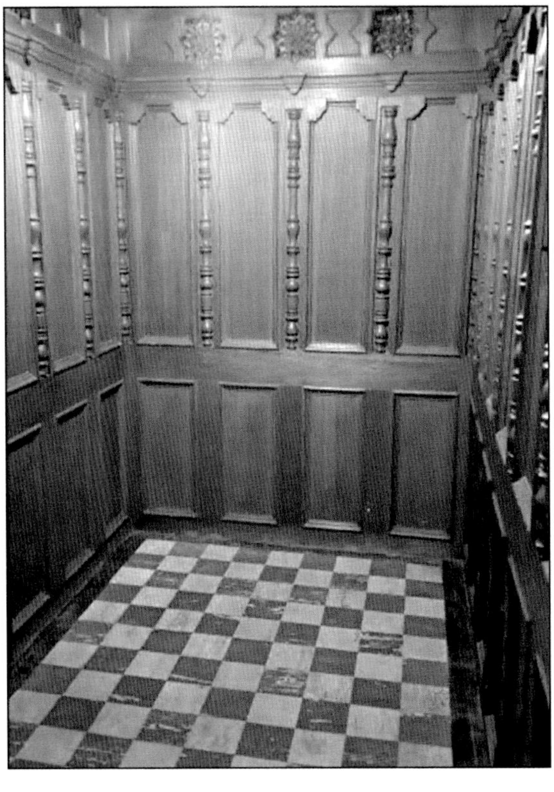

Many features of the cemetery focused on the convenience of mortuary and burial services at one elegant location for a cost most families could afford. Waiting parlors were decorated in the finest furniture. Flooring and crypt holders were made of the finest marble. Colorful fountains and lily ponds surrounded the chapel. (LBPL.)

Sunnyside Mausoleum was the first to be equipped with Degan Tower chimes, a pipe organ, and echo organ. For many years, the public was invited to concerts. Easter sunrise services drew tens of thousands. KGER radio frequently broadcast concerts from the site. It was also the first to be equipped with a silent elevator, invented by Cecil Bryan.

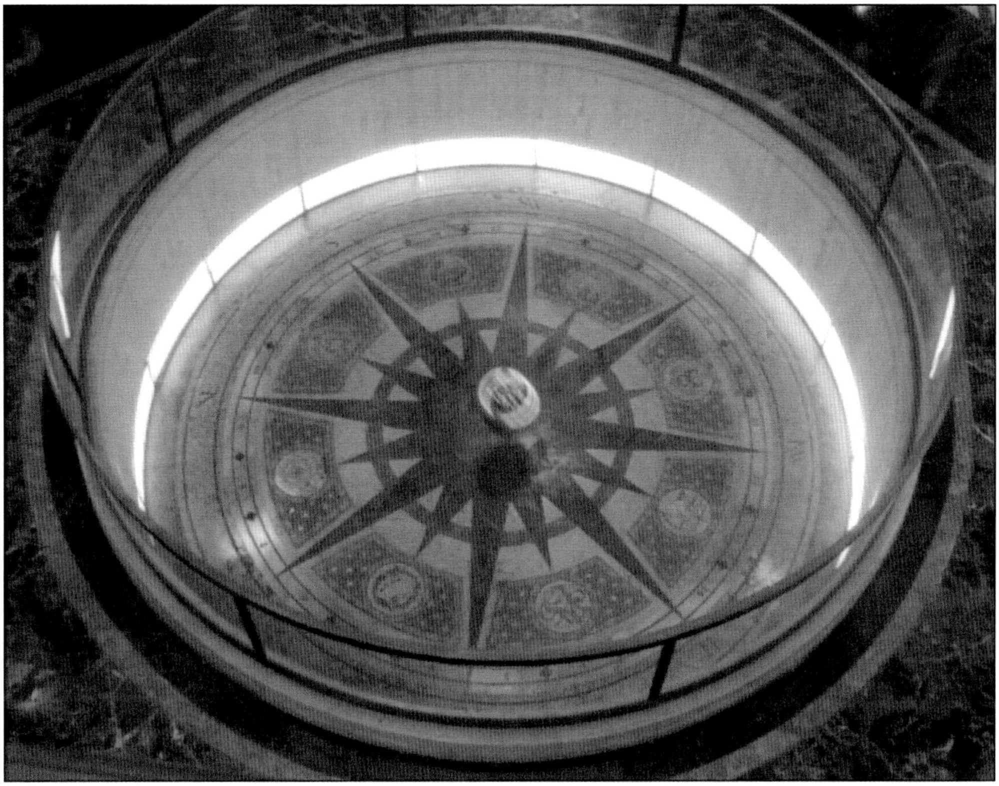

In 1851, French physicist Jean Bertrand Leon Foucault designed a pendulum to demonstrate how the earth rotates on its axis. A Foucault's pendulum is located on the ground floor of the mausoleum and is one of two in California. The Foucault pendulum is suspended five stories and can be viewed at several levels. A plaque overlooking the pendulum below explains how it operates. It takes 42 hours and 48 minutes for the pendulum to make a complete revolution. Lighting around the pendulum helps viewing. Foucault is also credited for experiments determining the velocity of light.

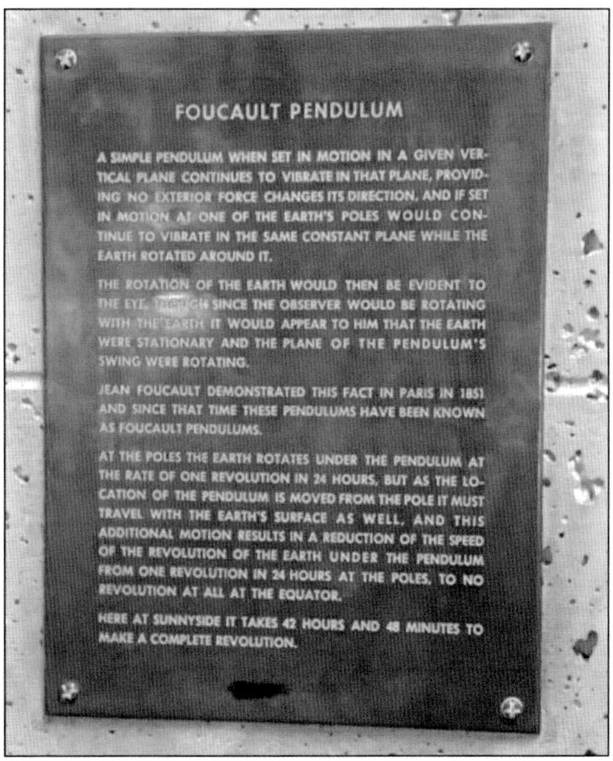

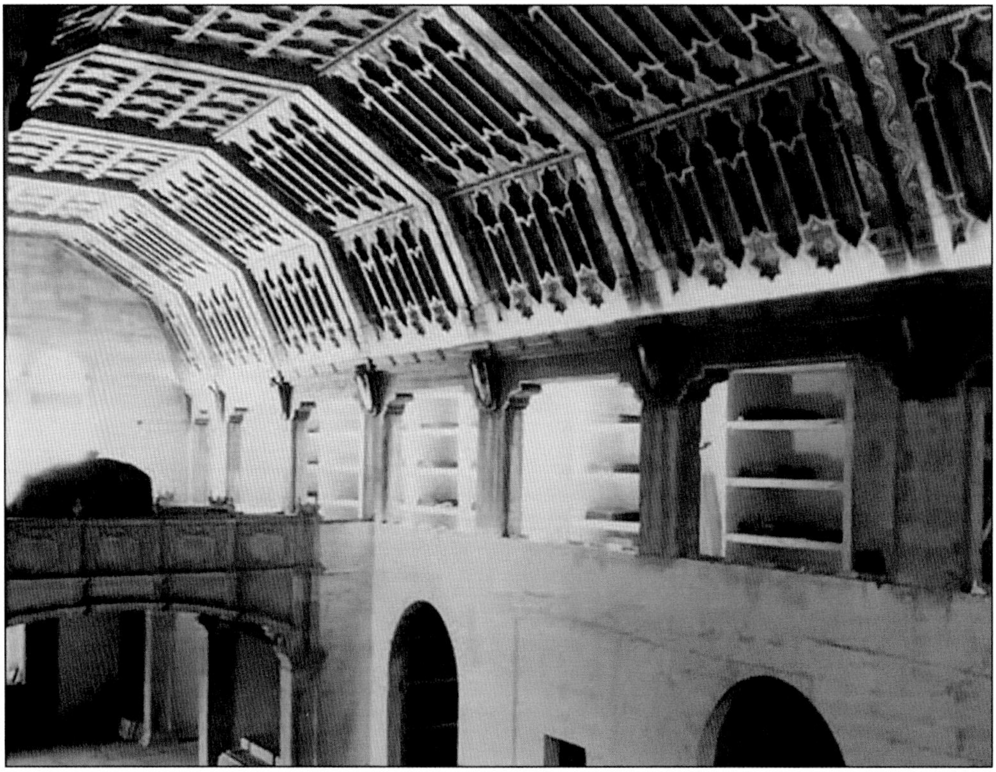

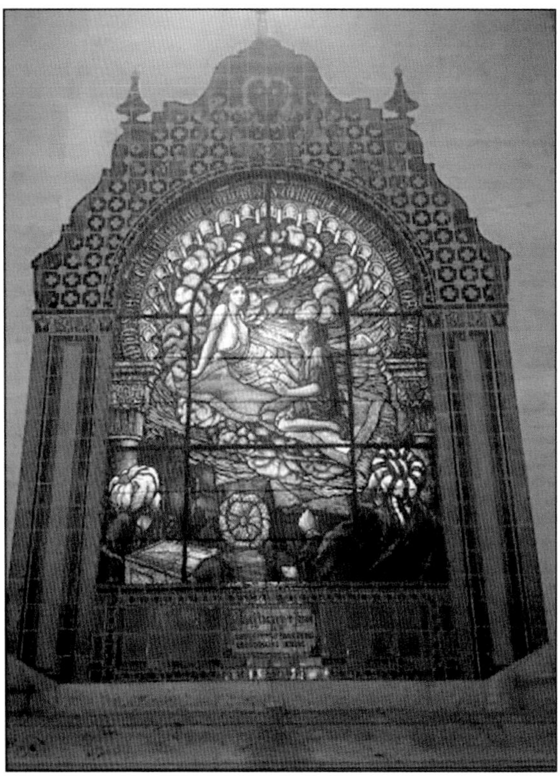

This photograph was taken in the 1930s and shows empty crypts. Once a casket is placed inside, the crypt is sealed. Crypts need to be tilted inward with drain holes to allow bodily gases and fluids from decomposing bodies to escape out the back and not the front. Crypts also need to be ventilated. (LBPL.)

The elaborate stained-glass "Pilgrim of Love" window depicts the story by Washington Irving of Sleepy Hollow fame. In 1897, Irving wrote a story based on the legend of Prince Ahmed Al Kamal. The prince is the son of a Moorish king who falls in love with a Christian princess. The window sets the theme of the "Galeria Alhambra" Moorish design of this part of the mausoleum.

The dark velvet draperies have been removed from the mausoleum. Ceilings and lighting have been updated throughout. Additional statues of religious pioneers have been placed in marble-lined hallways. However, the overall appearance and ambiance of the facility have remained essentially the same as in this 1930s photograph. (LBPL.)

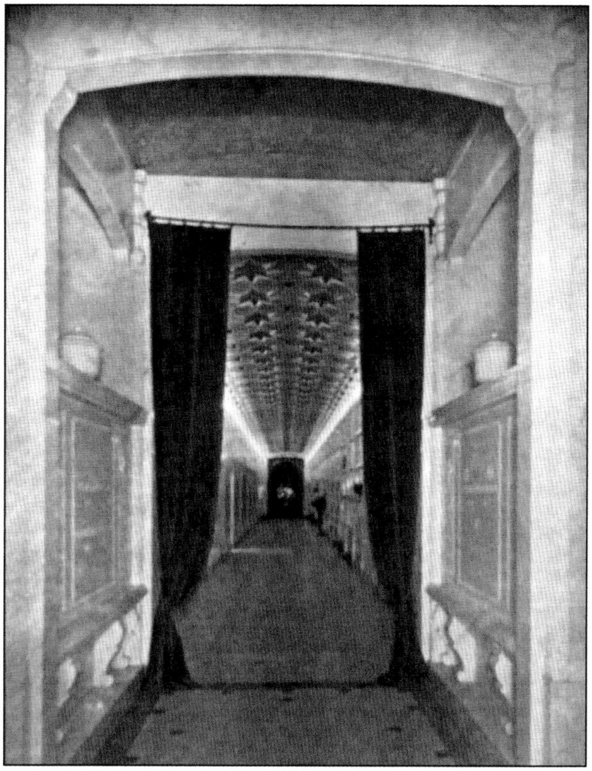

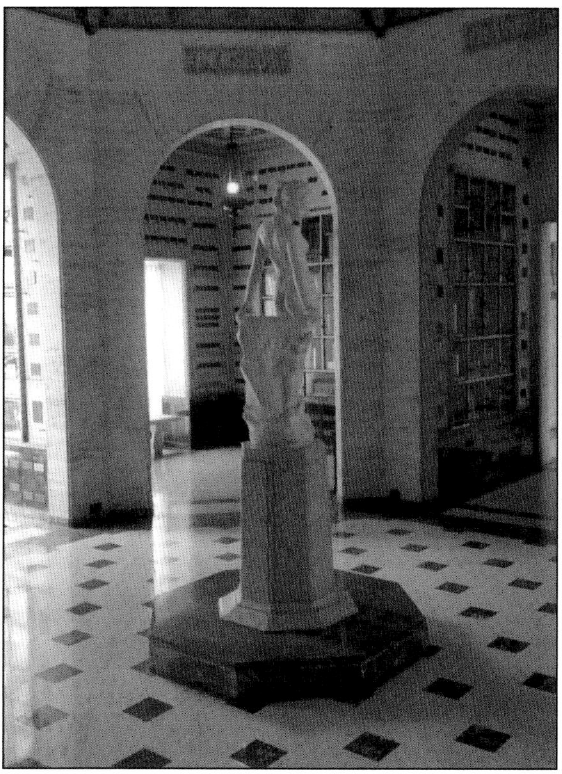

Danae, the mother of Perseus in Greek mythology, stands in the middle of a rotunda, surrounded by hundreds of niches of the columbarium. Each wall is inscribed with the names of other figures in mythology. The glass plates and shelving give the look of being inside an elegant library.

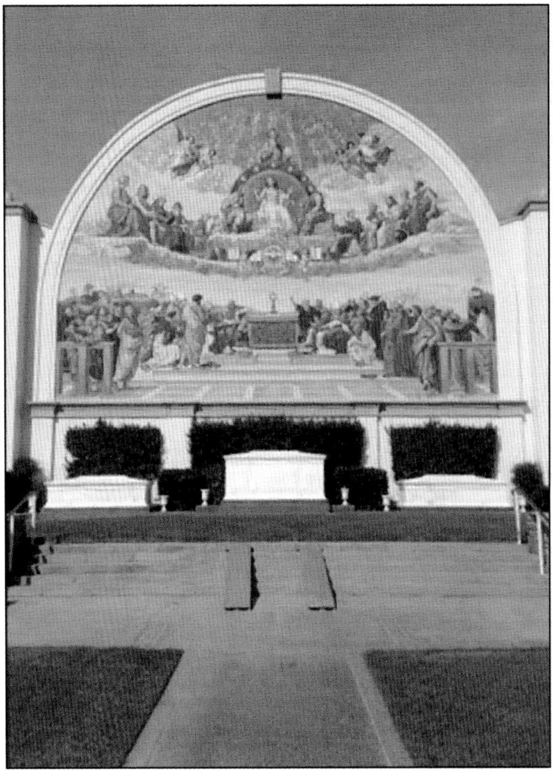

Outside the mausoleum is a massive mosaic re-creation of Raphael's fresco in the Vatican, *The Disputation of the Holy Sacrament*. Forest Lawn refers to theirs as "Paradise." Installed in 1980, it is composed of 2.8 million pieces of Venetian glass in 1,500 different hues. It is 45 feet high by 32 feet across.

Much of the original decor remains, including the letters "SM," inscribed in mosaics as well as on crypt gates. In 1974, a portion of the grounds were consecrated for entombment of people of the Jewish faith. The area is called Rose of Sharon Memorial Gardens.

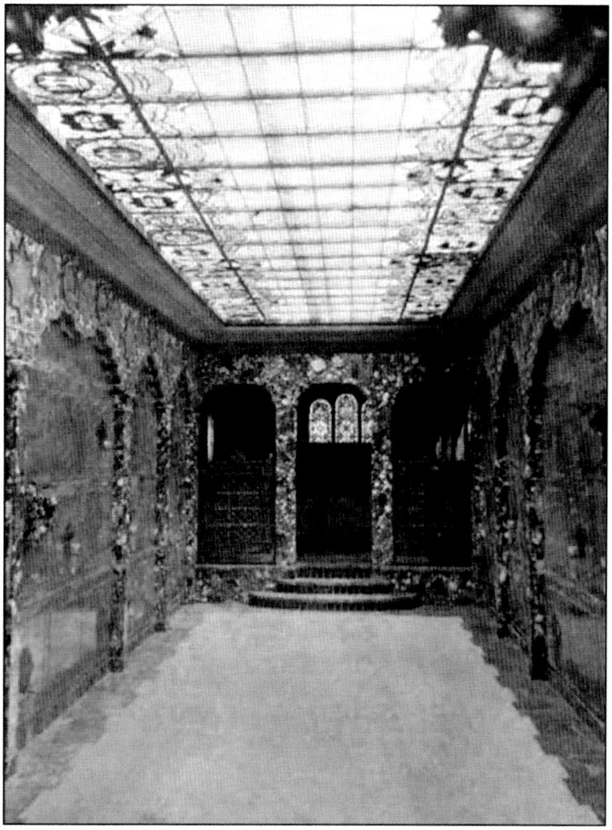

Families have the choice of burying their children in the "Little Lambs" section of the cemetery grounds or in the mausoleum alcove dedicated to children. The alcoves, like many in the mausoleum, are finished in Botticino marble and lit with sunlight coming through an imported art glass window. Botticino marble is a beige marble found in Italy and Turkey. It is the same type of marble found in the US Supreme Court. During the holidays and on the birthdays of a child, families gather and elaborately decorate graves and niches, while visiting for several hours. (Right, LBPL.)

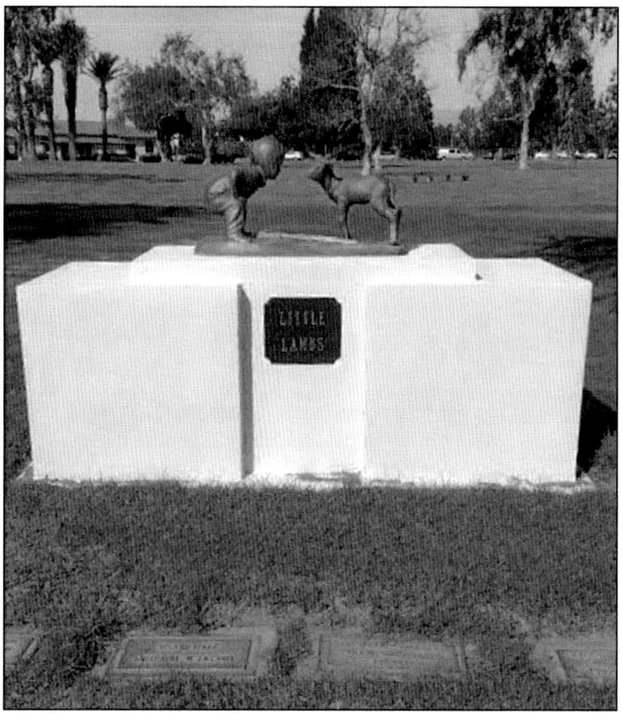

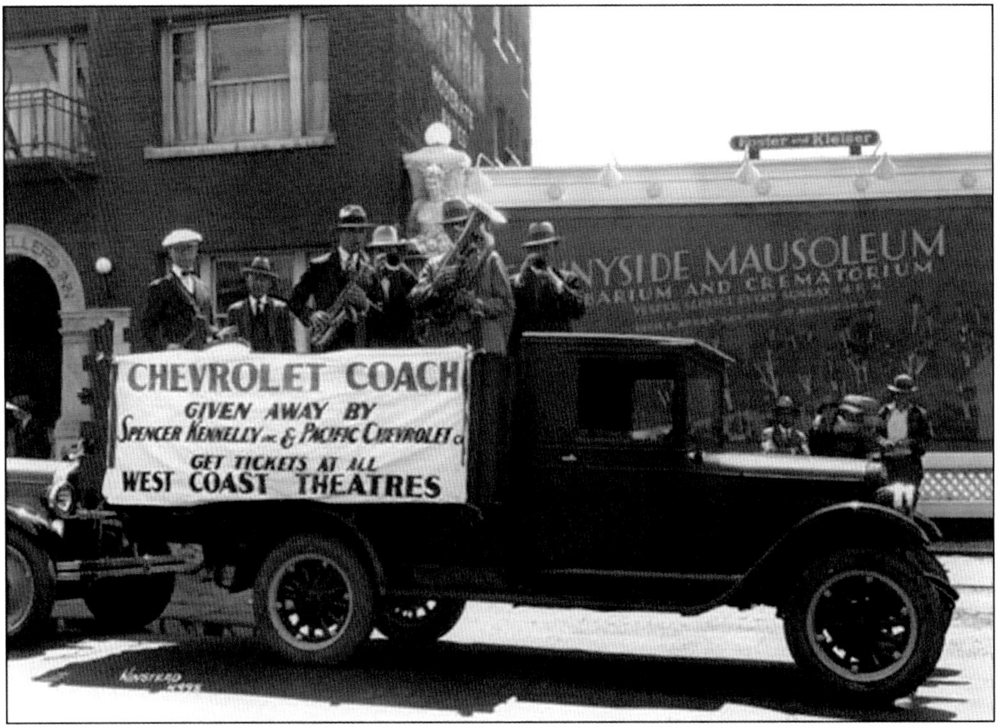

Cemeteries and mortuaries advertised to a growing city. This 1928 photograph of a Long Beach parade shows a large Foster and Kleiser billboard advertising the Sunnyside Mausoleum, Columbarium, and Crematorium. It also announces "Vesper Services Every Sunday at 4 pm," which allowed visitors to hear the beautiful pipe organ. (LBPL.)

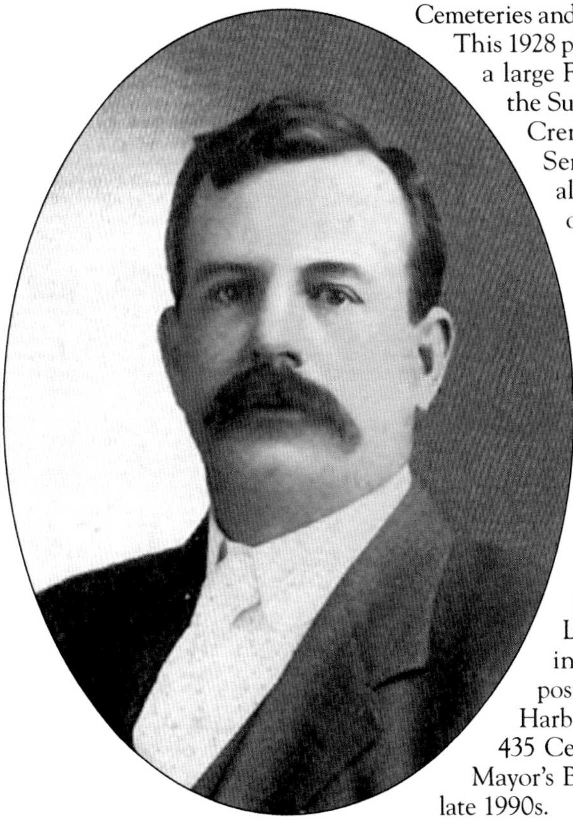

As both the Municipal Cemetery and other Sunnyside cemeteries fell into disrepair, more burials and entombments took place in the new Sunnyside. Many Long Beach notables are buried there, including former mayor, city manager, postmaster, and "father of the Long Beach Harbor," Charles H. Windham. His home at 435 Cedar Avenue was turned into the Lord Mayor's Bed and Breakfast, which closed in the late 1990s.

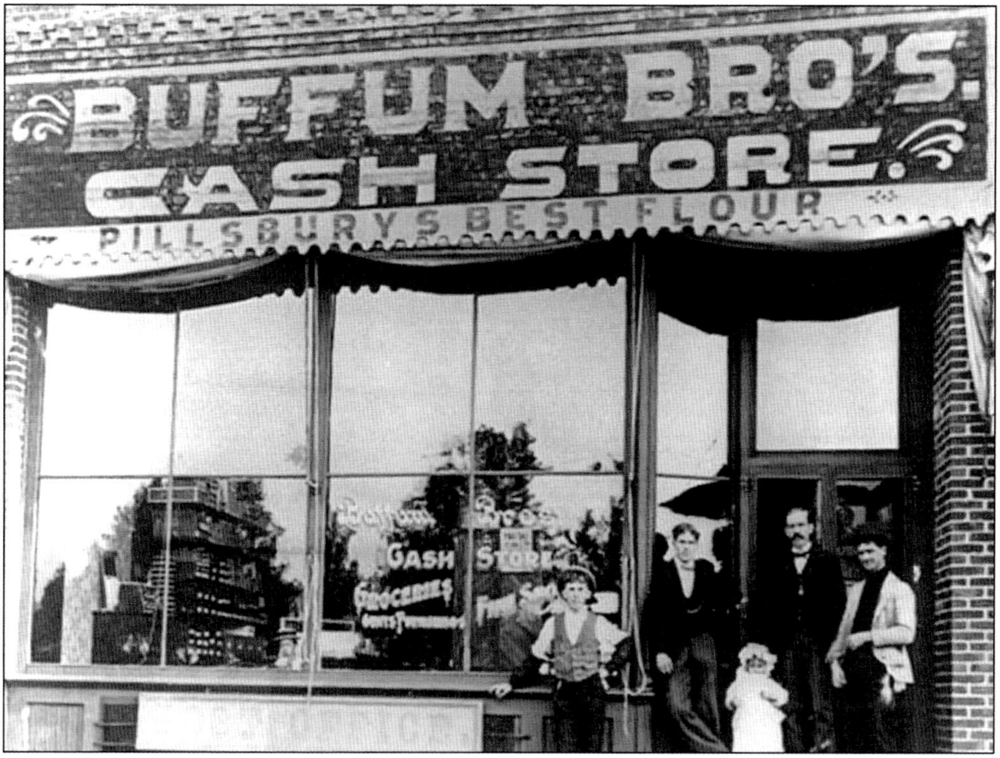

For many years, Buffums' department store on Pine Avenue was the place to shop. Charles Buffum and his brother Elmer founded it in 1904 as a dry goods store. Charles served on the city council and as mayor from 1921 through 1924, later serving on the Southern California Edison Company Board. His daughter Dorothy married Norman Chandler, whose family founded the *Los Angeles Times*. (LBPL.)

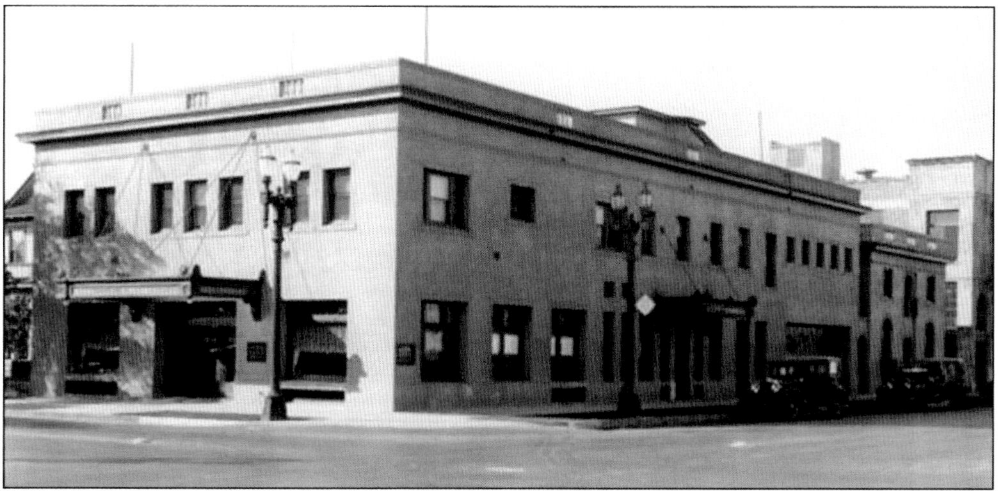

This 1920 photograph shows the Patterson & McQuilkin Mortuary funeral home, located at 555 Locust Avenue. The mortuary was founded by James W. Patterson and his wife, Effie M. Patterson, in 1914. James was an evangelist who organized the Patterson Class, a revivalist form of preaching, in the First Methodist Church. He was also a member of the Scottish Rite Lodge 327. James and Effie are interned in Sunnyside Mausoleum. (LBPL.)

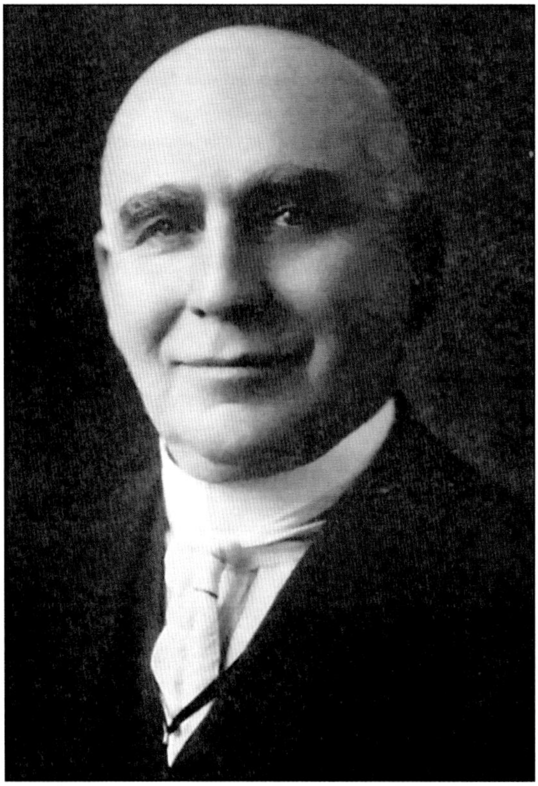

In 1934, Republican Frank Finley Merriam defeated Socialist Upton Sinclair to become Long Beach's first resident elected governor. Merriam's campaign was considered the dirtiest of its time. Merriam had a long political career before his election as governor. In Iowa, he served in the state legislature and as state auditor. He was publisher of the *Iowa Hopkinton Leader.* Merriam served in the California State Assembly and as lieutenant governor. He had one term as governor due to his unpopularity after sending National Guard troops to stop union organizing on the San Francisco docks. The Guard killed two men on what is known as "Bloody Thursday." (Both, LOC.)

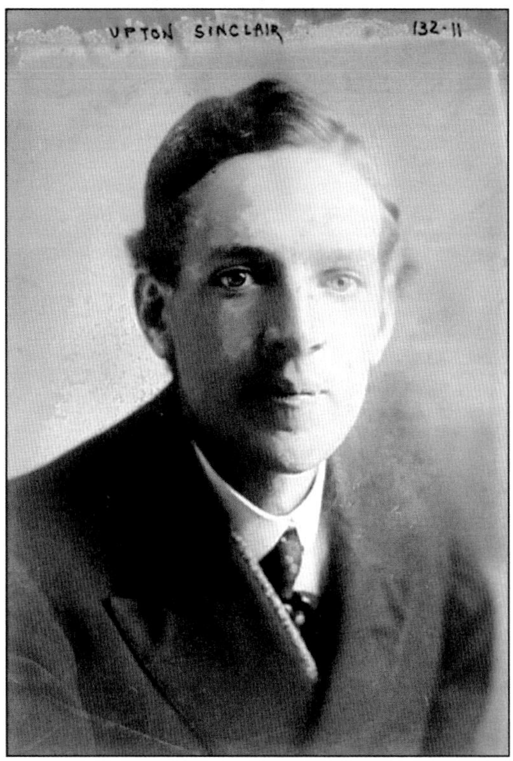

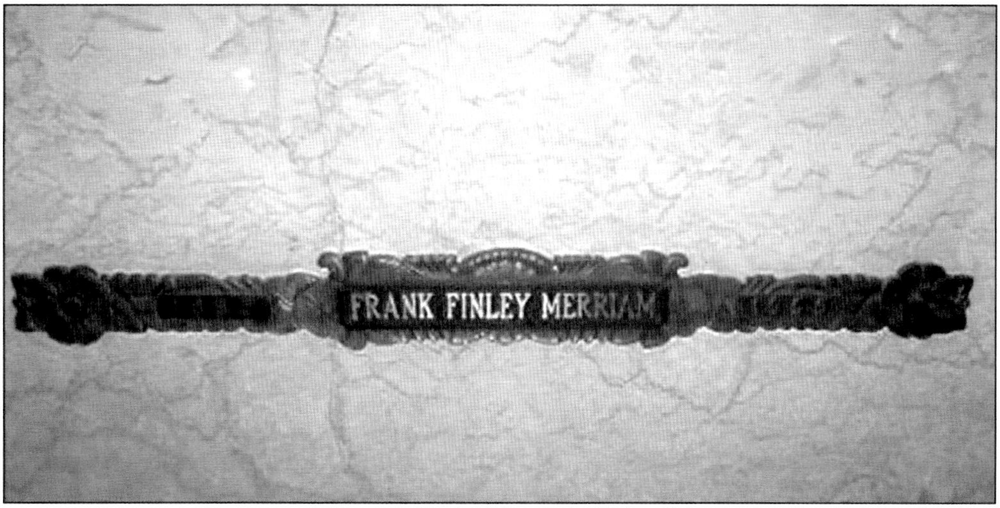

Frank Merriam married three times. Two of his wives are buried in the same place. First wife Elnora Nancy Hitchcock Merriam, who he divorced, is buried in Clarinda Cemetery in Iowa. Second wife Mary Ella "Nellie" Bronson Merriam died in 1931. He then remarried Jessie Stewart Millisack Lipsey Merriam, an activist for women's education and healthcare. She is buried between Merriam and her first husband Amasa Lipsey.

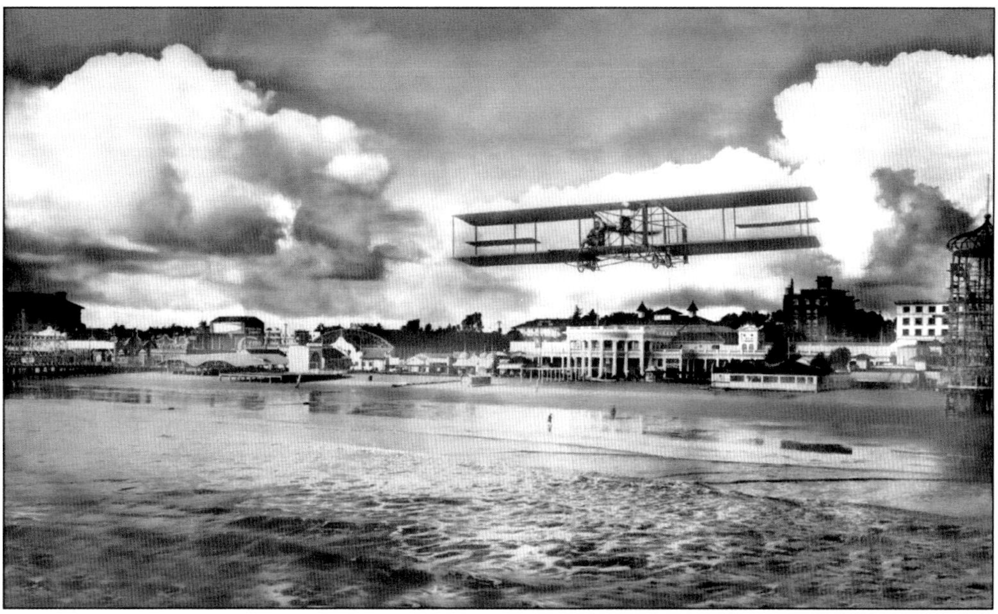

On December 8, 1928, pioneer aviator Earl Daugherty flew Warren E. Montfort, *Long Beach Press Telegram* city editor, and Elmer Starr, owner of the Pacific Engraving Company, in his new Laird airplane. Daugherty, a flight instructor and aerial stunt performer, is credited with establishing Long Beach's first airfield. Montfort and Starr were aviation enthusiasts and often took flights with Daugherty. (Long Beach Airport.)

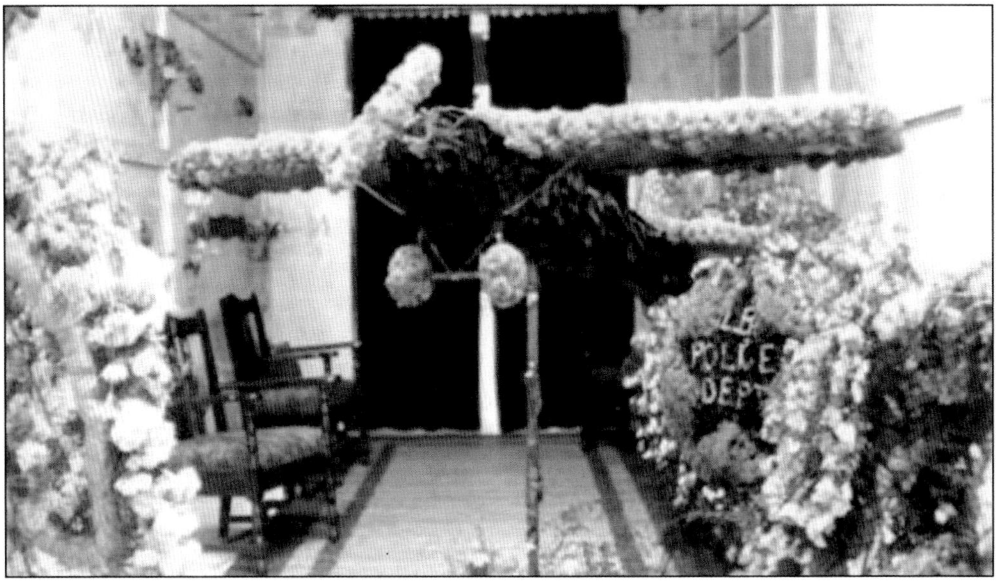

Several hundred people watched at the Long Beach Airport as Daugherty performed a series of barrel rolls, when suddenly a wing broke off and the airplane plummeted 3,500 feet, killing Daugherty, Montfort, and Starr. Newspapers reported that 50 planes flew overhead for Montfort's burial at Sunnyside Mausoleum. However, official records do not show that he is buried there. Daugherty is buried at Angeles Abbey Mausoleum, and his funeral flowers are shown here. It is not known where Starr is buried.

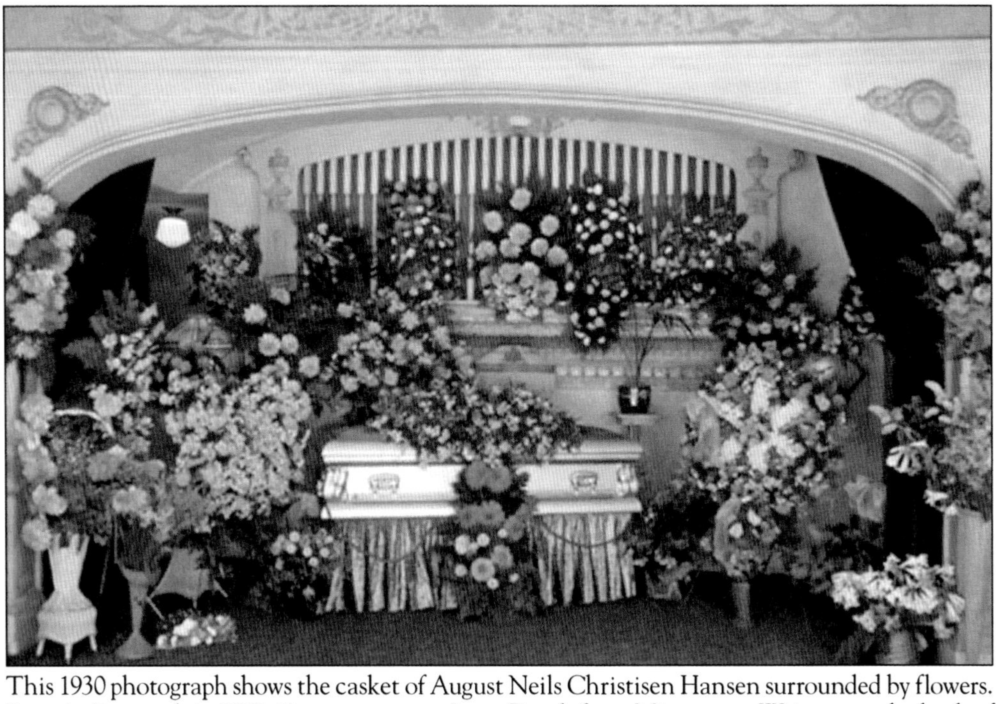

This 1930 photograph shows the casket of August Neils Christisen Hansen surrounded by flowers. Born in Denmark in 1857, Hansen came to Long Beach from Minnesota. Written on the back of the photograph are details of costs for being entombed at Sunnyside Mausoleum: metallic casket ($395) and double-sized "De Luxe Crypt" ($900). (LBPL.)

Thomas M. Eaton was born in Illinois in 1896 and served in the Navy during World War I. He moved to Long Beach in 1921, where he established an automobile business. Elected to the city council in 1934, he served as mayor in 1936. Eaton won the 18th Congressional District in 1939 and served only eight months before he died. (LBPL.)

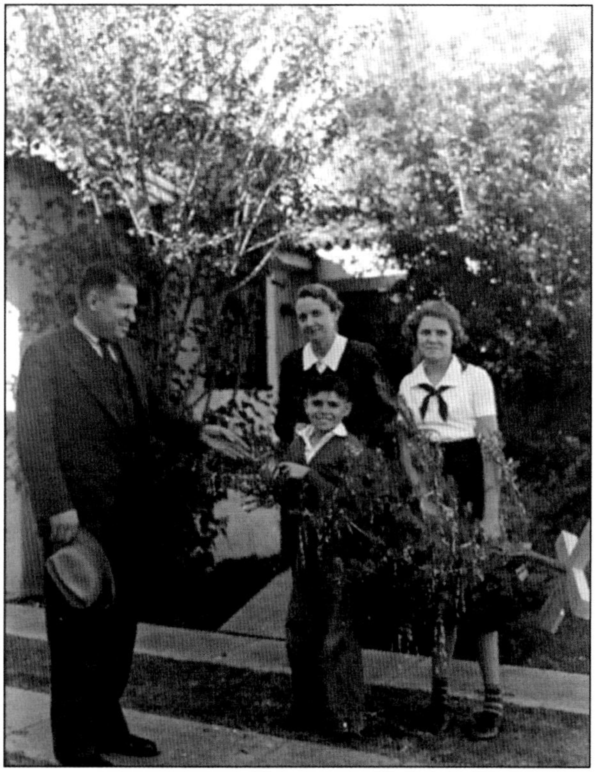

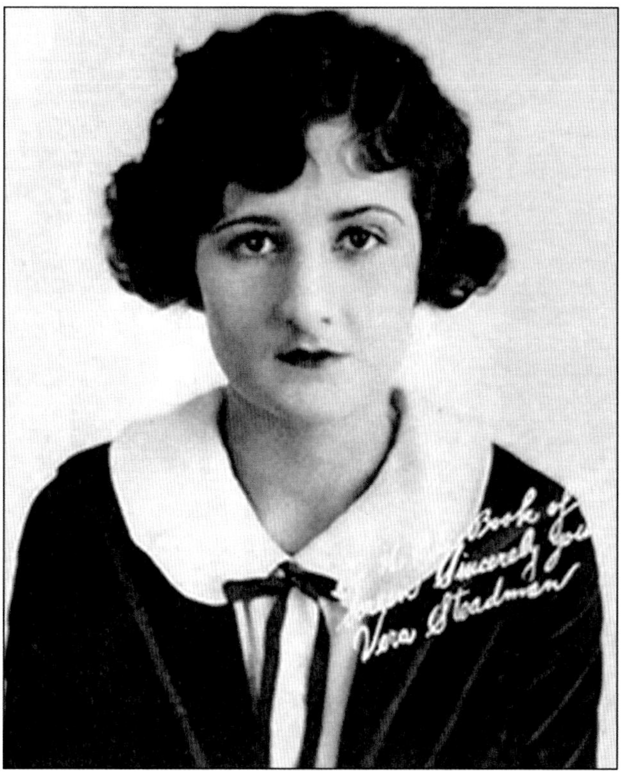

In 1917, movie producer Mack Sennett rented the Balboa Amusement Producing Company studios in Long Beach. This independent studio produced many movies from 1910 to 1921. Sennett included several young ladies in scant beach attire for his "Sennett Bathing Girls" movies, including comedienne and actress Vera Steadman. Steadman is credited with 99 films. She died in 1966.

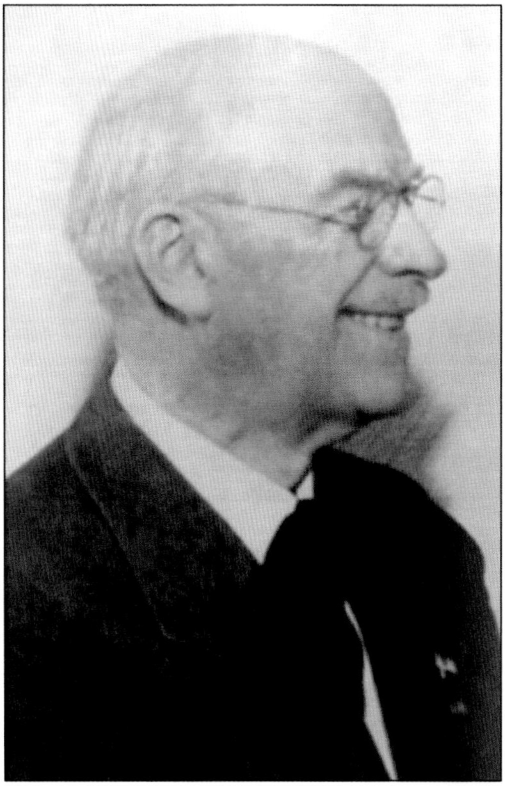

Charles Heartwell, a commissioned colonel in the California National Guard, served on the first Long Beach Water Commission. He suggested the purchase of land from the Montana Land Company and placement of water wells on the property that, in 1939, became a 122.5-acre park named in his honor. Heartwell Park is located on Carson Street, from Clark Avenue to the San Gabriel River.

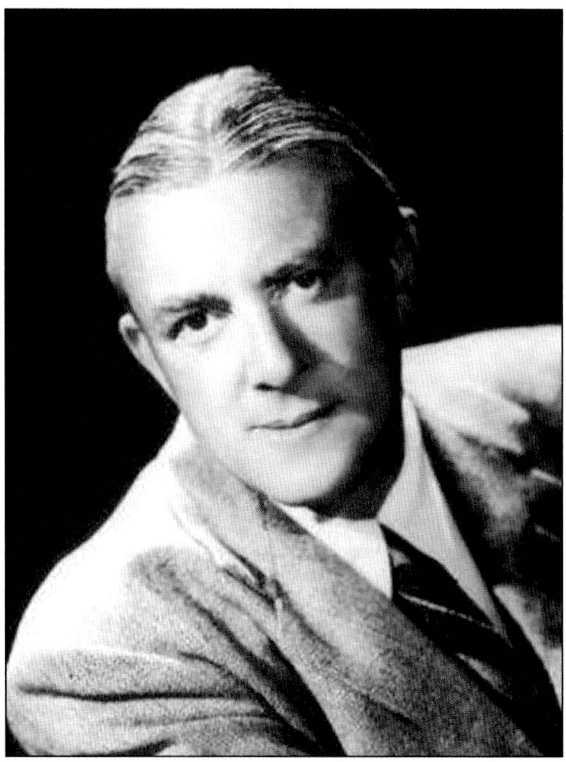

Novelist James Hilton told the press in the 1940s he moved to Long Beach because "it puts me closer to the feel of America." He was the author of several popular novels, including *Lost Horizon* and *Good-bye, Mr. Chips*. He won an Oscar in 1943 for his screenplay *Mrs. Miniver*. Hilton died in Seaside Hospital in 1954 from complications of liver cancer.

In conjunction with the PACIFIC SOUTHWEST EXPOSITION

AMERICA'S GREATEST MOTOR BOATING and YACHTING REGATTA

LONG BEACH, CALIF.

(Home port of Miss California)

AUGUST 4th to 12th

AHOY! The Pacific Southwest of America, mecca of Yachtsmen, invites you to the 8th Annual Regatta of the Southern California Yachting Association, sponsored by the thirteen boating and yachting clubs of Southern California.

This mammoth program, which has been approved by all the national yachting and power boat associations, includes races for starboats, R class boats, 6 meter boats, 45's, sloops, yawls and schooners of all classes. The power boat division includes races for hydroplanes of the 151, 510 and 725 classes, gold cup boats, all classes of outboards and all types of runabouts and power cruisers.

Championship boats of all classes have been entered. The regatta committee is now arranging an International Rudder Trophy challenge.

For further information and entry blanks, communicate with the Regatta Committee, Chamber of Commerce Bldg., Long Beach, California.

See the Big Pacific Southwest Exposition

This mammoth International event is the greatest Exposition held on the Pacific Coast since the San Diego Panama-Pacific International. It will portray the commercial and cultural advancement of the Pacific Area on a 60-acre site in the heart of the Long Beach-Los Angeles harbor district. More than twenty foreign nations are participating. The Pacific Southwest Exposition is Federally recognized and has the endorsement of the eleven Western states. Of particular interest to boatsmen will be the Division of Yachting and Motorboating at the Exposition. The dates of this brilliant attraction are July 27th to August 20th, inclusive

Richard Loynes came to Long Beach in 1886 and worked for the Bixby family. He opened a brickyard near Recreation Park and moved it to Fourteenth Street and Chestnut Avenue. His yard provided the clay pipes that transported water to the homes of Long Beach's first residents. Loynes constructed many of the brick homes in Long Beach. His son, "Smiling Dick," was best known for winning the Gold Cup racing his hydroplane *Miss California*. The boat was displayed at the 1928 Long Beach Pacific Southwest Exposition, as shown in the advertisement at right from *Motorboating* magazine. He helped establish the Long Beach Yacht Club in 1929 and served as president of the Long Beach Chamber of Commerce and as the first chair of the Long Beach Marina Committee in 1956. Loynes was appointed to the State Shoreline Planning Association, which strongly opposed use of tidelands revenues for any purpose "other than acquisition and development of beaches and parks."

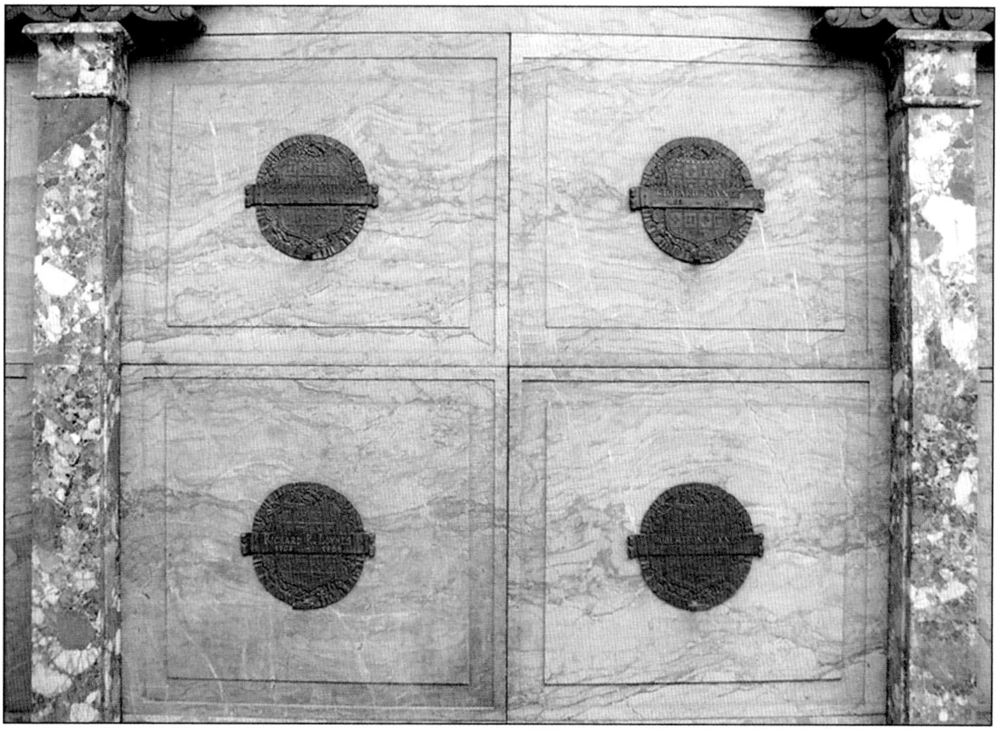

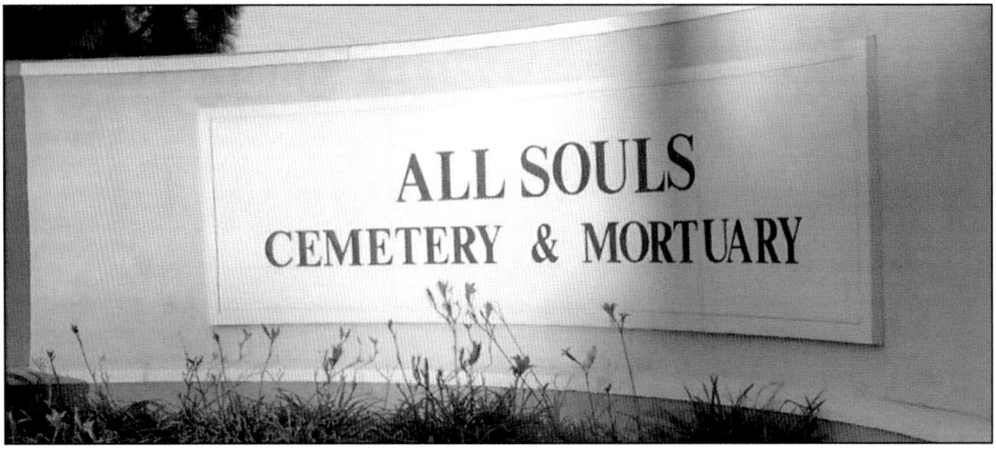

The large vacant land across from Sunnyside Mausoleum remained available for many years. In 1934, sixty acres were approved by the County of Los Angeles Regional Planning Board for a cemetery and an additional 30 acres was recommended to be added later. In 1945, developers proposed a Rose Hills Memorial Park Cemetery, which infuriated local homeowners from Lakewood Village and Los Cerritos; they formed the Bixby Highlands Property Owners Association to protest. Three years later, as a way of placating residents, the county board of supervisors negotiated with developers the contribution of 10 acres south of Sunnyside Mausoleum on the west side of Cherry Avenue for a city park. In 1950, a Catholic All Souls Cemetery was established on 78 acres.

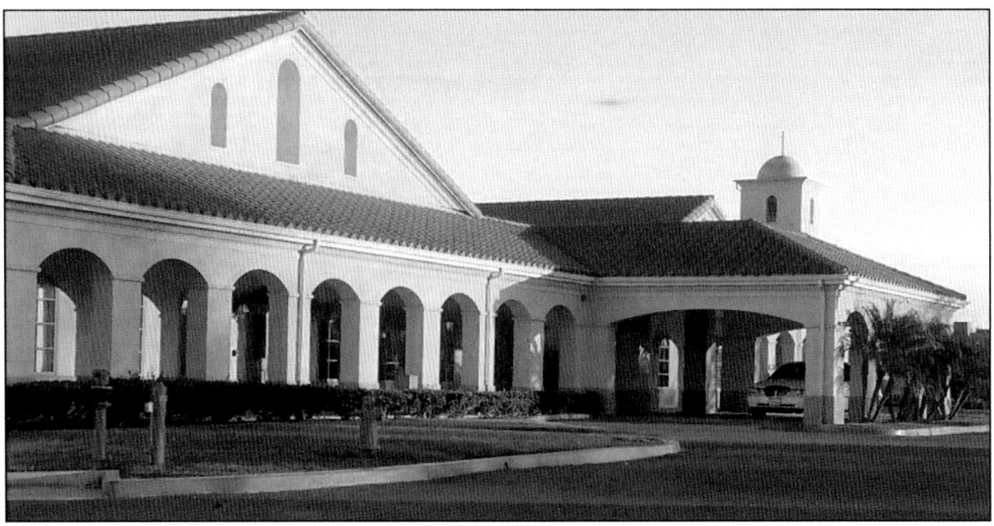

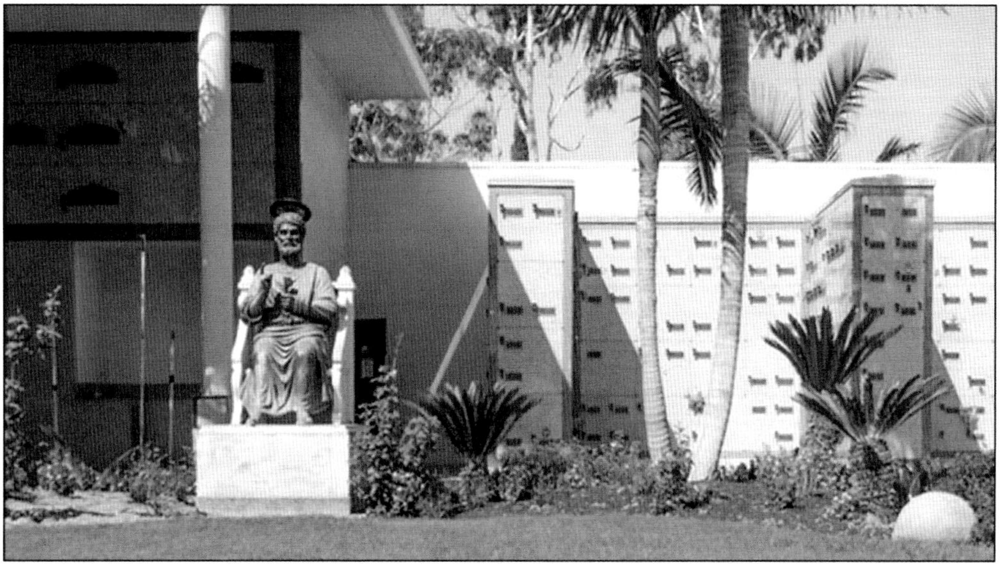

For many years, non-Catholics and those who committed suicide could not be buried in Catholic cemeteries. The church banned cremation until 1963. The Second Vatican Council of 1970 brought many changes, including utilizing white instead of black vestments and casket palls. All Souls Cemetery includes a mortuary, chapel, crematorium, and lawn crypts. Several columbaria hold the bone fragments of the deceased.

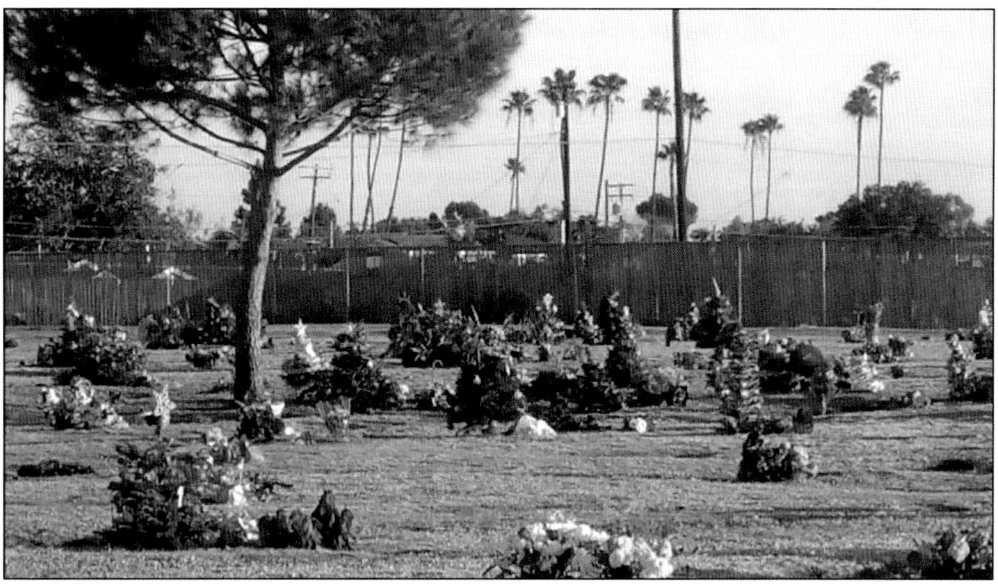

During most major holidays, the gravesites at All Souls are decorated by families. At Christmas, trees and decorations adorn many graves. Family members erect sun shades, bring music and food, and make a day of visiting. The cemetery posts regulations regarding when decorations need to be removed.

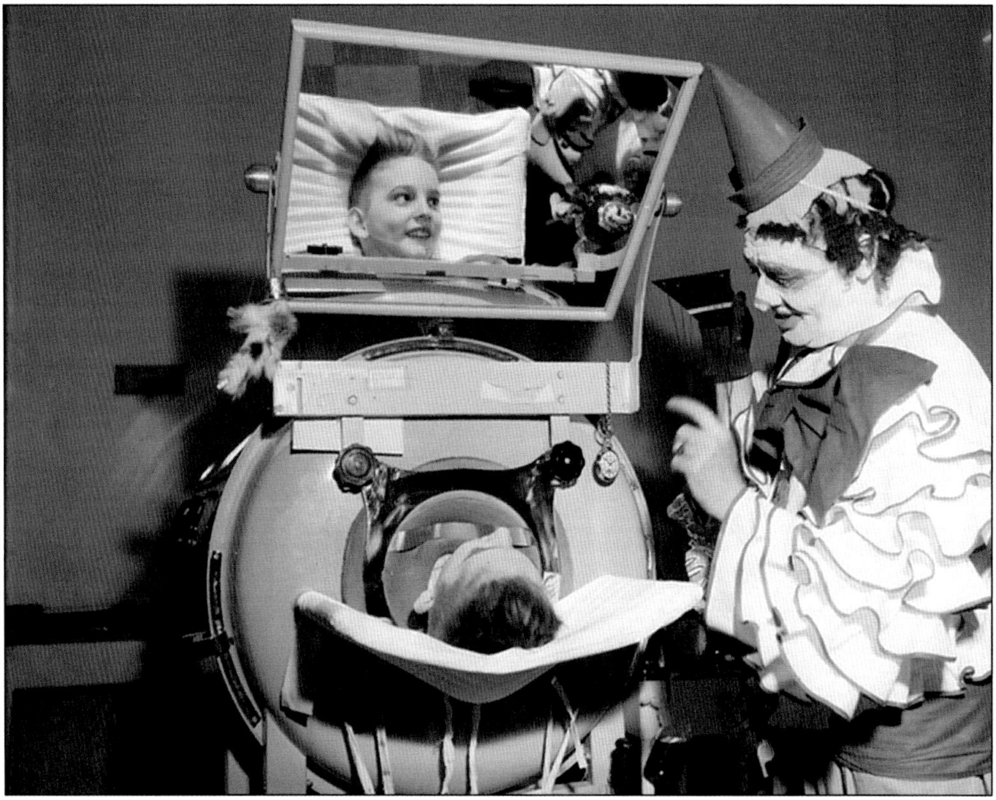

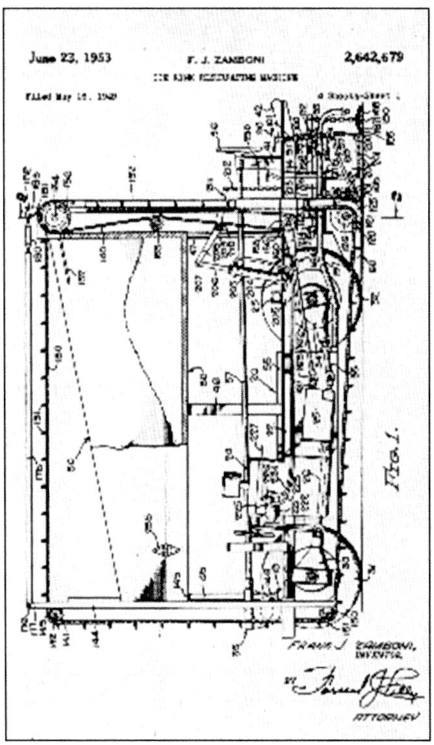

One of the earliest burials was Ed Ellsworth Boyle, also known as "Bobo the Clown." Boyle appeared in the "clown alleys" for Ringling Bros. and Barnum & Bailey and other circuses. He was known for his generosity in visiting sick children. After his burial in 1951, Chester "Bobo the Clown" Barnett complained that the death of Bobo had been "greatly exaggerated" because he was Bobo. Both he and Ellsworth "clowned under the same name." (Rancho Los Amigos.)

There are several notable people buried at All Souls. Frank Zamboni invented the ice resurfacing machine that revolutionized ice skating rinks in 1948, illustrated here. Professional football player Jack Snow played football for 11 years with the Rams before becoming a sports newscaster. Long Beach native Dolores Janney "Jenni" Rivera was a popular Hispanic entertainer who died in a plane crash in 2012. (US Patent Office.)

Six

Tragic Burials in Long Beach

Although death is inevitable, and its circumstances mostly routine, in the case of some early Long Beach residents, the facts surrounding their deaths are truly tragic.

There is the infant placed on a chair on the beach and swept out to sea by violent waves. Two young boys drowned in an agricultural slough. The deaf doctor who did not hear the electric trolley come behind him as he bicycled. A man with blisters on his feet who wore stockings dyed with a black ink that poisoned him. The man who shot himself and left a grieving widow to deal with the loss of their five sons. The woman who, while taking care of a neighbor, so compromised her own health she died within days of the other woman's passing. A baby scalded to death in an incubator designed by his father. A husband, son, and daughter poisoned by the wife and mother, who killed them for life insurance. A bride who, after shopping for her wedding dress, stepped from a streetcar and was hit by another. There were numerous deaths of people who filled their pockets with sand and jumped off the Pine Avenue Pier, which became known as "Suicide Pier."

Several major accidents and epidemics in early Long Beach took many lives. In 1905, the Hotel Bixby collapsed, killing several workers. Eight years later, during the celebration of Empire Day, dozens of women and children were killed and injured when floors of the city auditorium collapsed.

The automobiles and trolleys were important in bringing visitors to Long Beach, but they also brought injury and death to many.

All Long Beach cemeteries have sections dedicated to babies and young children; they share plots with adults or are buried alone. Early records indicate they died from poor nutrition and a variety of infectious diseases that would later be prevented with vaccinations.

The 1918 Spanish influenza epidemic killed many. An oil well explosion in 1931 took several lives. The 1933 Long Beach earthquake shook brick buildings and killed 53 in Long Beach.

These cemeteries hold many tragic stories.

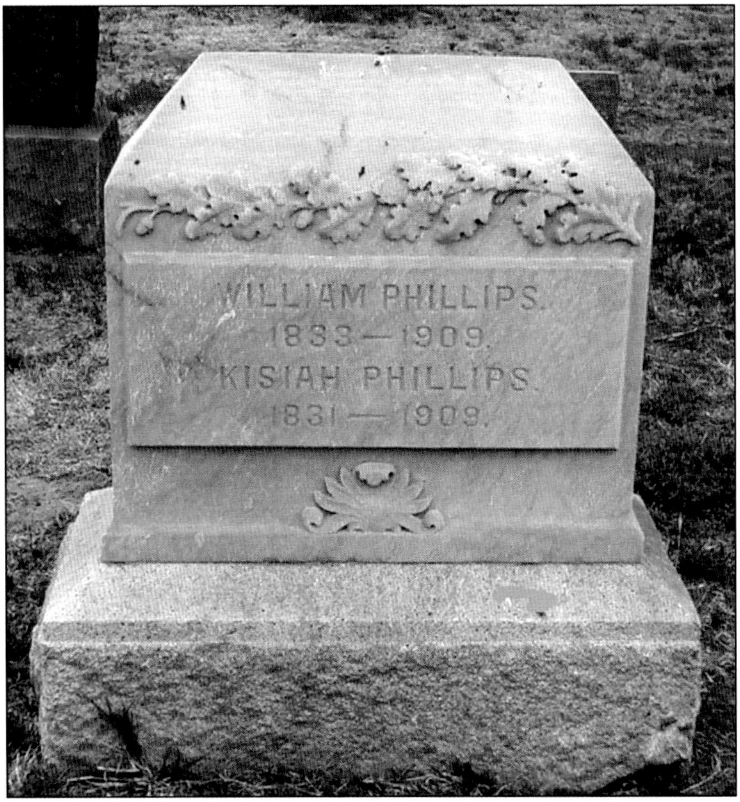

Kisiah and William Phillips were both in their late 70s in 1909. Kisiah, an invalid, became ill. Her husband, William, attempted to nurse her back to health. Instead, he wore himself down, contracted a cold, and died. Kisiah was so overcome with grief that 11 days later, she died. Both are buried in Sunnyside.

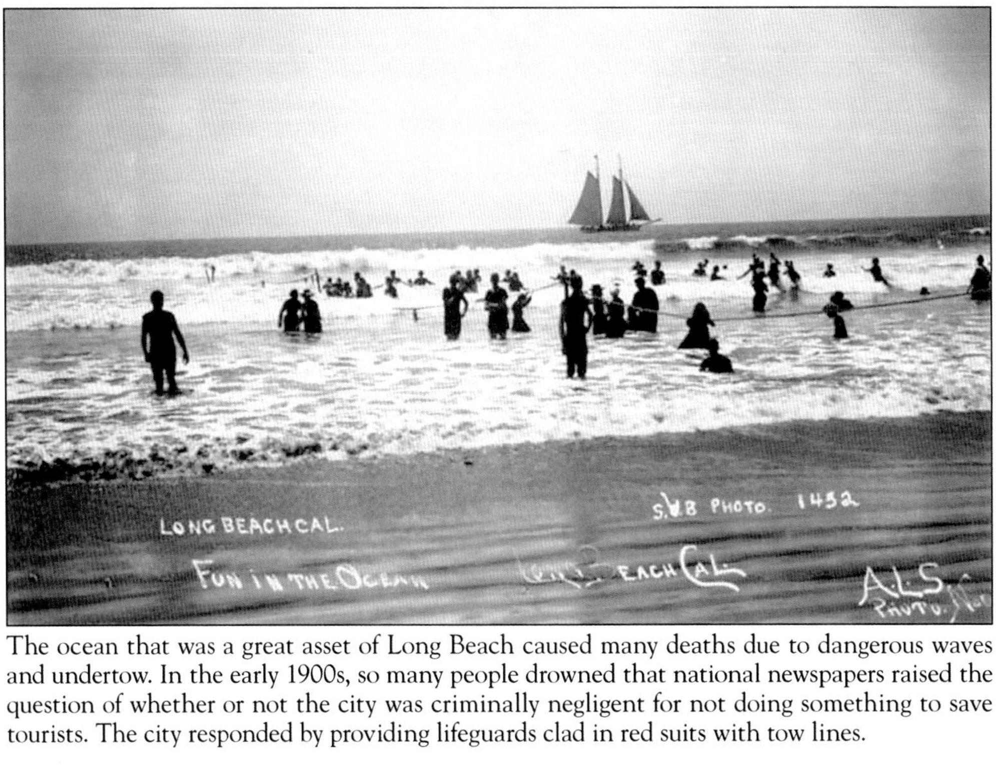

The ocean that was a great asset of Long Beach caused many deaths due to dangerous waves and undertow. In the early 1900s, so many people drowned that national newspapers raised the question of whether or not the city was criminally negligent for not doing something to save tourists. The city responded by providing lifeguards clad in red suits with tow lines.

The circumstances surrounding the drowning of many, like Jacob Griff, are unknown. It is known that, in 1910, police were asked to drag the bottom of the eight-foot-deep Cerritos Slough for the bodies of two young boys, Gerald Barbour and Raoul Mendoza, aged 11 and 13 years respectively. The boys had been reported missing by their parents. Police found the boys' hand-made skiff, which had capsized during the night. Both were buried in the Long Beach Municipal Cemetery. Victor Millard, who assisted in the search, cut his ankle and later died due to gangrene. Two years later, a tiny infant, wrapped in a ragged skirt and tucked in a shoebox, was found floating in the same slough.

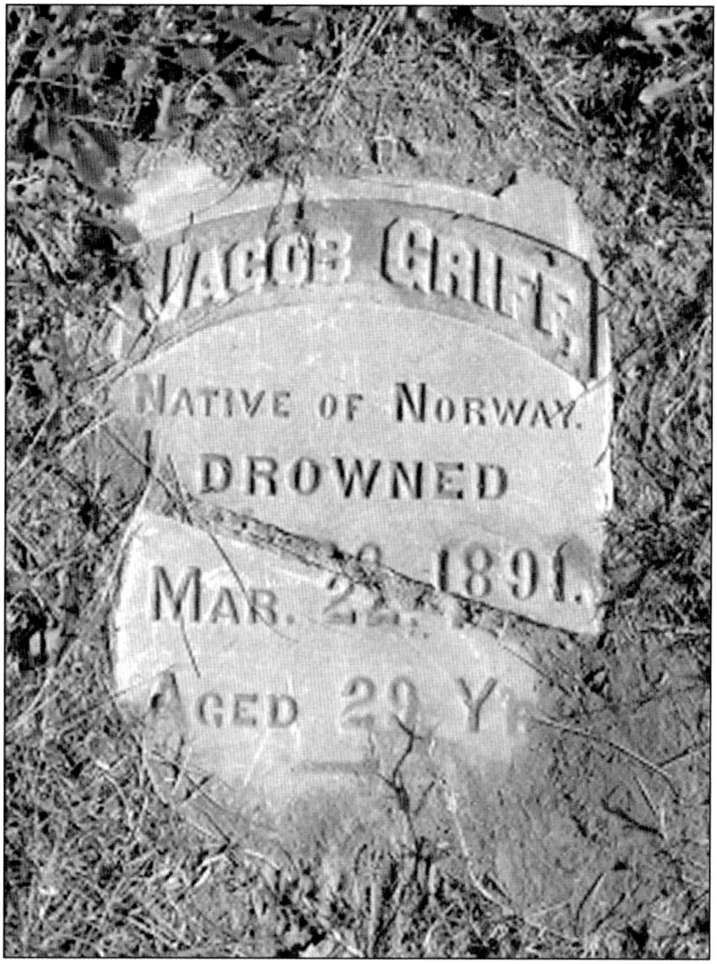

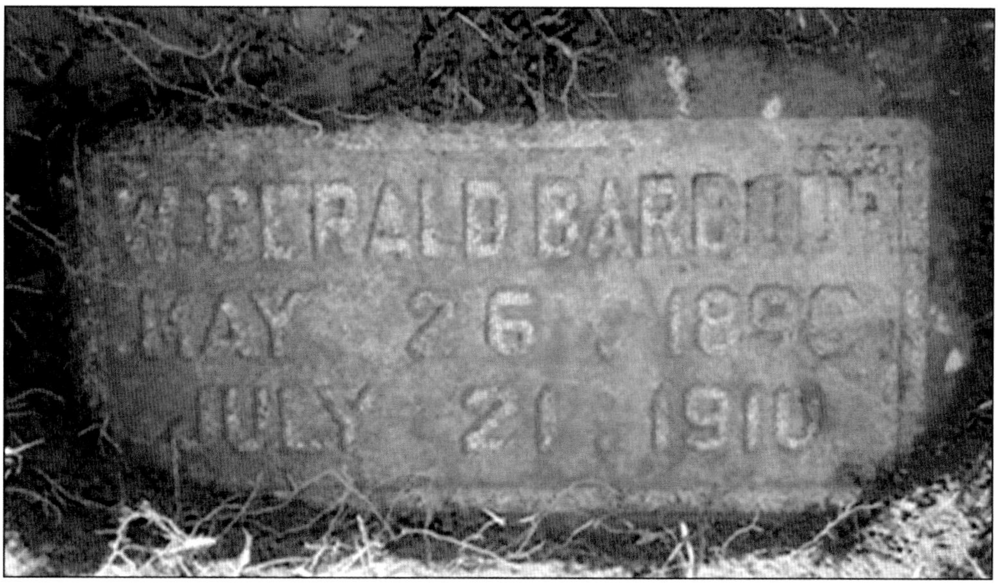

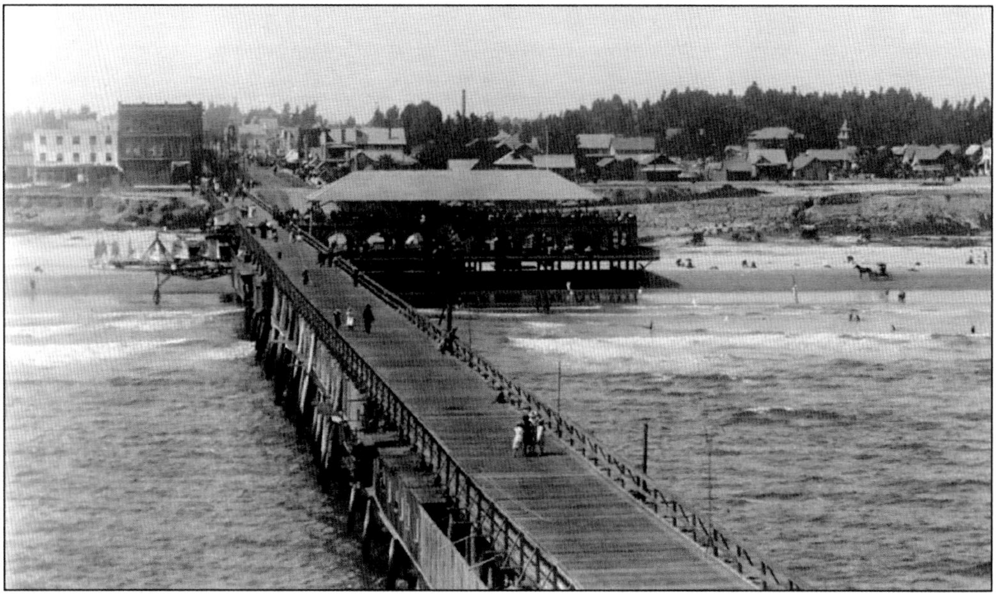

The early piers jutted several thousand feet over high waves and were convenient sites for people to take their own lives. Pine Avenue Pier eventually became known as Suicide Pier. In 1930, William O'Brien wheeled himself 18 miles from the county farm to Pine Avenue Pier. People reported seeing O'Brien go to the end of the pier. Only his wheelchair was found.

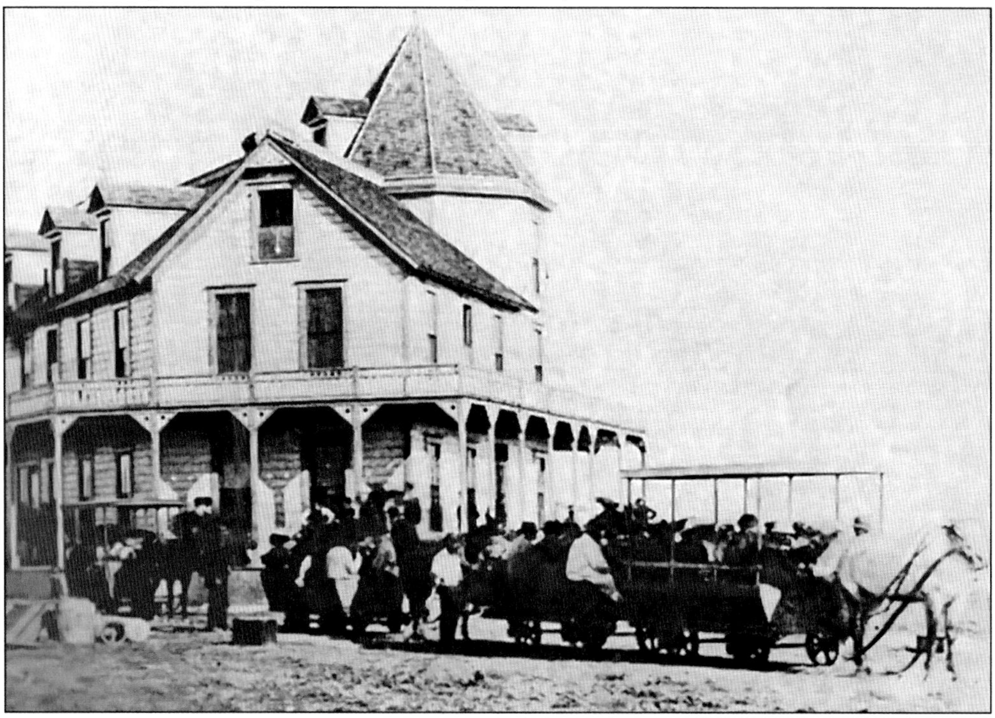

The introduction of the Pacific Electric Railroad trolley in 1902 to Long Beach enabled thousands to visit and was largely responsible for the city's fast growth in its early years. The electric trolley cars replaced the horse-drawn cars that were referred to as Long Beach's "Get Out and Push Railroad."

There were so many deaths because of trains, trolleys, and automobiles that the local press referred to them as an "epidemic." In 1895, Charles Hilton Williams was working as a brakeman and uncoupling cars at the Terminal Island Railroad when he apparently slipped and was run over by a train. The funeral for the popular 23-year-old was attended by many. He is buried at the Municipal Cemetery.

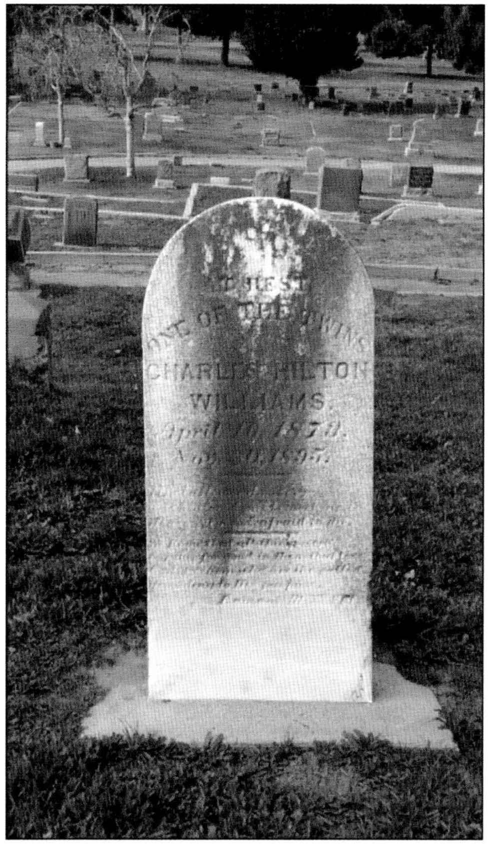

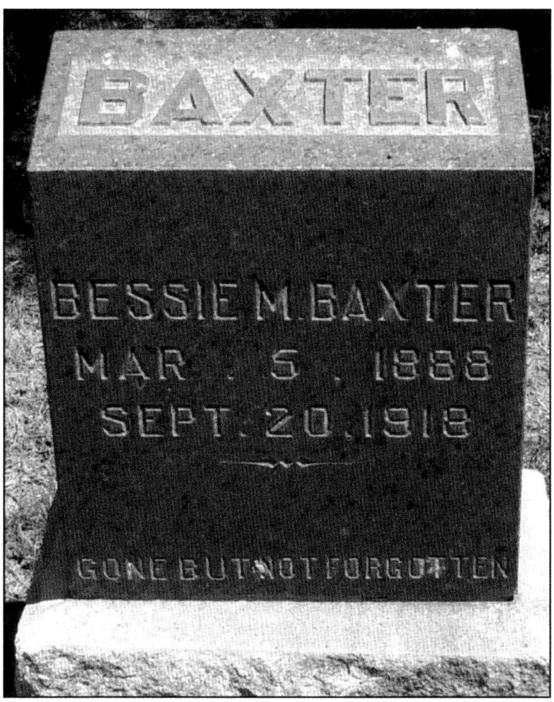

On September 20, 1918, Bessie McKensie Baxter boarded the trolley to go shopping for a dress for her wedding the next week to C.A. Tingley. She stepped off the street car at Burnett Street and American Avenue with her arms filled with bundles and was struck by another car. She died at Seaside Hospital and was buried in Sunnyside in her wedding dress, with the roses planned for the wedding.

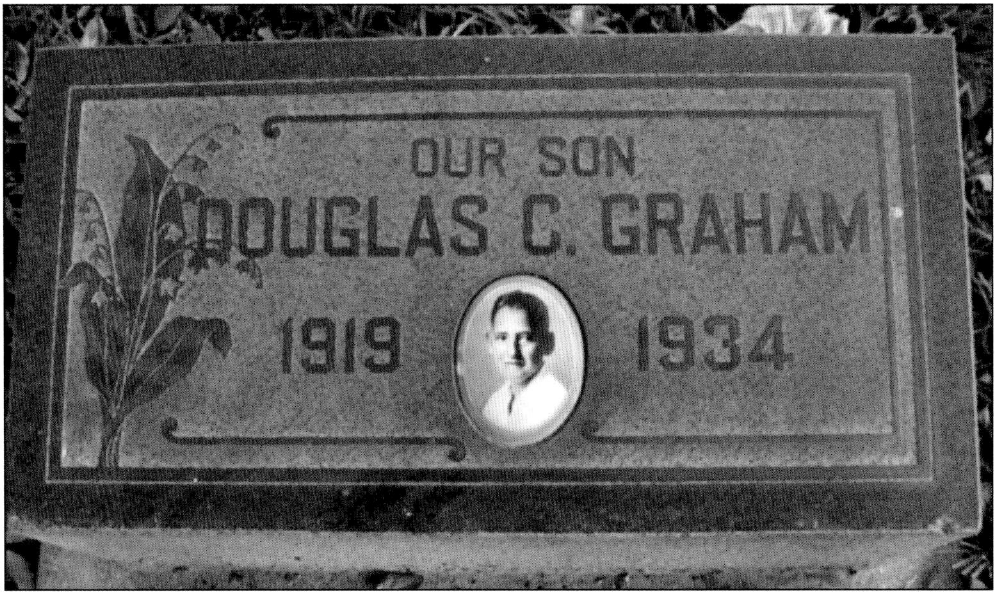

Douglas Graham was only 13 in 1934 when he was riding his bicycle and skidded underneath a truck. Douglas was crushed. The son of Andrew and Mollie Graham, Douglas has one of the few headstones with a photograph in the Sunnyside Cemetery.

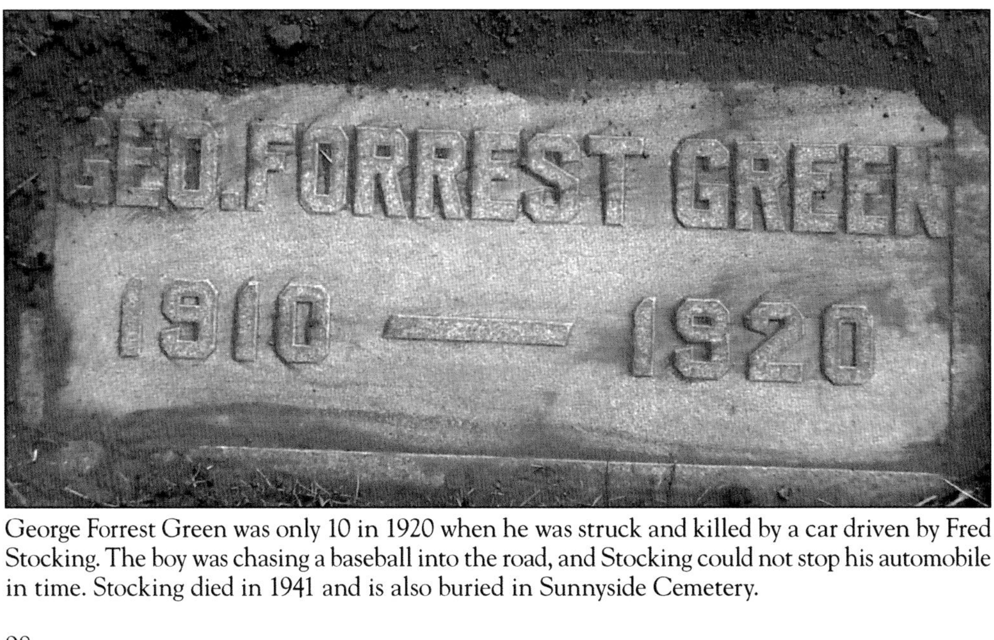

George Forrest Green was only 10 in 1920 when he was struck and killed by a car driven by Fred Stocking. The boy was chasing a baseball into the road, and Stocking could not stop his automobile in time. Stocking died in 1941 and is also buried in Sunnyside Cemetery.

Losing a spouse is tragic, but in the case of William Price, he was also the victim of burglary the day after his wife died. Not finding much to take, the burglar stole the sign from the front door that announced Kate Price's death on February 8, 1912. Kate is buried in the Municipal Cemetery.

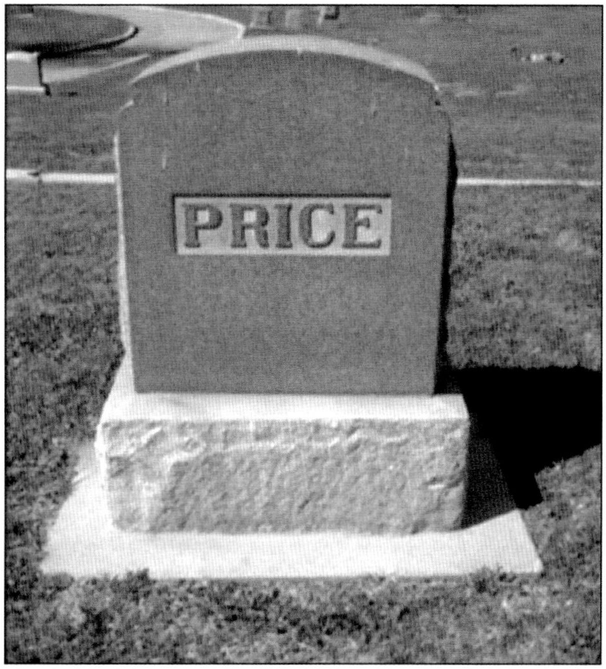

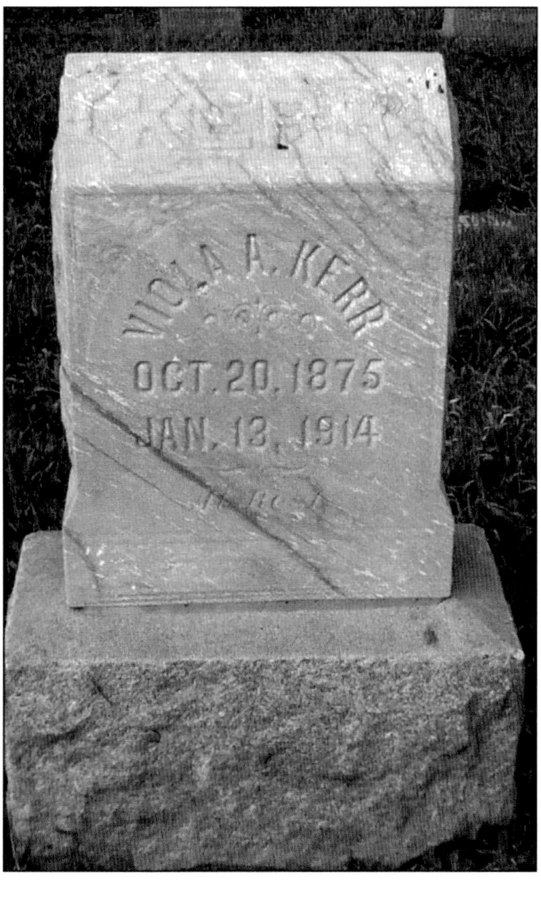

Effie Cunningham lost her spouse, Arthur, the father of her four young children, when he shot himself after killing his lover, Viola Kerr, in 1914. Effie told the press that Arthur was "most at fault and crazed by alcohol" and that it was "cowardice that sent that second bullet." Cunningham is buried in Municipal Cemetery and Kerr is buried in Sunnyside. Effie and her daughter are buried in San Gabriel Cemetery.

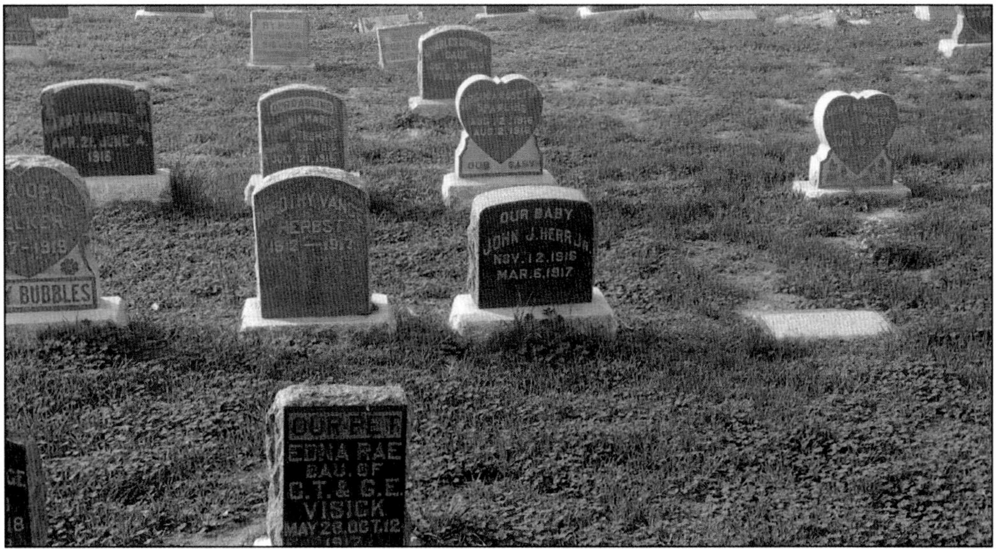

Infant mortality was quite high in early California. Babies often died of a condition called marasmus, which essentially means "wasting." Marasmus was usually caused by prolonged diarrhea brought on by unsanitary conditions and poor nutrition. Infectious diseases also took a toll. Each Long Beach cemetery has dedicated space for infant and child burials such as the one seen here at Sunnyside.

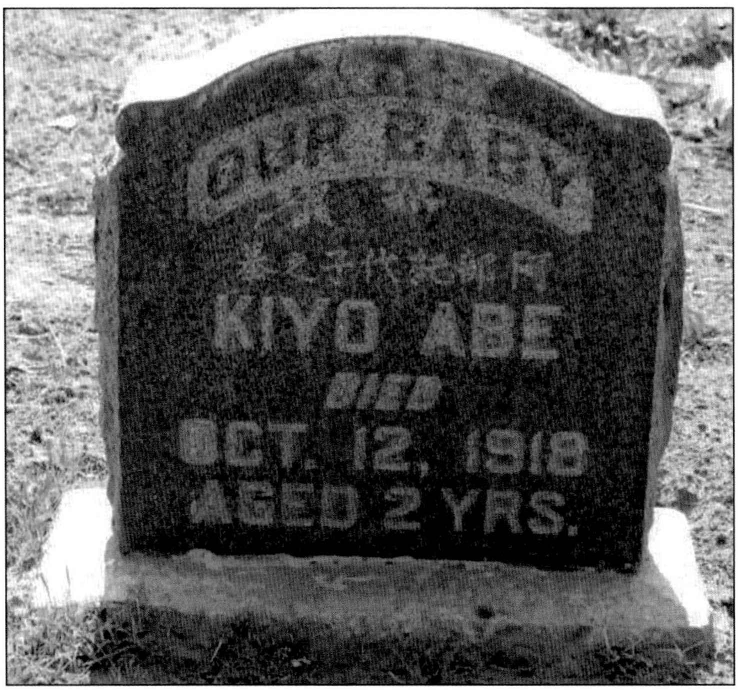

In 1918, the world was devastated by the Spanish influenza. Long Beach helped minimize the spread by closing its schools, churches, theaters, and amusement area for several weeks. Long Beach reported 57 people dying from influenza in November 1918. Kiyo Abe was just two when he died from influenza and pneumonia. He is buried in Sunnyside Cemetery, as are his parents, Rokuro and Akino.

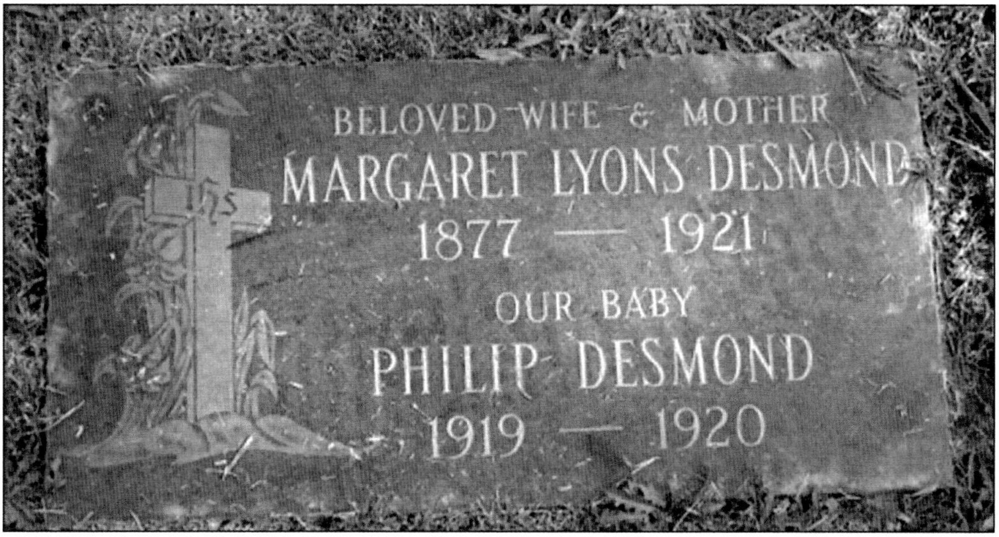

Infants were often buried in the same plot with parents, particularly mothers. Thirteen-month-old Philip Desmond, son of local postmaster Walter and his wife Margaret, died within five hours of contracting "membranous croup." He is buried with his mother in Sunnyside Cemetery. Walter served as public works commissioner and superintendent of the cemetery. He spearheaded efforts to stop oil drilling in the Sunnyside Cemetery. Later, he was appointed to the bench. He remarried and is buried with his second wife, Eleanor, in Holy Cross Cemetery. His son Gerald was a city councilman and city attorney and the namesake of the Gerald Desmond Bridge. Gerald is buried in All Souls Cemetery. (Below, US Department of Transportation.)

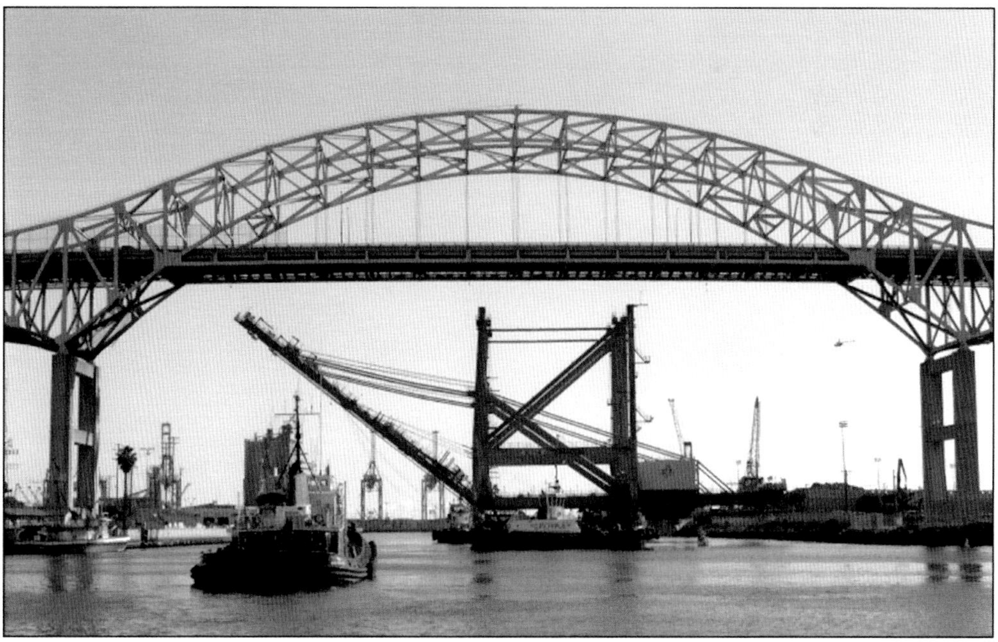

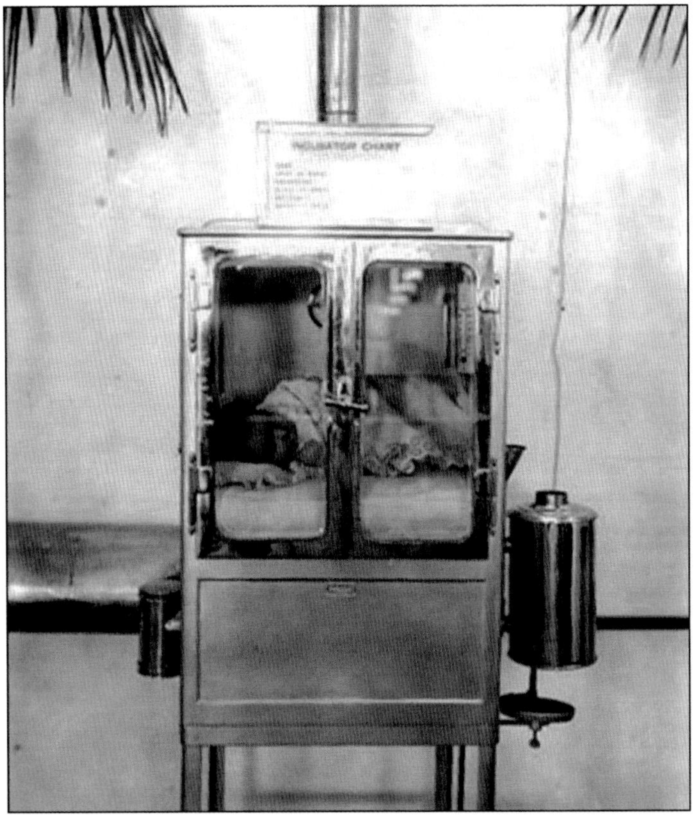

In 1909, a number of contraptions were being used as incubators for newborn babies. Richard De Spain placed his two-month-old son Ardirine into an incubator he had invented, which was heated with a bottle filled with hot water. The cork blew off the hot water bottle, and the baby was scalded to death. He is buried in Sunnyside Cemetery. (LOC.)

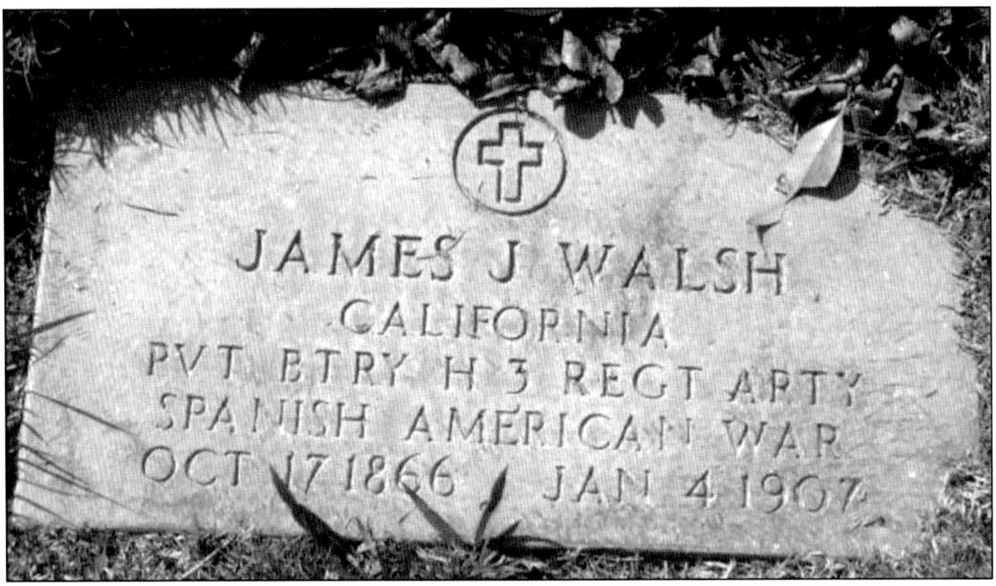

In 1906, five stories of the Hotel Bixby collapsed due to faulty construction, killing 11 workers and injuring many others. J.J. Walsh, a 35-year-old laborer and veteran of the Spanish-American War, was crushed under the collapse. He languished two months completely paralyzed before he died, leaving a widow and three small children. The public rallied to pay his mortgage. He is buried in the Municipal Cemetery.

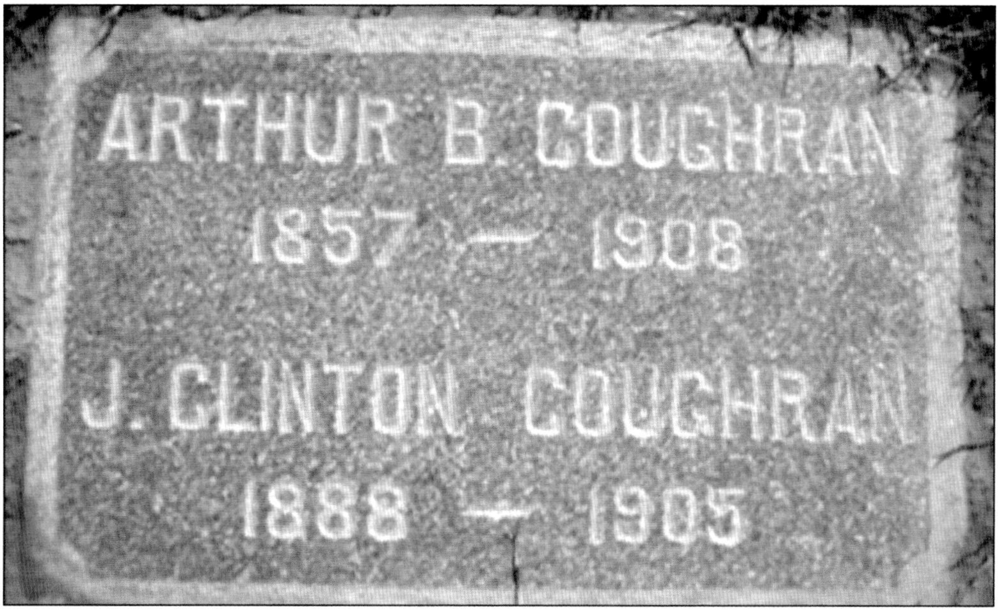

Arthur Coughran shot himself near his brother's Buena Park farm. Arthur was despondent over his failed investment in a "freak calf" in a local amusement show. Both he and his widow had lost five children over the years. Three years prior, in 1905, Arthur's 17-year-old son James fell to his death at the Los Alamitos Sugar Beet factory. Both are buried in the Municipal Cemetery.

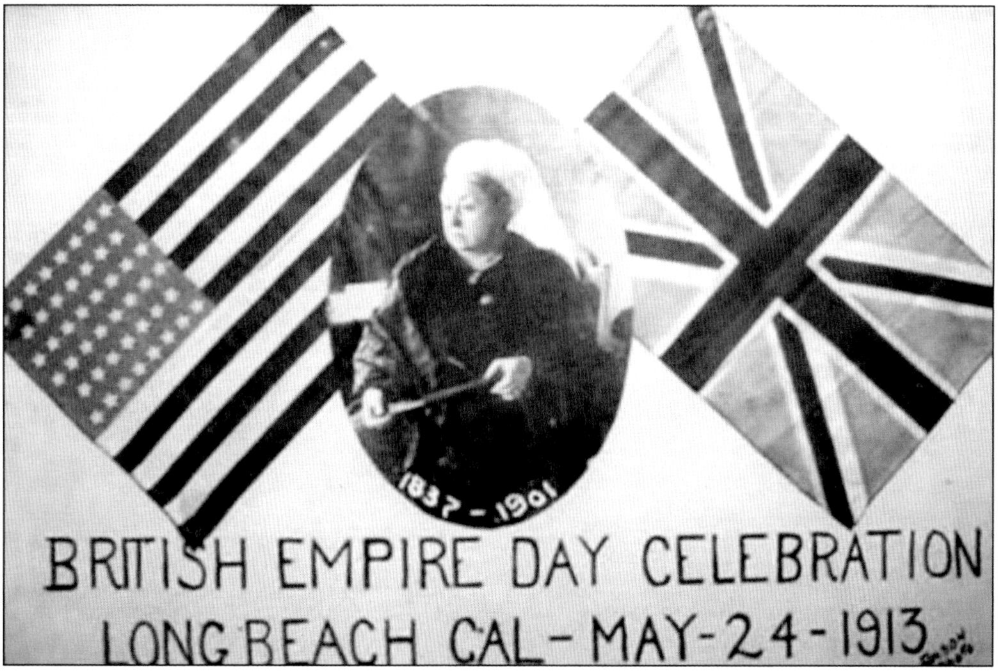

On May 24, 1913, approximately 20,000 gathered to celebrate Empire Day. The women, children, and older men congregated at the pier and auditorium, waiting for the parade of men who marched down Pine Avenue. Suddenly, the floors collapsed, sending dozens to their death or serious injury. A total of 36 were killed and 174 injured. Most who died were women, such as English-born Ada Mary Humphries Helps. She is buried in Sunnyside.

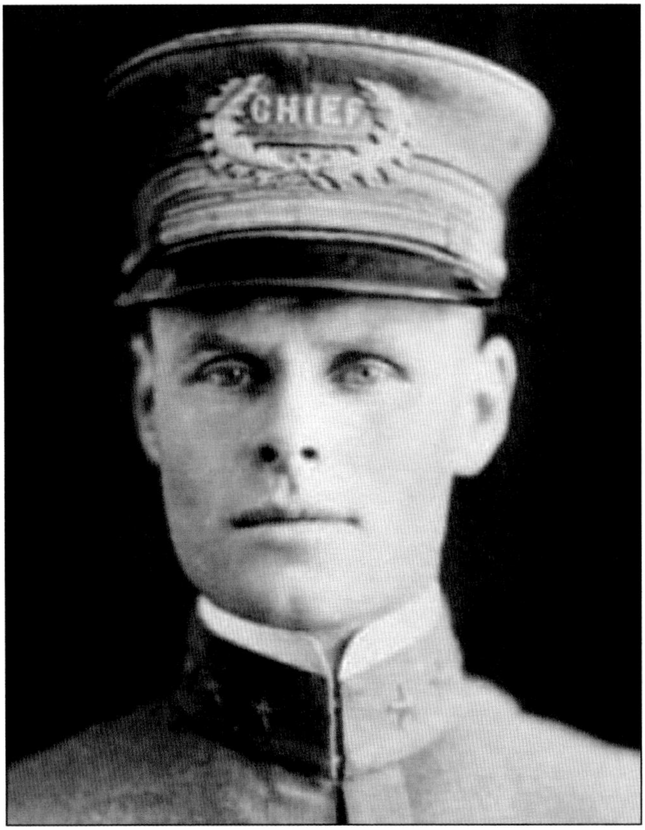

James L. Butterfield came to Long Beach from Missouri in 1911 and rose up the ranks of the police department from sergeant to chief by March 1920. Butterfield asked the county grand jury to investigate the police department. He lasted eight months before being removed for incompetency by the Civil Service Commission. Butterfield was later charged with involvement in a Ku Klux Klan–organized disturbance. He is buried in Sunnyside.

People were warned, as shown in this excerpt from the 1887 *The Sanitary Era*, that one could get blood poisoning from the ink in stockings. In 1906, Charles Down developed blisters on his feet. He died of blood poisoning caused by his black stockings. Down was a partner in the Down & Sinclair glove manufacturing company. He is buried in the Municipal Cemetery.

Dyed Stockings, Corns, etc.—W. H. Beach, chiropodist, Springfield, Mass., sends the suggestion that the aniline dyes (and we may add, many other dyes) in undergarments are poisoning people at wholesale by absorption through the skin. Many instances have been reported, and some have been copied into the Sanitary Era. Where abrasions take place from chafing or blistering the feet, which so commonly happens, or where corns, bunions, etc., have been removed, our correspondent states that many cases have come under his observation of painful and obstinate ulcers, crippled limbs, lockjaw, and blood-poisoning, from absorption of deleterious chemicals from the stockings, at the exposed part of the flesh. He thinks it criminal to remove corns, by salve or otherwise, without skillfully protecting the place until the skin has time to grow. It is no idle caution to reject all fancy undergarments and stockings, though the fashionable rage be for barbers' poles within the skirts.

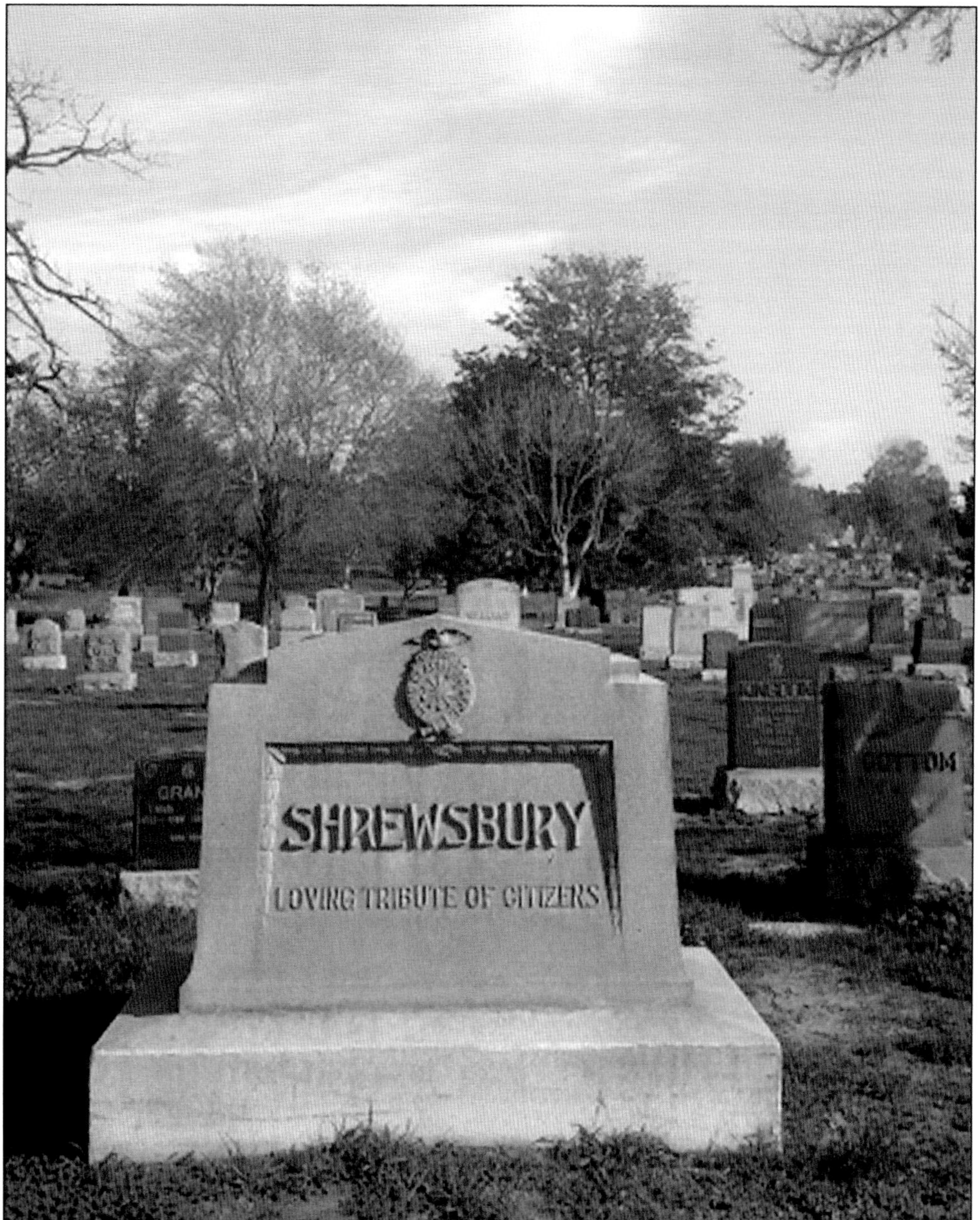

In 1916, Long Beach's first fire chief, Joseph Shrewsbury, responded to a false fire alarm, and his vehicle was struck by a chemical truck. He was thrown head first to the pavement and later died of his injuries. His funeral was attended by hundreds of mourners, including early aviator Earl Daugherty, who flew overhead as a tribute to the beloved chief. Joseph Eugene Shrewsbury was born in Minnesota in 1867 and came to Long Beach in 1902. He served as the city's first plumbing inspector and then became involved in the fire department due to his prior experience as a captain of a fire truck company in the state of Washington. In 1906, he was elected fire chief by the department and set about to modernize the city's firefighting services. His wife, Magnhild, is buried with him in Sunnyside.

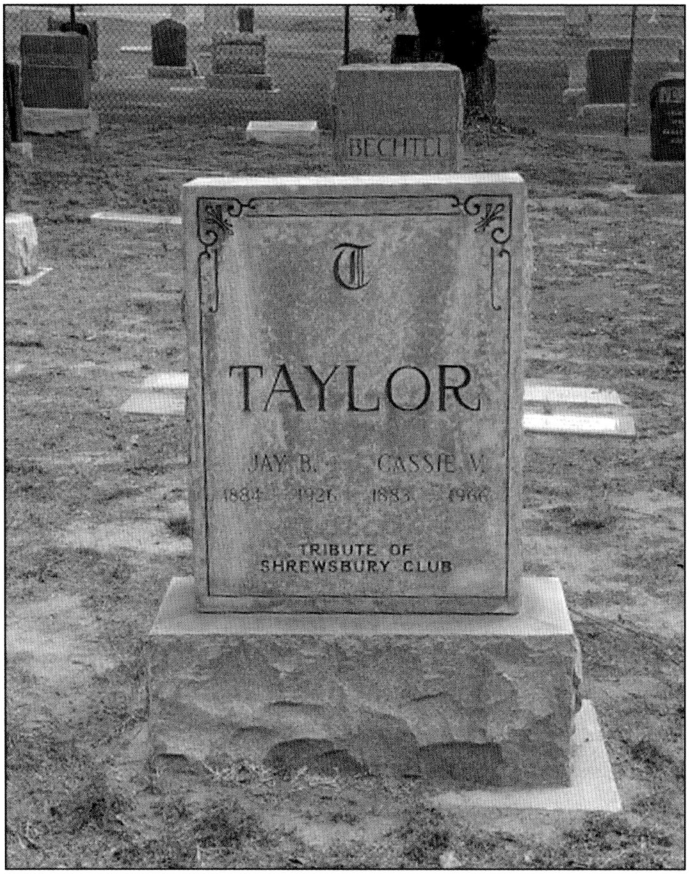

Fire Battalion Chief Jay B. Taylor slashed his throat in 1926 because he was distraught about infighting in the department concerning the promotion of a younger fireman over one more senior. Taylor wrote his wife, Cassie, he had "been double crossed and have double crossed others." Taylor served 20 years as a firefighter and was very popular. His headstone in Sunnyside bears the inscription, "Tribute of the Shrewsbury Club."

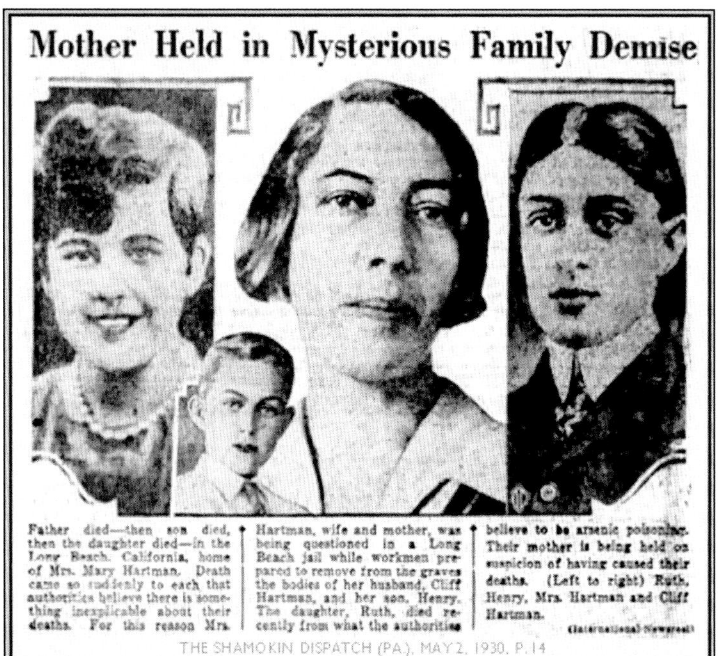

Mother Held in Mysterious Family Demise

Father died—then son died, then the daughter died—in the Long Beach, California, home of Mrs. Mary Hartman. Death came so suddenly to each that authorities believe there is something inexplicable about their deaths. For this reason Mrs. Hartman, wife and mother, was being questioned in a Long Beach jail while workmen prepared to remove from the graves the bodies of her husband, Cliff Hartman, and her son, Henry. The daughter, Ruth, died recently from what the authorities believe to be arsenic poisoning. Their mother is being held on suspicion of having caused their deaths. (Left to right) Ruth, Henry, Mrs. Hartman and Cliff Hartman.

(International Newsreel)

THE SHAMOKIN DISPATCH (PA.), MAY 2, 1930, P. 14

Before dying, 14-year-old Ruth Hartman complained that her mother gave her grape juice that had "a bad taste." Her mother, Mary, used arsenic to poison Ruth and her brother Henry. Ruth's father, Oluff, died from a head blow by "mysterious attackers." Ruth had purchased life insurance policies on her victims. She was found insane and placed in Patton State Hospital in 1930. Her family is buried in Sunnyside Cemetery.

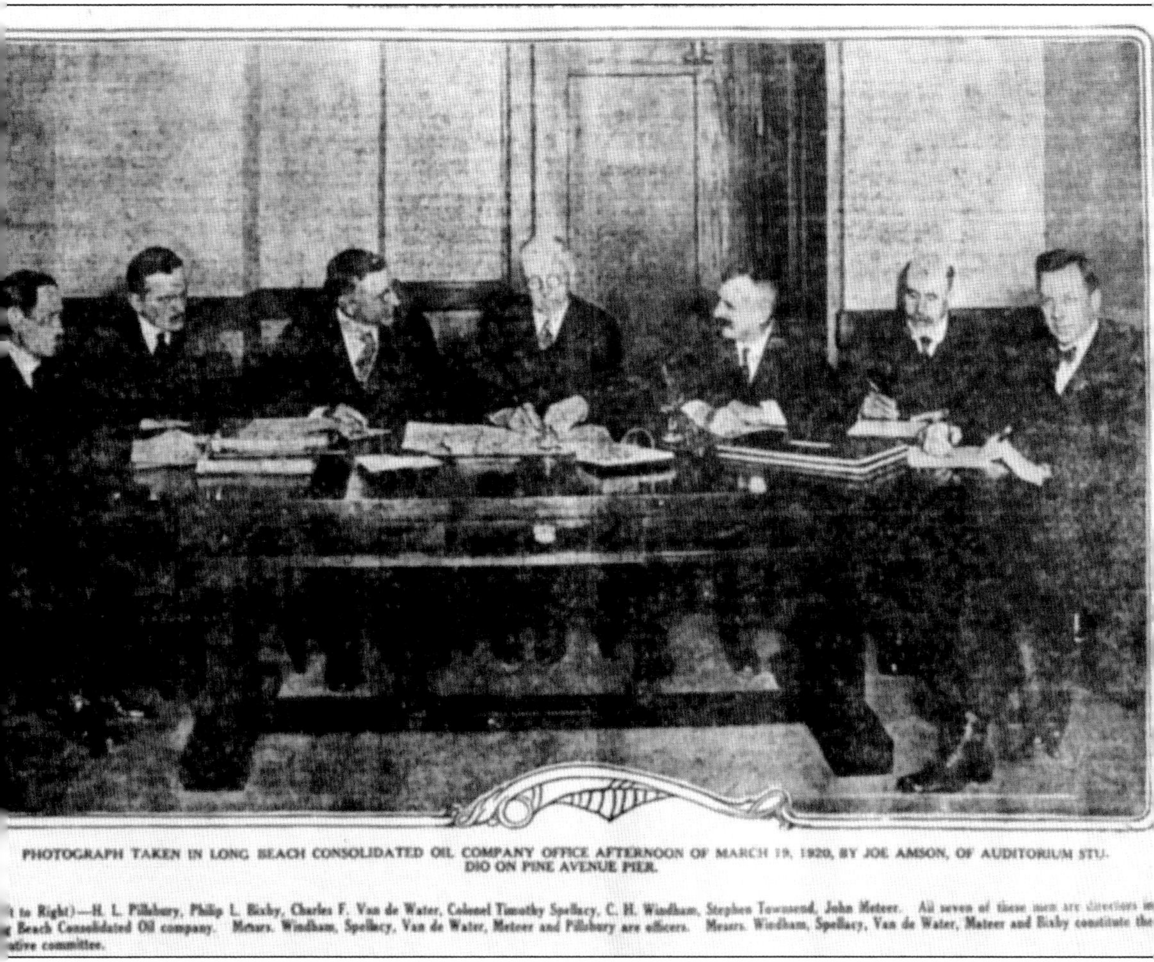

On November 20, 1920, newly elected congressman (and Poly High graduate) Charles F. Van de Water (third from left) and his 19-year-old secretary Janice Luebben were driving back to Long Beach from a celebration in Pomona. It was foggy, and Van de Water did not see a truck, driven by Carlyle Hughes, which was stopped on the road without lights. Van de Water and Luebben were killed. Edith Van de Water and Nina Cuthbert Jackson were injured. Hughes was later convicted of manslaughter. Van de Water and Luebben are both buried in Sunnyside Cemetery. Before his election to Congress, Van de Water was a prominent oil businessman and served as the vice president of the Long Beach Consolidated Oil Company. His wife, Edith, lived until 1961 and was elected the first president of the California Council of Republican Women. (LOC.)

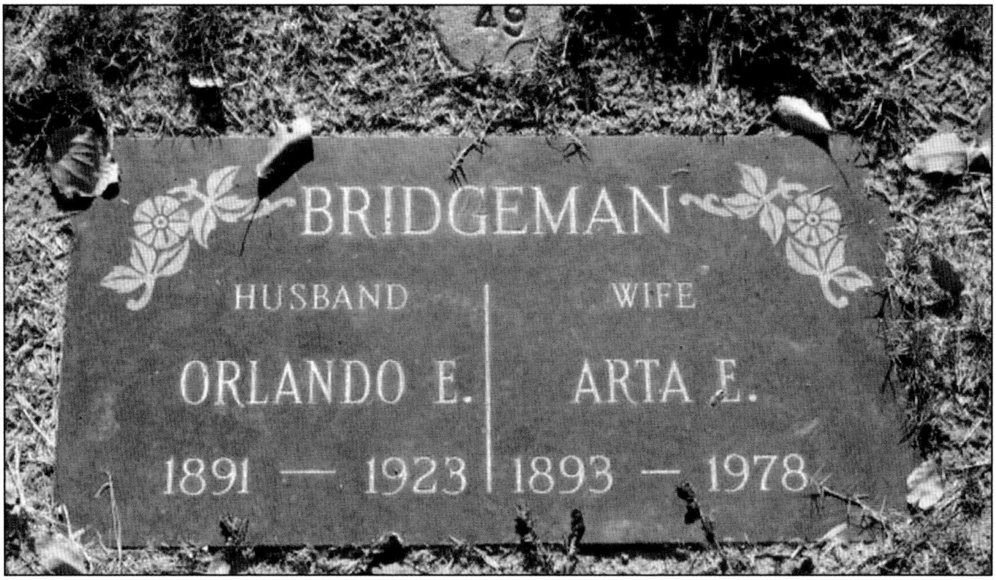

Orlando Edwin Bridgeman was the first Long Beach police officer to lose his life in the line of duty. In 1923, while helping a motorist, his gun fell from his holster to the ground, discharged, and shot him. Because the police did not have pensions, the other officers raised money to buy Bridgeman's widow, Arta, and five children a duplex. The family is buried together in Sunnyside.

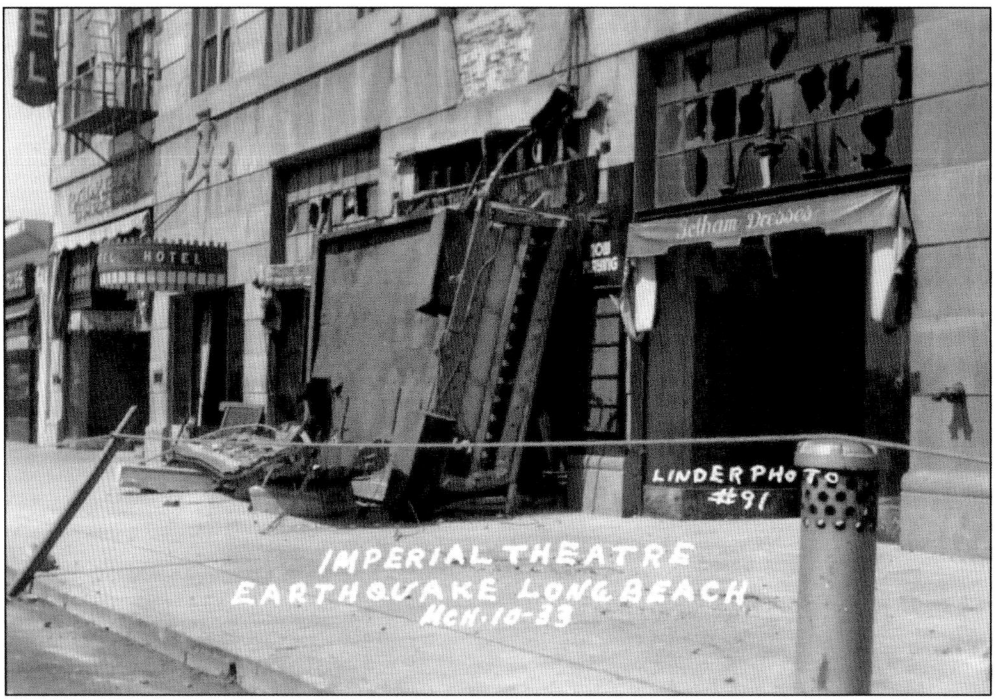

At 5:55 p.m., on March 10, 1933, a 6.4-magnitude earthquake hit Long Beach, destroying 98 percent of its schools and killing 125. Fifty-three of those killed were from Long Beach. Twenty-eight-year-old James Brodie, assistant manager of the Imperial Theater at 315 Ocean Boulevard, was killed when the heavy front canopy, seen here, fell on him. Brodie is buried in Sunnyside. (Michelle Gerdes.)

Seven

The Blue and Gray Club

Early Long Beach was a real estate developer's dream. The railroads had surplus property to sell, and also wanted to get rid of the Chinese workers they had exploited as cheap labor. So, they formed the California Immigrant Union with help from landowners like Jotham Bixby. Ads specifically targeted white, Christian American and European men who had at least $1,000.

New residents came from all parts of the country. Many came from the Midwest, which earned the city the name of "Iowa by the Sea." Land was set aside in the American Colony/Willmore City for the Methodist Chautauqua, which drew thousands to Long Beach each summer. The Women's Christian Temperance Union had a strong presence in Long Beach promoting Prohibition. Long Beach quickly earned the reputation of being a conservative, god-fearing, "dry" city.

The good weather and promise of farmland and peaceful surroundings attracted men (and their families) who had served in the Union or Confederate armies.

So large were the group of Civil War veterans who came to Long Beach, they formed the 181 Post of the Grand Army of the Republic (GAR), a national organization of Union veterans. A chapter of the Women's Relief Corps, which served as an auxiliary to the GAR, also was active. One of the major roles of the GAR was to preserve the memory and graves of those who had served in the Civil War. Large ceremonies were held in Long Beach for Decoration Day (which became Memorial Day) at the pier and at the cemeteries. The Long Beach GAR lobbied for special markers and designated space in the local cemeteries. Long Beach was one of the few cities that had a Blue and Gray GAR Drum Corps composed of both Union and Confederate veterans. It is one of the few cities where a cemetery holds so many who fought in the Civil War.

There are an estimated 1,200 veterans of the Civil War buried in both Sunnyside and the Municipal Cemeteries, including Medal of Honor recipient Nelson Ward and former slave Abraham Cleag.

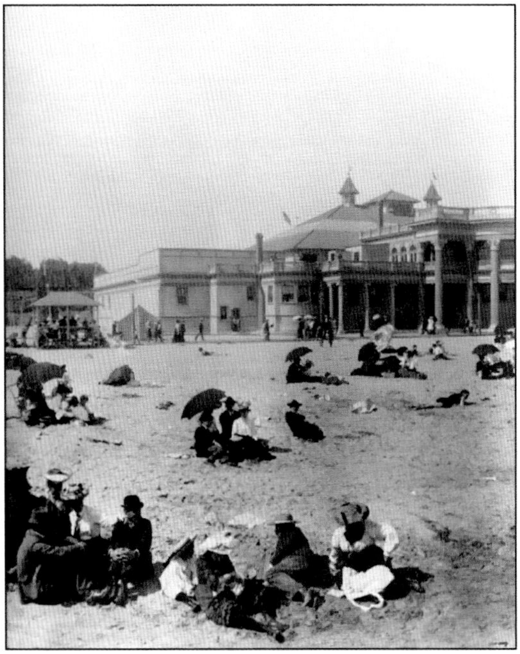

A lack of jobs after the Civil War and the desire for warmer climates drove thousands to the West. Long Beach attracted so many Civil War veterans that it became the home of one of the largest chapters of the Grand Army of the Republic. The GAR was a national veterans' organization dedicated to improving conditions for veterans and to fostering remembrance in local cemeteries.

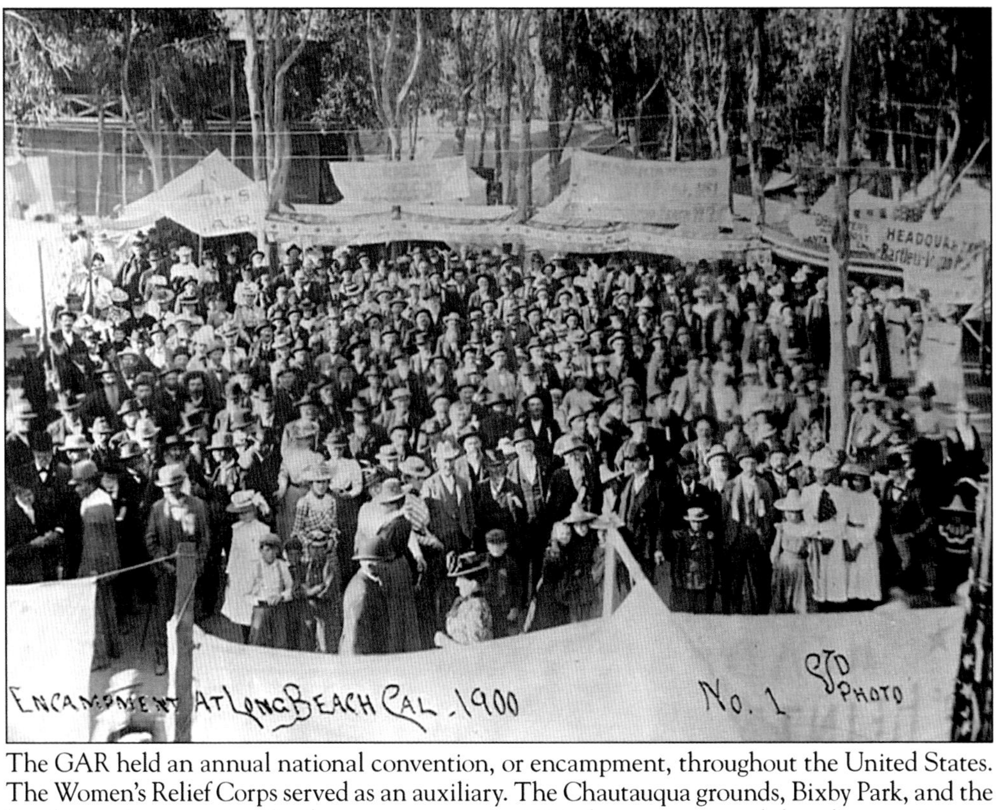

The GAR held an annual national convention, or encampment, throughout the United States. The Women's Relief Corps served as an auxiliary. The Chautauqua grounds, Bixby Park, and the beach were frequent sites for the encampment. In 1892, the press reported that the activities got out of hand when veterans burned down the tent of a "Chinaman" (who probably was serving as a cook) and then painted a white stripe down his pants.

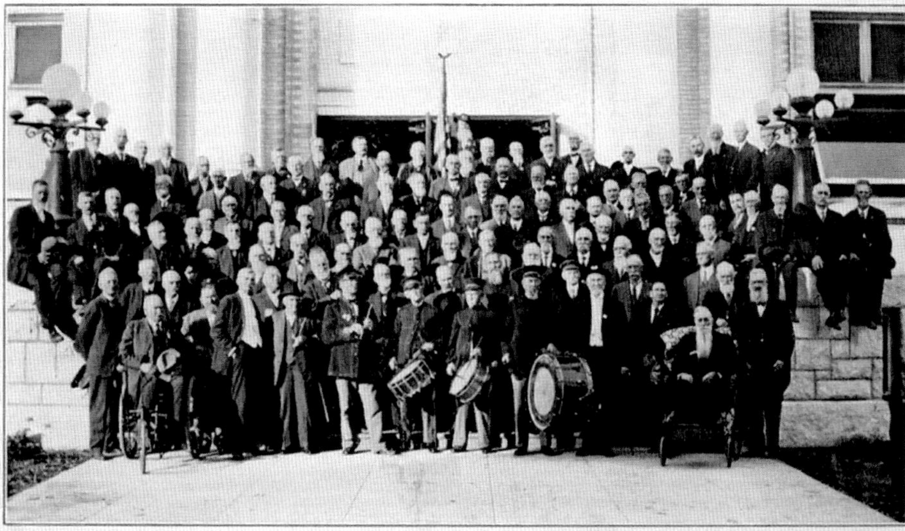

BLUE AND GRAY G. A. R. DRUM CORPS
J. K. Marsh, H. R. Tennant, H. Durkee, A. L. Russell

Long Beach was home to a Blue and Gray GAR Drum Corps, which gave its members enamel "Johnny and Yank" pins. The group practiced in the municipal auditorium. On June 28, 1915, the cornerstone was laid in Pacific Park for the Abraham Lincoln GAR memorial monument. It took the Citizens Monument Association 10 years to raise funds for the eight-ton granite statue, which was a copy of the figure in Illinois sculpted by Augustus St. Gaudens. Made by the F.E. Brittain Long Beach Monument Works, it includes the names of famous Civil War commanders and the battles in which they fought. A replica of a Springfield musket used in the Battle of Chickamauga is on the base. A cannon was sent by the Benicia Arsenal for the dedication ceremonies. Approximately 20,000 attended the July 1 dedication. In 1920, Pacific Park was renamed Lincoln Park.

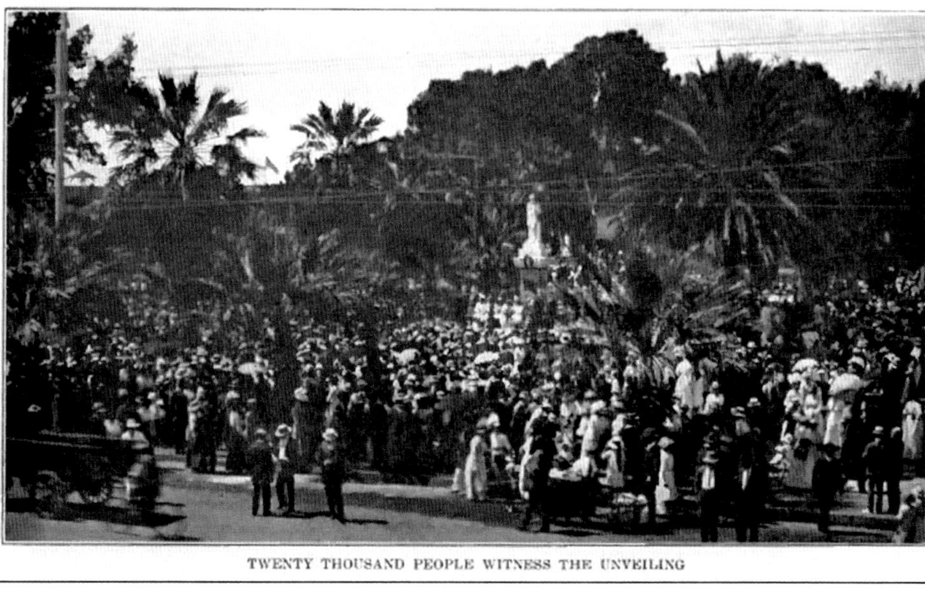

TWENTY THOUSAND PEOPLE WITNESS THE UNVEILING

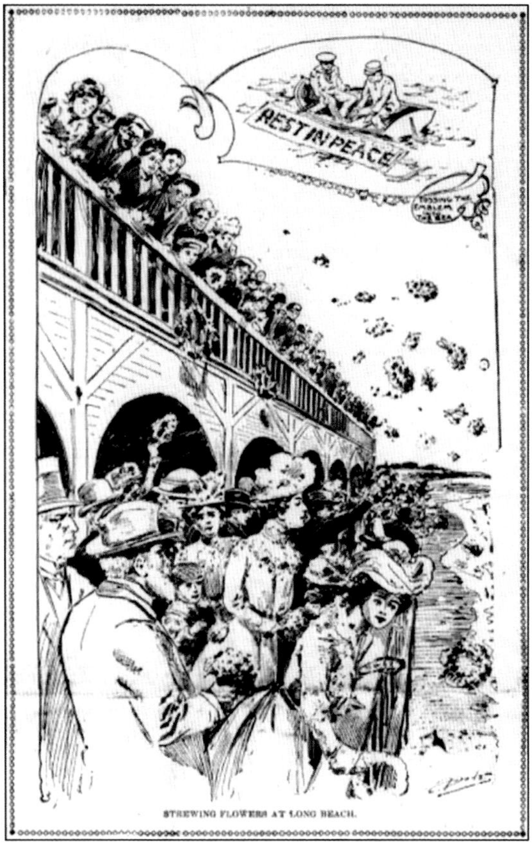

The GAR was primarily responsible for the designation of May 30 as Decoration Day. Flowers were strewn off the Pine Avenue Pier (as shown in this 1901 newspaper drawing), followed by a parade on Pine Avenue. Participants proceeded to a ceremony and decoration of graves on the "sunnyhills in back of Long Beach."

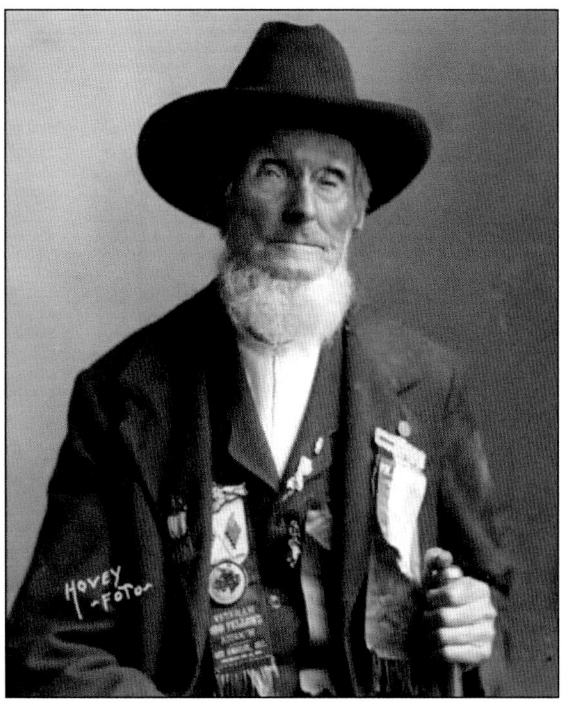

John J. Overton lies in the Municipal Cemetery. He was born on October 5, 1797, in Pennsylvania, and enlisted at age 15 to serve in the 1812 Black Hawk War and the Mexican-American War, and at 66, he served in the Civil War. He was the oldest living Odd Fellow at his death in 1904. Overton had a farm in Long Beach and then sold popcorn at the oceanfront.

In 1873, the US War Department adopted the first design for headstones for Union troops: a slab of marble or durable stone four inches thick, 10 inches wide, and 12 inches in height above the ground, with a sunken shield in which the inscription appeared in bas relief. The part above the ground was polished, and the top was slightly curved and contained the name and unit. An estimated 1,200 veterans of the Civil War are buried in both Sunnyside and Municipal Cemeteries. While the headstone is supposed to be raised, most in the Municipal Cemetery have been laid flat, as pictured in the image at right of the headstone of Josiah Bare of Company B, 28th Pennsylvania Infantry. In Sunnyside, most Union headstones are erect, as shown in the photograph below of the marker for David Bartshe.

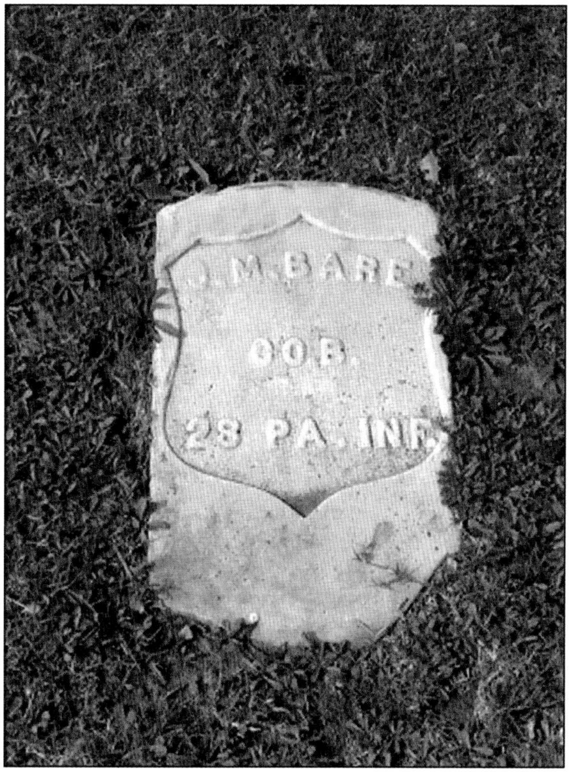

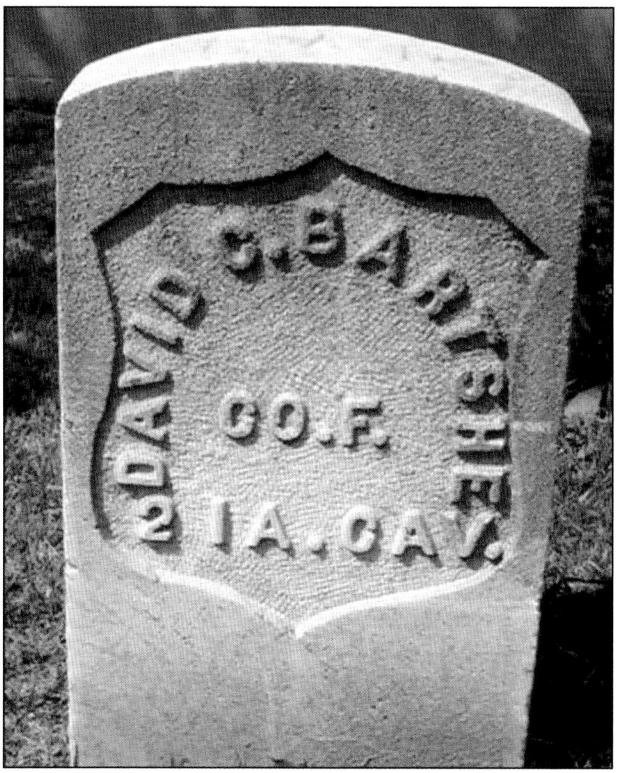

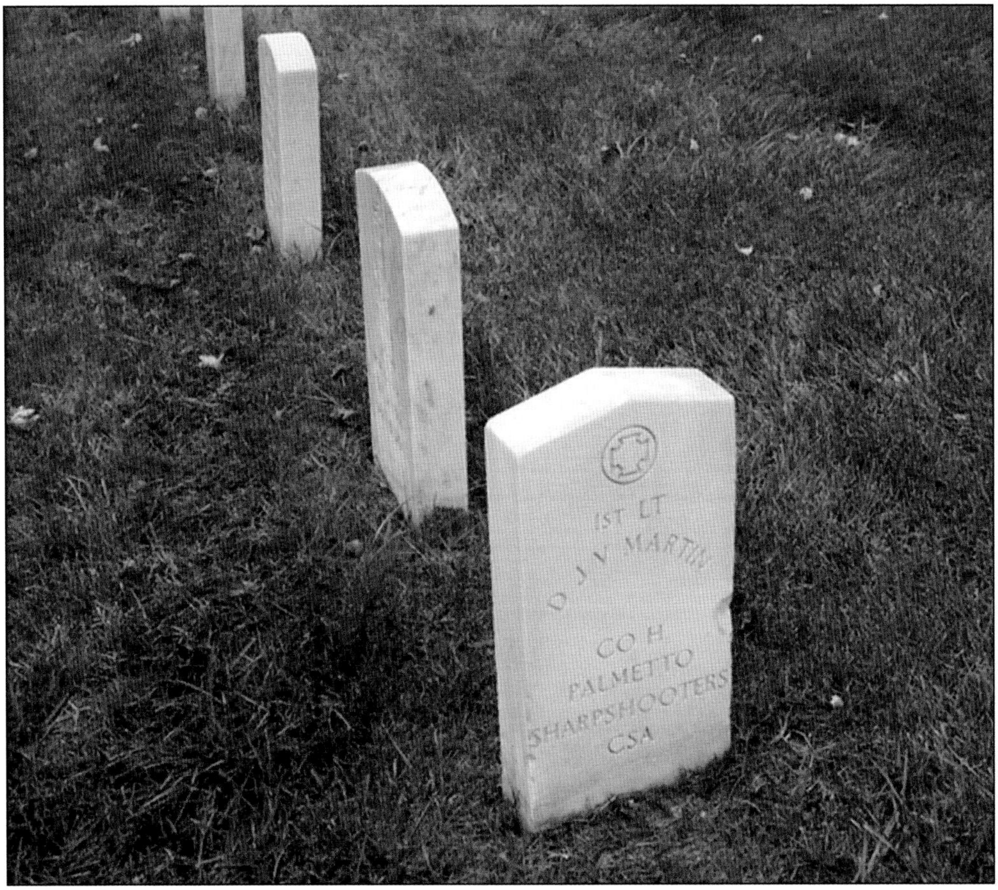

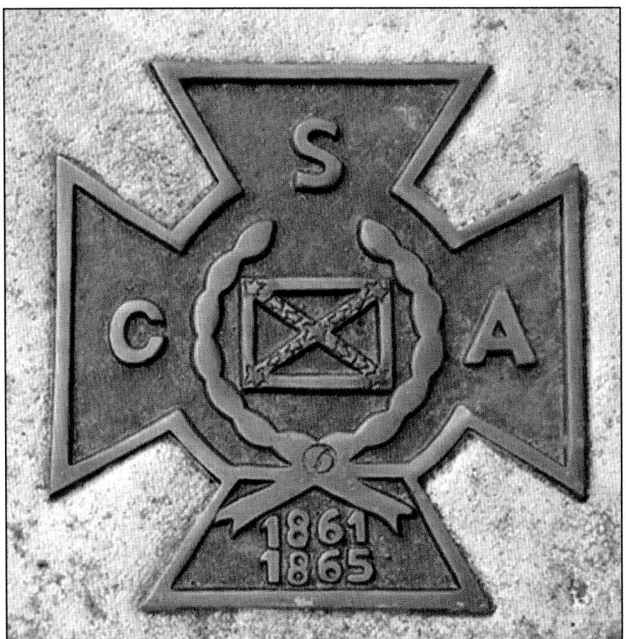

Confederate headstones were designed in 1909. The same materials were to be used without an inscribed shield. The tops were pointed instead of rounded, allegedly to prevent Yanks from sitting on them. By 1930, the Confederate Cross of Honor was allowed on the headstone. None of the headstones in Long Beach cemeteries are the official Confederate markers, as shown in this Library of Congress photograph. The Gen. Joe Wheeler Chapter of the Long Beach Daughters of the Confederacy hosted national conventions. Burial records indicate two Confederate soldiers are buried in the Municipal Cemetery and five are in Sunnyside.

Wives who became members of the GAR Women's Relief Corps (WRC) were given honors at burial and had headstones carved in the same style as their husbands who had served. Anna Spencer's headstone in the Municipal Cemetery has the Union shield and the insignia for the WRC.

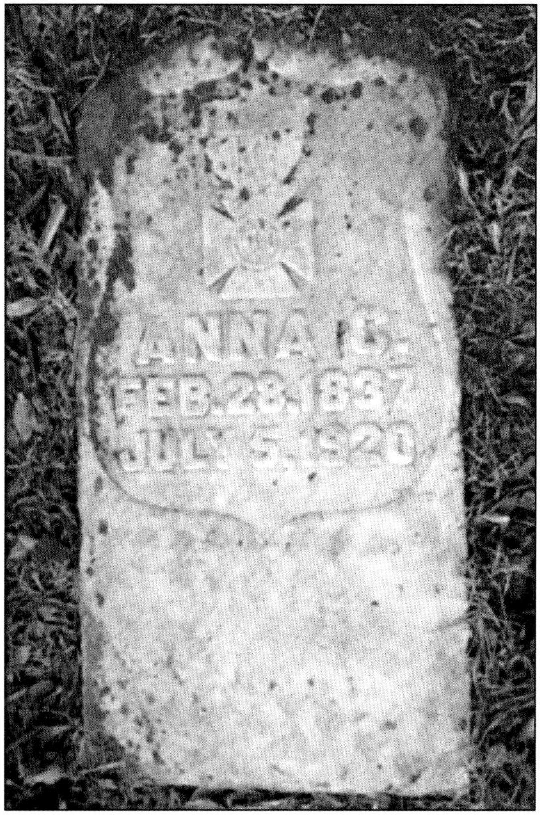

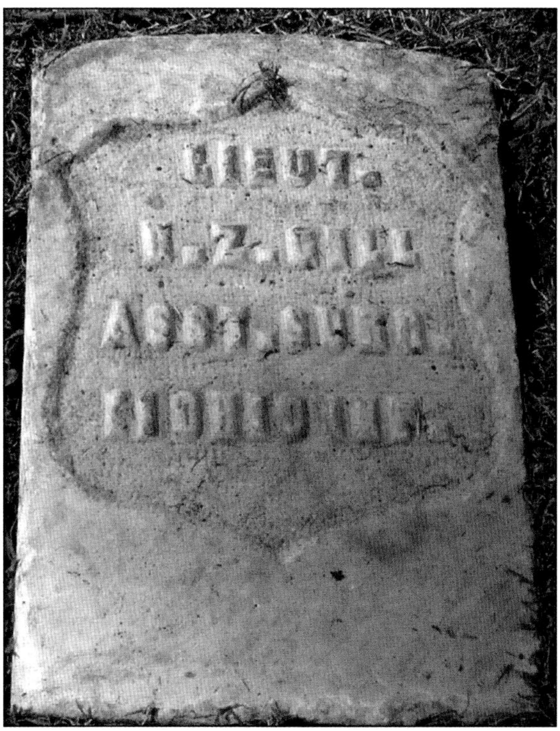

Civil War surgeon and expert on diphtheria, H.Z. Gill, was buried in the Municipal Cemetery in 1907. Gill was originally from Ohio. He was chief surgeon of the First Division of the 20th Army Corps. While in Long Beach, he served as commander of the 181 Post of the GAR. The GAR handled his funeral services.

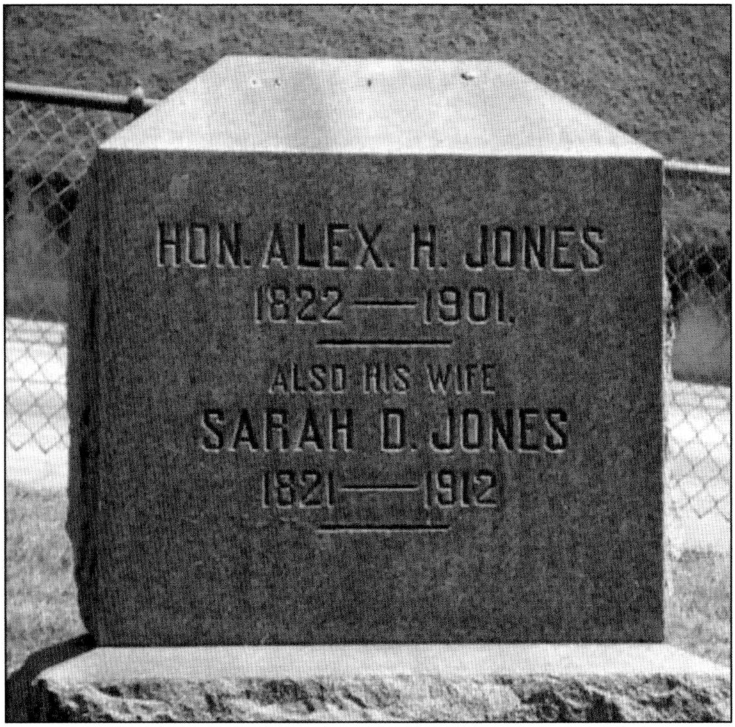

The Honorable Alexander Hamilton Jones lies in the Municipal Cemetery. Born in North Carolina in 1822, he enlisted in the Union army and was captured fighting in Tennessee. He escaped and rejoined. In 1868, he was elected to the US House of Representatives and served until 1871. In 1895, he came to Long Beach and died in 1901. He is buried with his wife, Sarah, who died in 1912.

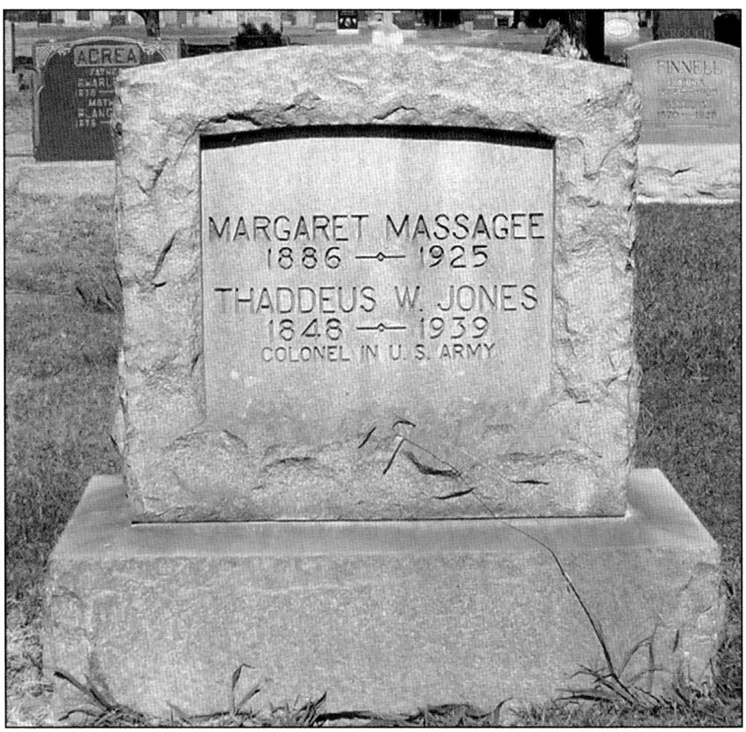

Congressman Jones's sons Thaddeus and Otho are buried in the Sunnyside Cemetery. Thaddeus, a West Point graduate, served as a colonel in the 1907 Battle of San Juan. He advocated for including African American soldiers in artillery companies, noting their bravery and low levels of desertion. He is buried with his daughter.

John Ricker Hurd was brevetted a brigadier general, US Volunteers on March 13, 1865, for his meritorious service at the battles of Shiloh, Stone River, and Chickamauga. Brevetting gave a rank but not the authority. Hurd was a war prisoner at Richmond Libby Prison but escaped. He is buried in Sunnyside.

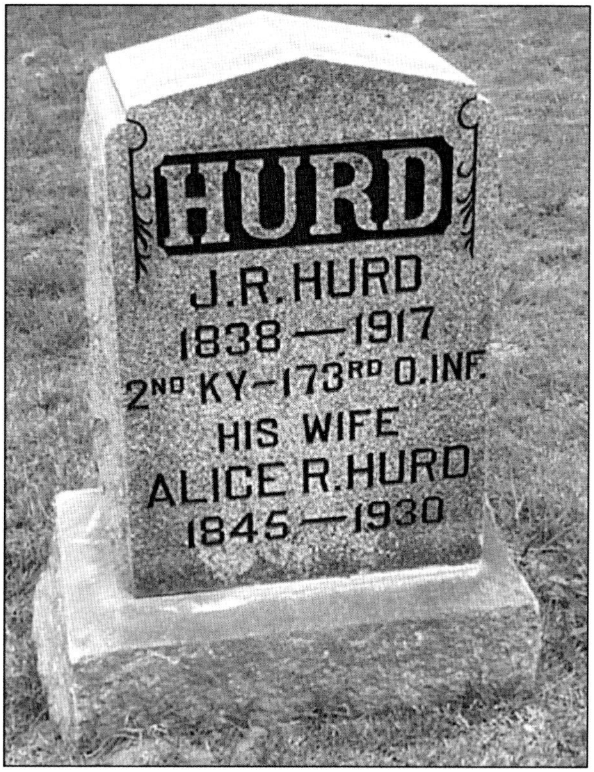

In December 1935, members of the Lawton Camp No. 10, Sons of Union Veterans and the Anna Etheridge Tent No. 58, Daughters of Union Veterans, dedicated a flag standard and bronze plaques at Sunnyside Cemetery in the area designated as the Civil War section. In 2011, vandals stole the bronze plaques from the standard.

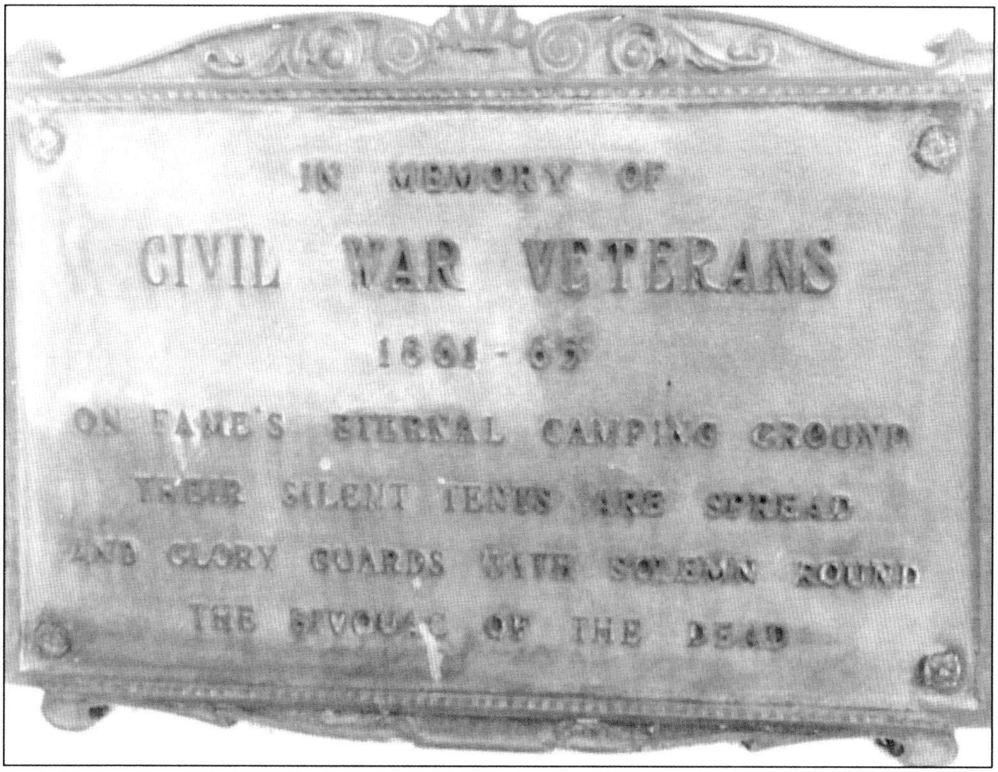

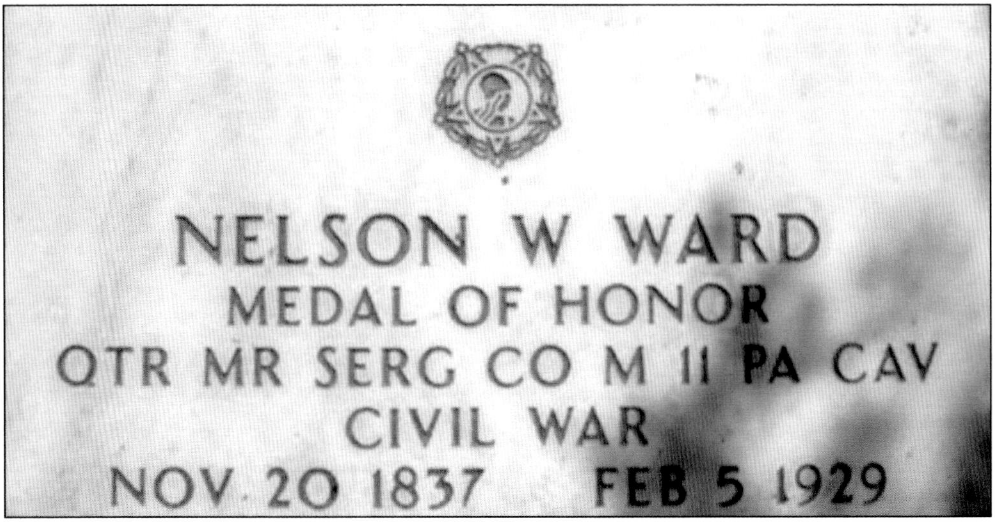

On September 10, 1897, Nelson Ward received the Medal of Honor for extraordinary heroism performed on June 25, 1864, while serving with Company M, 11th Pennsylvania Cavalry, in action at Staunton River Bridge, Virginia. His original headstone at Sunnyside Cemetery did not include his Medal of Honor. A separate marker was installed later.

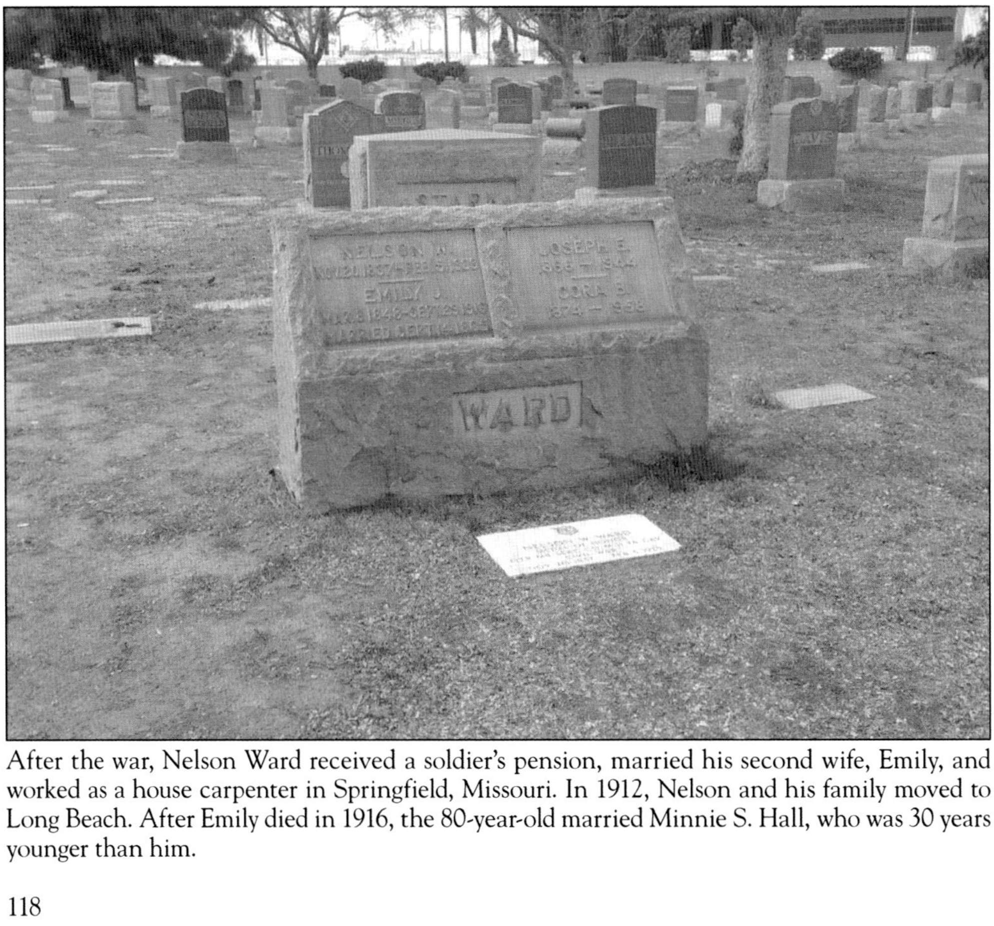

After the war, Nelson Ward received a soldier's pension, married his second wife, Emily, and worked as a house carpenter in Springfield, Missouri. In 1912, Nelson and his family moved to Long Beach. After Emily died in 1916, the 80-year-old married Minnie S. Hall, who was 30 years younger than him.

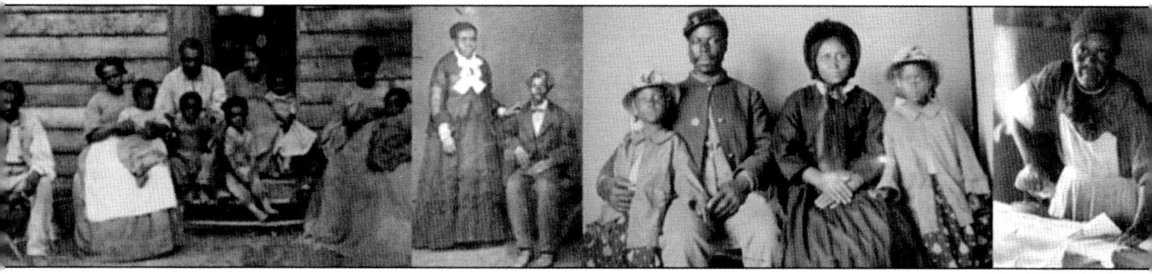

Abraham Cleage, born into slavery in 1838 on the Cleage Plantation in Tennessee, enlisted as a private in Company A of the 1st Colored Heavy Artillery Regiment in Knoxville. After he mustered out, Abraham and his wife, Amanda, moved to Texas and then Long Beach, where he worked as a city hall janitor until he died in 1908. He is buried in the Municipal Cemetery; however, his marker is missing. This photograph collage is from the genealogy website that is tracking those who were slaves on the Cleage Plantation. More details can be found at findingeliza.com/archives/19253.

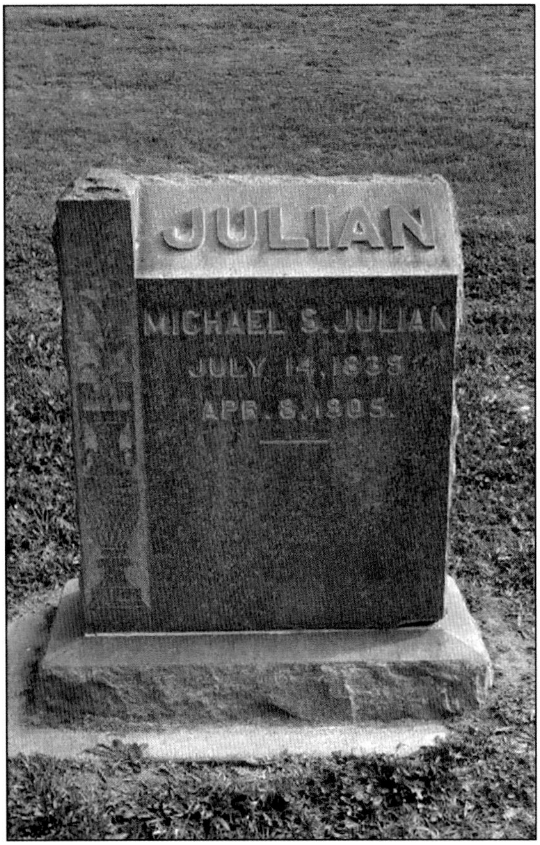

Confederate veterans Michael Sherrill Julian and cousin Drury Bailey came to California in the 1860s in search of gold. Julian served as a sergeant in the North Carolina Infantry and claimed to have been captured at the Battle of Gettysburg. Julian and Bailey founded a mining town in Northern San Diego County, which was named Julian after Michael because he was considered "the most attractive male in the community." Julian was elected assessor of San Diego County and then moved to Long Beach. He and his wife, Margaret, opened Hotel Julian in 1897 on Cedar Avenue between Ocean Avenue and First Street. The hotel faced Pacific Park and was known as a family hotel. Julian died in 1905 and is buried in the Municipal Cemetery.

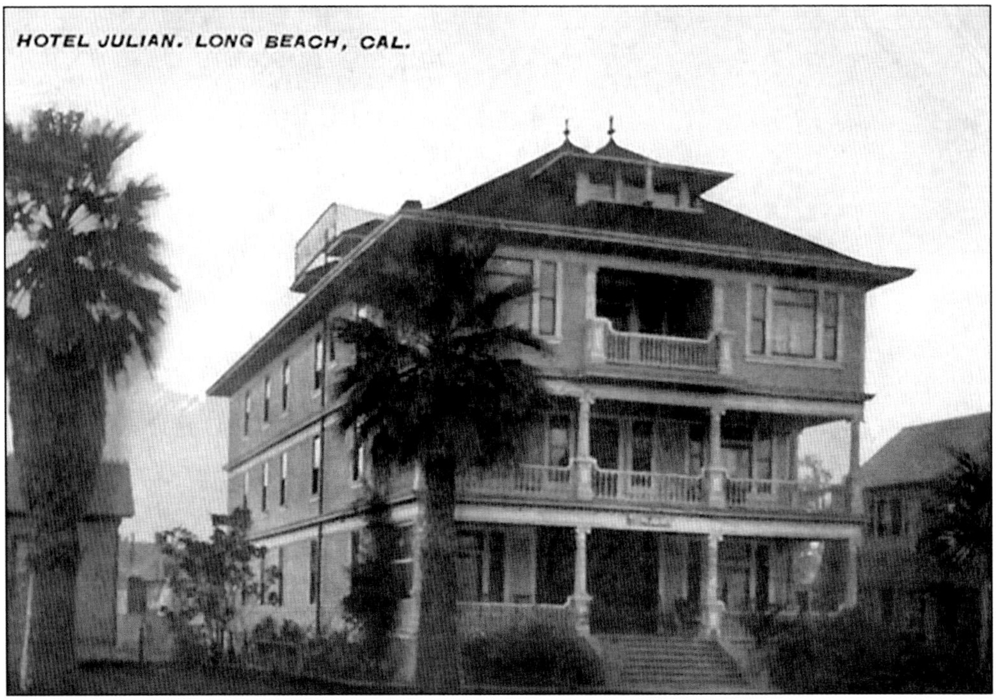

Alabama-born Nathaniel Washington Tolle is the other Confederate veteran buried in the Municipal Cemetery. The five Confederate soldiers identified in Sunnyside are John Addison Booty, John Dean, Capt. Tyler Calhoun Jordan, Derrill Wingard, and Judge Alexander Lawson, who served as the third city prosecutor of Long Beach.

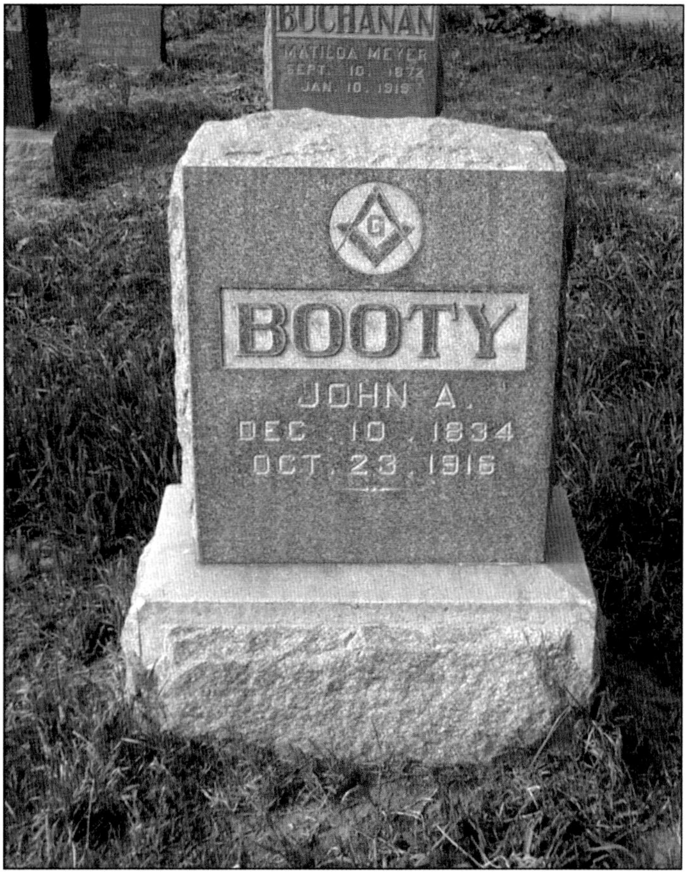

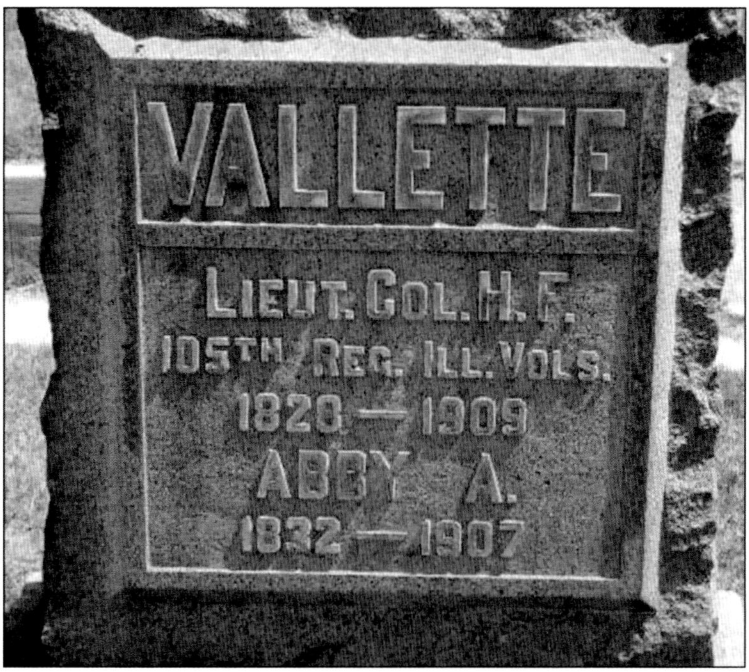

Henry Franklin Vallette served in the Civil War as a lieutenant colonel and then practiced law in Chicago for over 40 years. He and his wife, Abby, moved to Long Beach in 1891. She died in 1907. In early 1909, the totally blind Vallette, at age 86, married a 25-year-old. He died several months later and is buried with Abby in the Municipal Cemetery.

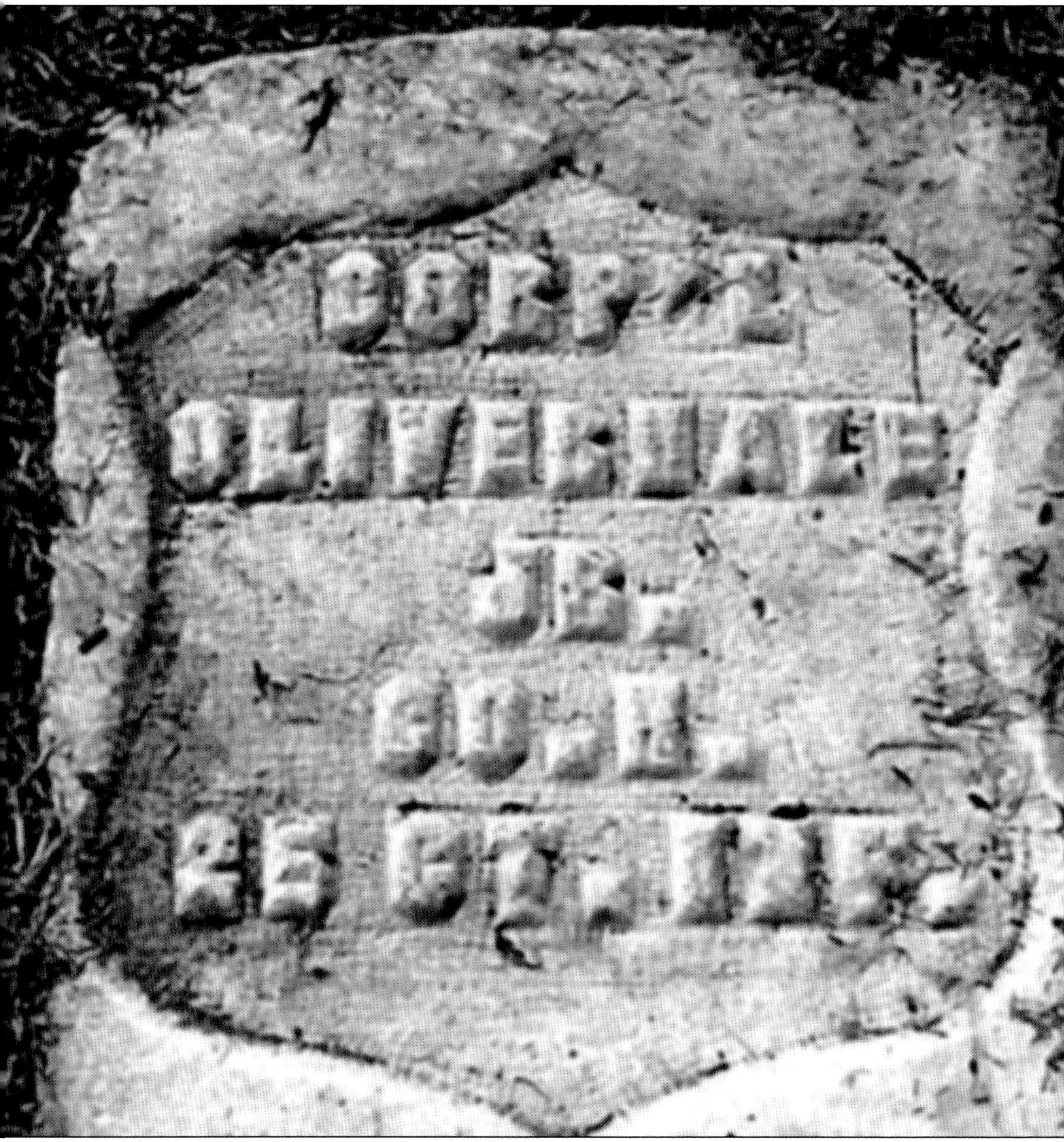

Corporal Oliver Hale was born in Connecticut on July 4, 1841. A direct descendant of Revolutionary patriot Nathan Hale, he enlisted in Company H, 25th Connecticut Infantry, Union army, and served until 1866 as a color bearer. During the Battle of Vicksburg, one of the standard bearers was killed, and another went insane. Hale was never the same. He and his wife, Alwida, moved to Long Beach in 1902 because of his health. He owned considerable real estate when he died in 1904. The GAR arranged for burial in the Municipal Cemetery. Their son Revilo (Oliver spelled backwards because of too many Olivers in the family), was an employee of the early Long Beach Water Department. He was killed while bicycling in 1932. Revilo is also buried in the Municipal Cemetery alongside his wife, Maude Catherine Fisher Hale.

Local papers reported that George Washington Wilcox died in 1921 leaving an estate worth more than $20,000. Wilcox enlisted at age 18 and served in Company D, 22nd Michigan Infantry until April 22, 1865. Buried in the Municipal Cemetery with his wife, Sarah, their headstone displays badges of the GAR and Auxiliary.

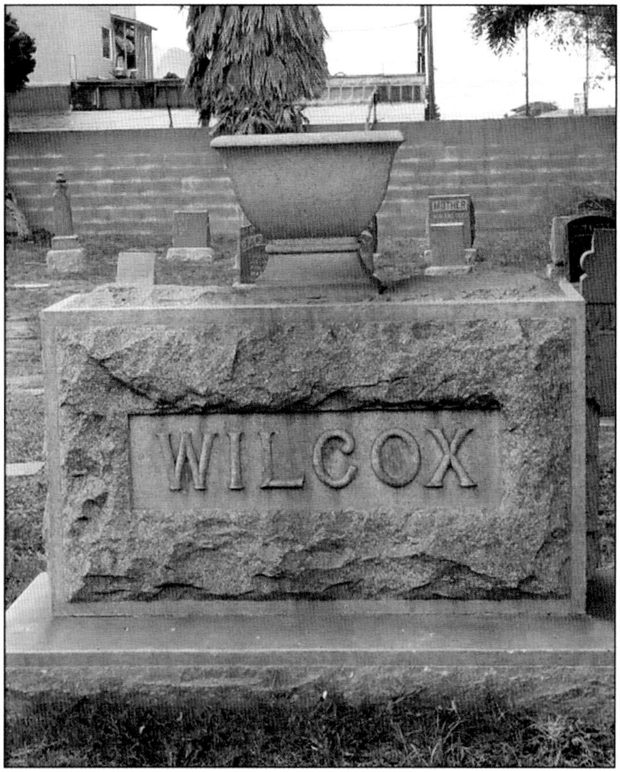

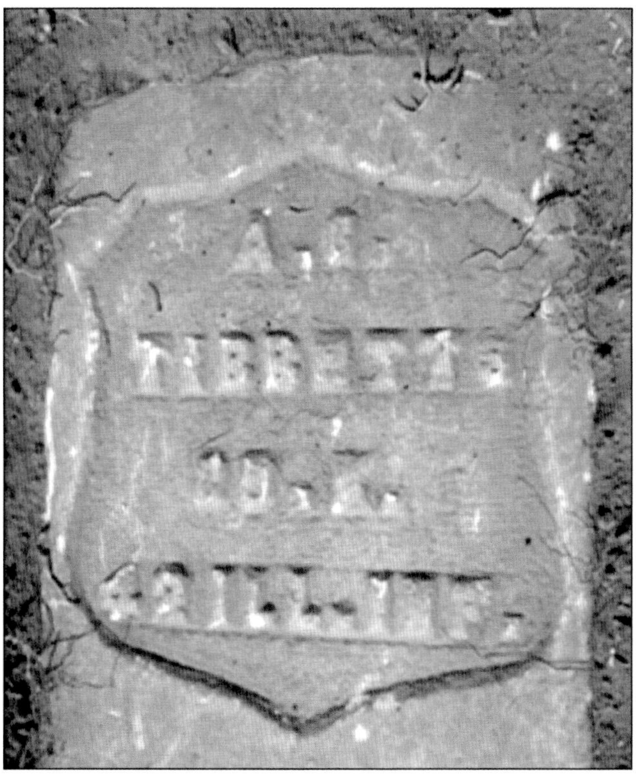

A.R. Tibbetts, of Company K, 42nd Illinois Infantry, was discharged in 1861 due to disability. Local newspapers call him "Captain;" however, official records indicate he was a private. Tibbetts killed himself after being jilted by his wife, who ran away with a man renting a room in their home. He had offered his life savings to make her stay, but she left. He is buried in the Municipal Cemetery.

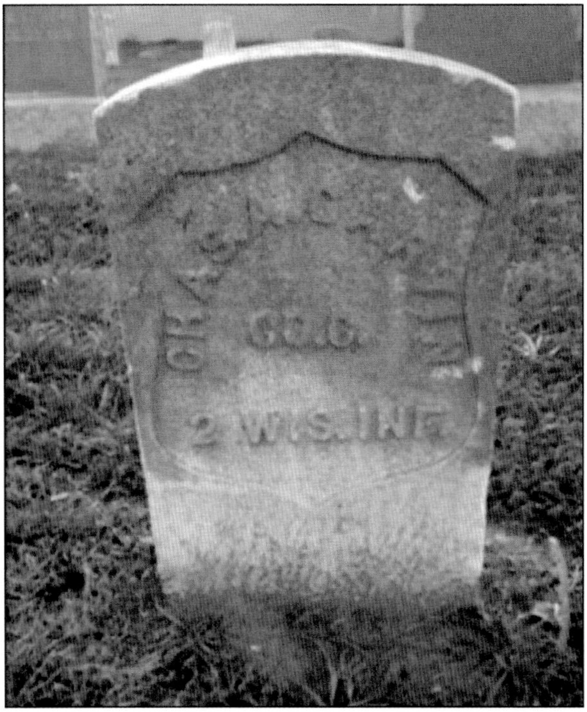

Charles Abraham Garvin kept a diary of his service in Company C, 2nd Wisconsin Volunteer Infantry, also known as the Iron Brigade. He claimed he was shot several times during numerous battles including Bull Run and Gettysburg. His brother James died in 1862. Charles married his widow, Mary, two years later, and they had six children. Mary died in 1882, and Charles is buried in Sunnyside.

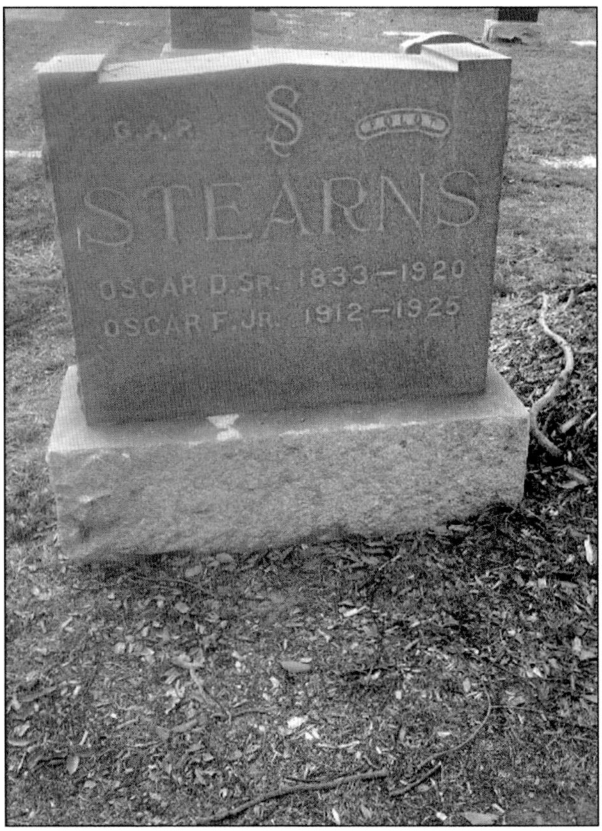

Pvt. Oscar Stearns and his son Oscar Jr. are buried in Sunnyside. Private Stearns served in the 150th Regiment Ohio Infantry (National Guard) that fought back Confederate troops trying to capture Washington, DC. He and his wife resided at 735 Freeman Avenue when he died in 1920.

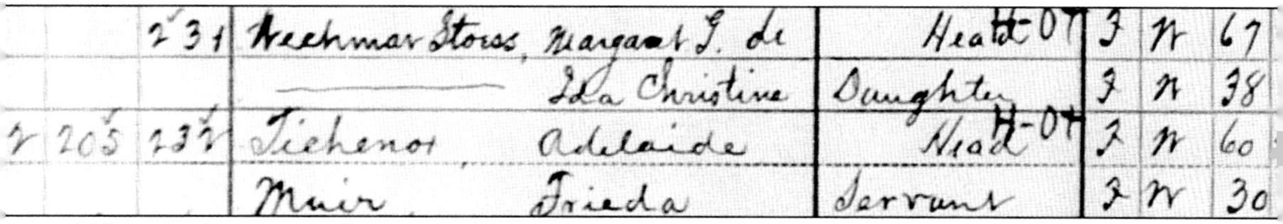

	231	Wechmar Stoess, Margaret G. de	Head	F	W	67
		—— Ida Christine	Daughter	F	W	38
205	237	Tichenor, Adelaide	Head	F	W	60
		Muir, Frieda	Servant	F	W	30

Although Margaret Graham Howell Davis Stoess is buried in nearby Compton, the sister in law of Confederate president Jefferson Davis died in Long Beach on August 17, 1930. Born in 1842, "Maggie" lived with her sister and brother in law in the White House of the Confederacy during the Civil War. When Jefferson Davis was imprisoned, the family fled to Canada and then Europe. Margaret met and married Carl De Wechmar Stoess, a native of Alsace-Lorraine and 20 years older. Margaret became Madame De Wechmar Stoess. She and her two children, Christine and Philip, moved from England to Victoria, Canada. Her husband died in 1894 and left the family "miserably poor." It is unclear how and why she moved to Long Beach, but the 1910 census shows her living with her daughter at 231 Ocean Avenue, next door to philanthropist Adelaide Tichenor.

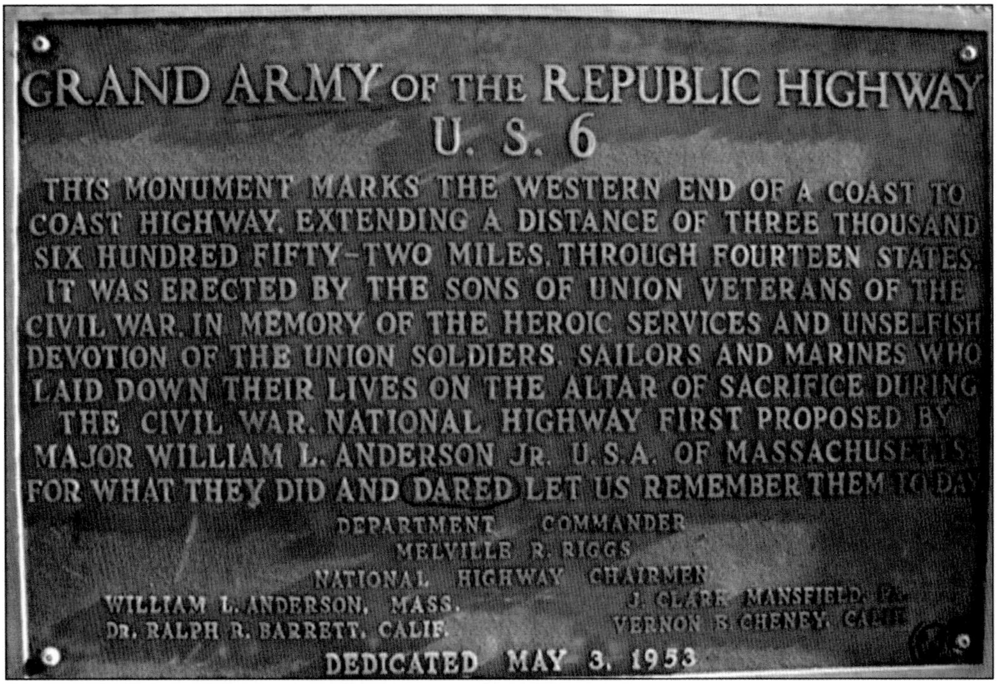

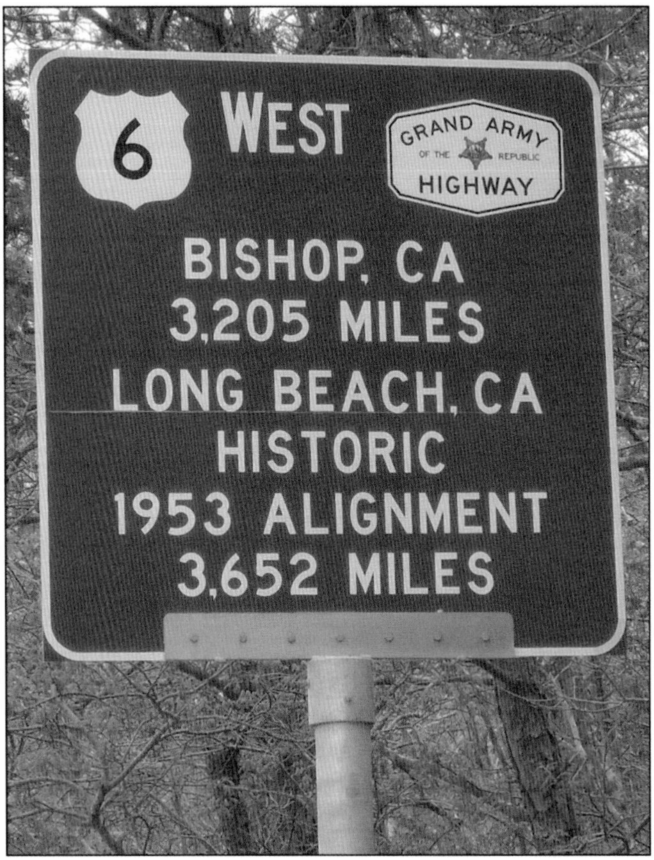

On June 21, 1937, US Route 6 became a transcontinental highway by extending it to Long Beach, California, 3,652 miles from Provincetown on Cape Cod in Massachusetts. The eastern terminus was at New Beach Circle; the western terminus at the intersection of the Long Beach Freeway and Pacific Coast Highway (US Route 101). On May 3, 1953, a dedication of US Route 6 as the Grand Army of the Republic Highway was held in Long Beach by five service organizations, including the Sons of Union Civil War Veterans, which sponsored a monument that was placed on the front of the old Municipal Auditorium. Today, the plaque is at the Long Beach Performing Arts Theater.

Additional Information Sources

All Souls Cemetery	4400 Cherry Avenue, Long Beach, CA 90807 562-424-8601 http://catholiccemeteriesla.org/location/all-souls-cemetery/
Forest Lawn Long Beach	1500 East San Antonio Drive, Long Beach, CA 90807 888-204-3131 http://forestlawn.com/long-beach/
Historical Society of Long Beach	4260 Atlantic Avenue, Long Beach, CA 90807 562-424-2220 www.hslb.org
Long Beach Municipal Cemetery	1151 East Willow Street, Long Beach, CA 90806 562-570-6634 www.longbeach.gov
Sunnyside Cemetery	1095 East Willow Street, Long Beach, CA 90806 562-595-9392

www.findagrave.com

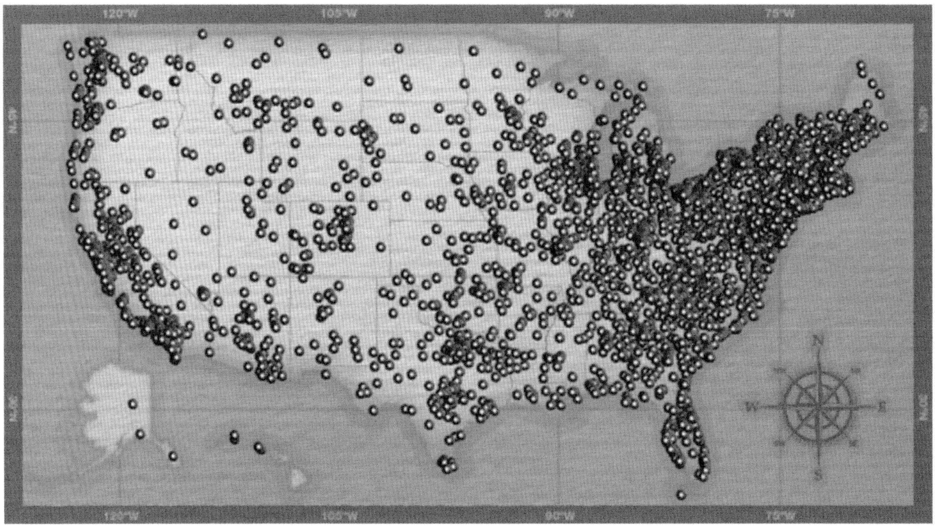